CW00539904

The Fun We Had

The Fun
We Had

Trials, tribulations and triumph
at the chalk face

Carrie Evans

Copyright © 2023 Carrie Evans

The moral right of the author has been asserted.

Apart from any fair dealing for the purposes of research or private study,
or criticism or review, as permitted under the Copyright, Designs and Patents
Act 1988, this publication may only be reproduced, stored or transmitted, in
any form or by any means, with the prior permission in writing of the
publishers, or in the case of reprographic reproduction in accordance with
the terms of licences issued by the Copyright Licensing Agency. Enquiries
concerning reproduction outside those terms should be sent to the publishers.

Troubador Publishing Ltd
Unit E2 Airfield Business Park,
Harrison Road, Market Harborough,
Leicestershire LE16 7UL
Tel: 0116 279 2299
Email: books@troubador.co.uk
Web: www.troubador.co.uk/matador

ISBN 978-1-80514-069-6

British Library Cataloguing in Publication Data.
A catalogue record for this book is available from the British Library.

Printed and bound in Great Britain by CMP UK
Typeset in 11pt Minion Pro by Troubador Publishing Ltd, Leicester, UK

Matador is an imprint of Troubador Publishing Ltd

To my mother Elizabeth, my friend Zoe
and my beloved husband Simon.

Contents

Chapter 1

Middle Eastern Musings

Hey ho, let's go! At long last I have a PC of my own, albeit someone's scruffy outdated cast-off, and there's no longer any excuse not to do what I've talked of doing for some time now – well, most of my life, really – simply to *write*. The keyboard is far from clean and I'm not wild about the rather obscene dayglow vermilion and black mouse pad I just dug out of the past-and-future presents box. However, I like the fearless, forthright colleague who gave to it me, my namesake, Caroline K; whenever we find ourselves in each other's company we somehow end up exchanging juicy details of our past love lives, which makes such a welcome change from the old, flogged-to-death, work at the chalkface gripes and groans. I love the artfully designed ring binder (retrieved from a wastepaper basket at my college at the end of last semester) that I intend using for my notes, featuring a white-gloved chortling Mickey Mouse, that pernicious symbol of American cultural imperialism, as he always reminds me of dear, delicate Marina, the Armenian beauty, who spotted a fellow soul in need of a quiet spot to retreat to at a Diesel gig in Paris one cold winter's night way back when in the late seventies. She took me in unquestioningly, introduced me to her circle of friends and gave me a wonderful, warm black sweater. I lived in that sweater until it fell apart, and later on, just before I headed off south for some much-needed Greek sun, she gave me her V-necked Mickey Mouse T-shirt, which she knew I loved and which I wore and wore until it too was in tatters. It lies beside the unpretentious little Dell screen now, the ring binder, that is, not the ragged T-shirt.

My desk is pushed up against the window in the end bedroom so I can gaze out as I reminisce, ruminate and compose. I love the view from here, from the seventeenth floor of Al Majaz Tower, out over the palm-fringed Sharjah corniche, which surrounds Khalid Lagoon, our view for almost five years now, with its multi-coloured neon lights, the never-ending stream of evening traffic (pretty much soundless, in fact, from this height), weaving slowly up towards the Blue Souq, dozen upon dozen of pairs of red tail lights on the right and a matching band of brighter, white ones on the left, with the new ivory-hued mosque looming up above, between the inky waters of the lagoon and the ever-creeping cars, its domes and minarets softly illuminated in orange, recently built for all the world as though to enhance the outlook from the spacious, though some might say characterless, flat we currently call home.

You may say it is the second glass of Rosemount Estate merlot that is simply having its desired effect after a gruelling week staving off fear and loathing at the gulag – and this may well come into it – but at this point in time, I do feel that life is sweet, despite my growing disquiet with the laws of this land, particularly those relating to women, and the uneasy feeling that Big Brother is constantly watching me at work. I am aware that I have so much; to begin with, I have a 'good man' (that really has to be said in an Irish accent, as it was my dear friend Barbara from Belfast, one of the witnesses at our Dubai wedding, who gave her candid opinion of Simon's merits in those precise terms). I have a quaint, but loving, family (Mum and two younger brothers), each member with their own brand of quirky humour. I have quite passable health for someone who's lived for over half a century. I am still able to enjoy locomotion, something I have come to appreciate more than ever since spending two weeks in bed with my leg in plaster, the whole duration of a holiday in Seville, where my main objective had been to improve my salsa steps in a local dancing class. I have encountered so many brilliant, hilarious, wild and wanton people in my life (or have at least read their words), I've seen such extraordinarily beautiful and such truly hideous places, witnessed and experienced such extremes of emotion, I know that the only way to do justice to it all is to try to put some of it down in writing. It's quite simple really: whether anyone reads it or not is pretty much immaterial; it just has to be done, and it has to start now – the keyboard can be cleaned up later.

Thursday 31 March 2005

Awoke this morning to the thickest pea-souper I believe I've ever seen in the Gulf. I remember first hearing about this phenomenon at Spring Gardens in London from a terribly plummy sort of a chap, who was supposedly interviewing me for a summer job teaching English at the British Council in Bahrain. I say supposedly, as I don't recall any probing or even remotely challenging questions that day, such as which tense I would set about teaching first to elementary-level learners, past simple or present perfect, but I do remember him explaining, almost insultingly when I come to think of it, that very few

teachers wanted to stick around in the Gulf in the summer
months, because of the searing heat of the desert combined with
the exceptionally high humidity, which he called the pea-soup
effect. Even after my foolish slip of the tongue, admitting, at his
enquiry about my self-perceived weaknesses in relation to work,
that I might be considered something of an alcoholic when
what I had meant to say, of course, was workaholic, he quickly
informed me that I seemed to be 'the right type' and that he
thought I'd get on very well over there. They were clearly quite
desperate for staff.

The reason I had been going to Bahrain back then in 1993
was not out of any particular interest in the Gulf area or in the
Muslim communities living there, nor out of a desire to enhance
my CV, but simply for a change of air and also to visit an old pal,
whom I shall call Mr T, a fellow 'tefler'(Teacher of English as a
Foreign Language), who, unlike me, was at that time wedded
to the Arab world. It made sense to try to earn a bob or two
while I was out there, hence my application to work at the
British Council. It was the first summer I'd spent without Rick,
a gentle man from whom I'd been inseparable for ten years, and
so, despite in many ways embracing my new life and looking
forward to new adventures and experiences, a part of me was
still in deep mourning for the loss of something treasured and
seemingly irreplaceable. On top of this, on my return to the UK
from New Zealand, a few months earlier, a close friend had had
a serious, extended psychotic episode, one in which I had felt
bound (though others assured me of the inadvisability of doing
such a thing) to take on what I saw as the key role of helper, if not
saviour, and had ended up crawling to the GP myself and being
prescribed some pretty hefty tranquillisers. My recollections of
that harrowing period are not surprisingly a little hazy; I spent a
fair bit of time wandering the grimy, gum-pocked pavements of
North London, feeling as though I was enveloped in thick wads

of cotton wool, searching for my ward, aiming to entice her away from the pulsating pubs of Pinner High Street and back to the sanctuary of her peaceful, book-lined flat, where I had prepared hot, nutritious food that I believed would help in her recovery.

As soon as my friend was out of hospital and back on her feet, off I went with Czech Airlines to steamy Manama-on-sea, soon realising that, while Mr T might have been capable of teaching thirty-odd hours a week and still have the time and energy for having fun, I certainly didn't. Much as I like children, I should have known, after my teaching debut in Crete in my tender youth, that I am not really cut out for teaching these small beings at all, creatures who in mere minutes manage to mangle materials that have taken hours to create and who seem to laugh at all the wrong things. I did get slightly better in time at teaching 'young learners' as we now call them, but really only when they behaved. I don't seem to have the mean streak that comes in so handy when dealing with juvenile villains, and, of course, in each class, there's always one. Let us just say that those Bahraini children might possibly have been better off without me. No one could say I didn't try, however, and the fairly fragile state of mind in which I entered the institution after I'd completed my course of tranquillisers must be borne in mind, should you ever happen to hear that I was the teacher who went down in the annals of the British Council as the one who dissolved into tears in the haughty Director of Studies' office, after her assistant Miss Bunny's unexpected lollop into the class of eight-year-old miscreants, whom I was clearly failing to manage or teach any of the basics of English grammar and usage.

Of course, I already had an idea about the unsatisfactory position of women in many Muslim countries; I had travelled up and down the Nile in Egypt in my early twenties and had been dismayed to find that one rarely saw anything more of the local women in public than their huge, kohl-lined eyes, peering out inquisitively from beneath swathes of black cloth as they scuttled by, children clasped to their sides as though fearful that we infidels might bite. Working in Crete in the seventies too had broken me in, so to speak, and prepared me for that vaguely insulting scrutiny one is sometimes subjected to when venturing out alone in countries where the men make the rules – in many places it just isn't something a respectable single woman would do. Perhaps I'd become more culturally sensitive but I found my awareness of the looks of disapproval directed at me in the Bahraini capital when I was out and about unaccompanied tended to take much of the pleasure out of my exploration of the souqs and back streets and I was not able to enjoy that fine feeling of anonymity one experiences in other distant and exotic foreign parts. Despite my admittedly sketchy knowledge of the culture, I was rather taken aback on the first day at the school when some of the youngest girls turned up in full Muslim adult attire, complete with gloves, stockings , head-scarves and ankle length *abaya*, not, thankfully, the face cover, the *niqab* or the *burka*, that to this day I find so unnatural and so deeply unsettling.

My co-teachers at the Bahraini British Council were friendly enough, the possible exception being a pale, reticent English woman with a striking figure and penetrating gaze who mainly kept herself to herself and whose rare remarks in the staff room tended to be dry or caustic. One weekend I happened to get into conversation with her at a party given by one of the permanent staff. I was treated to the most fascinating account of her days smuggling cocaine out of South America in small aircraft. The transformation due to alcohol and who knows what other drugs was quite extraordinary. Sadly, before I had fully satisfied my curiosity about her former persona and intrepid, illicit exploits, she passed out and was unceremoniously carried off by her husband, who apologised rather sweetly to me, explaining that, alas, this always tended to happen at parties.

Despite the stresses and strains of teaching Bahraini children, life was never dull chez Mr T and his dark, softly spoken flatmate – let's call him Mr X – in scenic Manama (in actuality the area was flat, featureless and deadly boring): dancing to old Tamla Motown numbers – The Four Tops' 'Loco in Acapulco' springs to mind – concocting culinary delights in the pokey, windowless kitchen after our weekly romp around the sprawling local supermarket, Carrefour, filling the trolley to overflowing, then adding a few more sweet delicacies at the check-out counter, watching candid-camera-type takes filmed at local weddings back at the flat – goodness knows where Mr T got hold of them. The funniest by far was of the sophisticated, stylishly dressed Middle Eastern matriarch gazing serenely around her at the younger ladies swaying their hair rhythmically as they performed an undulating Khaliji dance, then all of a sudden twisting her torso around to give her buttocks a good, long scratch, blissfully ignorant of the ingeniously positioned camera filming her every move a mere metre or so behind her. There was also a certain Mr Bean sketch involving a flying nappy at a funfair, which never failed to have us – Mr T in particular – doubling up in paroxysms of mirth each time we watched it.

The other activity that Mr T entered into, with a fervour that I later realised was probably motivated by a strong desire to get me out of the house a bit more in my free time, was scouring the island in search of a local beau for me. Early on in my stay, I was instructed to gather up my snazziest, skimpiest swimwear and flashiest accessories and accompany him to a certain remote expats-only private beach for an afternoon's sunbathing. A key spot, I learned, in this small exclusive area was the ice-cream kiosk, where free ice cream was handed out to anyone who asked. This, I was told earnestly by Mr T, was where I should linger in my bikini, making sure I turned to admire the view in either direction as I ate my ice cream. The reason for this bizarre charade was that the little platform in front of the kiosk was the precise spot where the current emir trained the telescope from his yacht, moored a little way out from the shore, in search of shapely young Western beauties to keep him company on board from time to time. Not only were such fortunate ones wined and dined and given the pleasure of spending a leisurely afternoon in the ruler's presence, but, on their departure, they were reportedly presented with a gold envelope containing a not insignificant sum of money for their trouble. Not having a lot of choice in the matter, I carried out the instructions to the best of my ability and even went up a second time for ice cream that I really didn't want, but no call to the yacht came that day, and the venture was duly abandoned.

Another prime pick-up spot, Mr T informed me on a different occasion, was a certain coffee shop in one of the more upmarket malls just outside the city, so there we sat over countless fruit shakes, hoping our similar colouring would suggest we were siblings or cousins rather than a couple, furtively appraising and eyeing up the male customers at the adjacent café. The local talent, however, in their Persil-white *dishdashas* and perfectly groomed beards, seemed far more interested in talking to each other than to a slightly reserved-looking Western woman, no longer in the first flush of youth. The fact was, it was Mr T's idea rather than mine to try to track down a good-looking local guide for me that summer; my heart simply wasn't in it, and, not surprisingly, the liaison never came about. There was a brief encounter with an Englishman we dubbed Egghead, not on account of his superior intelligence but rather on account of his peculiarly egg-shaped, balding head. Although I got to spend a weekend in the UAE and was treated to a guided tour of the country's cities, souqs, and desert valleys, it was all a bit of a disaster and taught me that when a heterosexual man talks about 'a short trip with no strings attached' the chances are he is lying through his teeth.

I was sorry to say goodbye to my gracious hosts when my visit to Bahrain came to an end – it was to be many years before I saw Mr T again – but I was not sorry to be leaving the Gulf, indeed it was a relief. Little did I think, as I boarded that alarmingly antiquated Czech aircraft, hard-earned wads of currency stuffed into my handbag and underwear, that I would return, but return I did, not, I hasten to add, because my ideas about the religion or the Muslim world had changed or because I had developed an interest in the flora and fauna of the desert, but simply because I felt the time had come to make some real money for a change. My South American trip and the MA TESOL I'd undertaken after leaving New Zealand had, between them, mopped up a tidy sum and I just hoped that the UAE 'package' everyone assured me was one of the 'best around' for an EFL teacher would make up for the lack of cultural stimulation and scenic splendour.

So now, as I sit here in Sharjah, six years on from my return to the Gulf, gazing out of my wide, dusty window, the mist before me starts to thin and I'm reminded of another student of mine who used to hide a part of his face. Actually, out of cultural sensitivity and extreme concern not to do anything that might be branded as in any way 'colonial' in attitude, we were not supposed to refer to them as students at all, but as 'trainees'. This was on an off-campus course I was employed to set up and run for an Auckland tertiary college, literally days after my arrival in New Zealand, sometime before my first Gulf experience. The 'trainee' in question went by the name of Starling.

Despite the fact that this burly and highly physical fifty-year-old from Tonga, a man who positively oozed sexuality, had worked in the capacity of bouncer for a number of years at clubs in and around Auckland, he was always courteous and sensitive and I'm quite sure an honest, good-hearted man – quite a contrast, you might say, to the paranoid, evil despot after whom he was named, a leader who wiped out a large section of the Russian population and yet shared a table with Winston Churchill, indeed was said to have got on famously with him. This unusual individual, the Tongan Starling, insisted on wearing a rather sinister pair of reflective aviator sunglasses indoors and out, come rain and shine, so that you rarely, if ever, got to see his eyes. I did, in fact, have this privilege on more than one occasion and what struck me each time was their intelligence and, at the same time, their sadness. I believe Starling had had a wife and family but was divorced, and perhaps because of this was considered the black sheep of the family, something he tended to joke about, but at these times the words of the song 'Tears of a Clown' came to mind. I never questioned this habit of his of wearing sunglasses indoors – nor, incidentally, his fascination with the sex life of African elephants, evidenced by the mainly pictorial book I once caught him engrossed in at the local library, just after a literacy class, in which I'd distributed library membership cards. I think given the choice I'd rather see a person's face with the eyes hidden than vice versa, though it's a tough call. The eyes, after all, are supposed to be the windows to the soul. It's all I can do sometimes in my more heated moments to resist whipping off the *niqab* (the Muslim female face covering) of some of my more affectedly retiring students and saying: '*Look*, missy, we're all women here in the privacy of our classroom, no one really cares about how we look, if our noses are too big or if we rival Cleopatra in beauty, please just *stop* being silly.' Of course, such talk would get one fired around here, and we enjoy our tax-free salaries and long paid holidays, so we toe the line and pay lip service to the antiquated aspects of the religion and tolerate what some would say is a few misguided individuals' interpretations of the Koran, with regard to women's clothing and demeanour.

Why the name Starling? Well apparently, the midwife at Starling's birth on the isle of Tonga, sometime in the late 1940s, was the sister of none other than the Russian premier, Stalin, himself. What she was doing on the remote Pacific Island at the time, working in a poorly paid job in the medical field, far from her native Russia, has always remained something of a mystery, but I have no reason to think he was joking when he divulged this information. Why would he invent such a story? Why was the 'g' added at the end of the name? I'm afraid these questions will remain frustratingly forever unanswered.

Most of the trainees on this 'pre-employment training course' had been taken from the unemployed lists at the local welfare office, and comprised a colourful collection of cheerful, skinny ex-refugees from SE Asian countries, predominantly Vietnam, but also Cambodia and Laos, and a group of more sedate and generously proportioned, for the most part recently arrived, immigrants from Pacific Islands such as Western Samoa, Tonga, and Niue. As in the case of Starling, many people of Pacific Island origin, who had been in New Zealand for a number of years, unable, supposedly, to secure jobs on account of their lack of English, had, in reality, become rather comfortable living on the reasonably generous government benefits distributed to larger families, and their wives – as in the case of another trainee on our first course, the punch-drunk, ex-professional Samoan boxer, Seti – would have hit the roof if they had forfeited their welfare cheques to take up low-paid employment in the local electronics factory (Seti told us this himself). In any case, one still assumed that with the majority of these folk there was not a great deal of money left after the bills had been paid, particularly as large get-togethers with copious amounts of food were almost weekly events in both the Pacific Island and the Vietnamese communities, although the former tended to be sober churchy sort of affairs, to which we were only occasionally invited, whilst the latter were generally jolly, informal garden parties, held in celebration of a child's birthday or the opening of a business, usually a bakery or perhaps a fish and chip shop. To these we were always invited, and invariably enjoyed, as everyone was so relaxed and friendly and people of all ages were there in equal number, the men putting the world to rights over beers and cigarettes around the barbecue, while the women beavered away and joked in the kitchen, appearing to have every bit as much fun as the men and children, and if they were exhausted from toiling over pots and pans since daybreak, they never showed it. We felt very privileged to be accepted so unconditionally by the Vietnamese community and always enjoyed the time we spent with these generous, hospitable folk, who operated from the heart. I admired their courage in undertaking perilous journeys to get to New Zealand and marvelled at their resilience and industriousness. Our closest friends, Hung and Dang, were very keen for us to become partners in their thriving French bakery business – they assured us that we'd make a lot more money with them than we did teaching, but we valued the friendship and didn't want to jeopardise that. We knew their four young children often worked in the bakery when not at school and foresaw problems over this, plus safety issues and the running of the business. Besides, while Rick seemed to manage to communicate with the husband, Dang, quite well, I barely understood a word he said and used to find it extremely tiring constantly trying to think of reasonable responses to all the unintelligible questions he put to me.

Returning to Starling, it was fairly early on in the twelve-week course that he suggested everyone come over to his place for a 'feed' after the day's classes one Friday afternoon. Although the Pacific Islanders and the SE Asians got on well enough at the centre and there was much camaraderie over cups of tea in the 'smoko' break – even poker or volleyball, weather permitting – they did not normally mix socially outside class, and I had my doubts as to the merits of the suggestion, not least as I found it hard to imagine how around sixteen of us, including teachers, would fit into our host's front room, should the weather turn nasty, and then there was the cost. In this, our first year in New Zealand, we would have been a little hard-pressed to put on a lavish spread for half a dozen people ourselves, and yet here was a single man living on a benefit proposing to cater for almost three times that number. Starling was gently persistent, however, and so towards the end of the course, a date was set, and off we all went after the last class of the week in search of his humble home. What Starling had not told us was that he lived with his brother, who was a wealthy Mormon, conveniently away at that time on a visit to Tonga. The modest home we had expected turned out to be comparatively palatial, a bungalow admittedly, but with a number of large, rather grandly furnished rooms, including a massive living area with all the furniture pushed back against the walls should people get the urge to dance. Sometime after this, I had occasion to visit Seti the ex-boxer's home too. His living room, similarly, was generously proportioned but lacked the grandeur of Starling's home. It only had the barest essentials when it came to furniture, but it must be said that this was compensated for by an impressive gallery of stern-looking family elders, gazing down at one from each of the four walls, as though daring the house dwellers to break the code of abstinence and modesty taught by the missionaries in their sincere yet hopelessly misguided zeal for passing on the teachings of the good Lord to 'primitive beings' in far-flung places.

Once people had had a few beers beside the barbecue in Starling's garden and had started to mingle, the party got going and everyone got on famously. Contrary to expectations, the whole thing was a roaring success. The evening summer sun shone down and as we gathered around the pool for photos, pleasantly sozzled and replete with hot dogs, lamb chops, sausages, ice cream and apple pie, and even the young Mormons, who had been trying without much success to do a bit of proselytising in the kitchen, came out to join us, I remember thinking how remarkable life could be and I believe it was then that Starling came up beside me and told me confidentially that he had been watching me and my 'better half' over the past couple of months and that he had a word of advice for us. He proceeded to say that we were a lovely couple, that we obviously had a good relationship and that he thought it was high time we had some children – I wouldn't have been surprised if he had offered to show us how it was done. The seriousness and urgency of this message struck me and, though I thanked him and promised to think about what he had said, it was probably a good two years before we decided to put his advice into practice, which, as it turned out, was rather too late.

The mist over Sharjah corniche has all but evaporated now and I have a feeling it's going to be a scorcher. I shall mop the floors and do the usual weekend chores, then perhaps a spot of marking – there's always marking to be done – and think a bit about the course I'm supposed to be writing. How heavenly to be able to do things at one's own pace and simply potter, pore and ponder all day long. Funnily enough, I have come to like the routine of the working week. I remember my brother Richard once waxing lyrical about the joys of routine as we walked the dogs along the towpath at Henley-on-Thames, and I just couldn't see the appeal – a peripatetic lifestyle seemed the only one for me and I wondered if I would ever cope with the rigours of a demanding full-time, *permanent* teaching job. My old friend Jude once suggested, in that sweet, most tentative way she has, that for once in my life I might try *staying* in one place for a while – *that* would be the true test of my mettle. She knew quite well that for me deciding on an interesting destination, packing a bag and sticking my thumb out – or jumping on the first cheap flight to a new continent – and thinking about a job when I reached my journey's end was easy. It didn't take courage, as some people thought; I was just following my nature. What really took courage was signing a three-year contract to work in the UAE for the Higher Colleges of Technology – in fact, it may well have been the bravest thing I've ever done. Some might say I'd sold my soul to Mammon, and adapting to the situation hasn't been easy, but, against all expectations, the routine aspect of my life here has turned out to be rather pleasant.

Thursday 7 April 2005

Yesterday was a surprisingly enjoyable day at work – at times I felt positively exuberant – and though I was well and truly done in by the time I stumbled over the doorstep at getting on for 9 pm, my normal weekday bedtime (just as well Simon wasn't here or he'd have given me a right roasting for working so late), laden with carrier bags plus Calvin Klein jumbo-sized leather hold-all, bulging with weekend work – no slim and stylish briefcase would suffice in this job, I'm afraid – I had a sense that things were somehow going to be alright, that the extensive dry rot they've just discovered in the lovely Regency flat we bought last year in Hove, something we've been told is going to require a 'substantial sum' to rectify, is a matter we will simply take in our stride; my poor little Brighton flat, with its ever-recurring damp and tedious tenant-trials, will be patiently and lovingly cared for and kept within the family, no matter what the cost. Goodness, when you've forked out the best part of twenty grand in less than half that number of years and find yourself contemplating the expense of scaffolding for the third round of roof works in the same time span, there is only one thing for it, it seems to me – to tell oneself that one is on a divine mission to provide small, aging properties in the south of Britain with top quality, sturdy roofing, roofing that will withstand the buffetings and lashings of fearsome Atlantic gales and make citizens for miles around green with envy, roofing that will see in the 22nd century.

I was not unaware, as I was writing the last two monster sentences, that they were getting rather long for comfort, that the full stop key was starting to jiggle uneasily on one leg, and that a certain English school teacher I recall from my youth would be getting that glint in his eye and preparing to write in bold authoritative letters '*Punctuation*! Break down this sentence into smaller, more digestible pieces!' It was only this morning, ironically, that I was reading my student Zamzam's last exam essay on the problem of overcrowding in the UAE's cities and wondering how I could drive it home to her, without crushing her burgeoning writer's spirit, that very often the best way to say something is the simplest way. One of the best writers in the English language, many would agree, is Graham Greene. You don't get him rambling on and on, clocking up subordinate clause after subordinate clause, without a care in the world for the comfort or the comprehension of the poor reader. Who am I to give such advice when, as you can see, I am a prime culprit myself? I am, however, fully aware of this tendency of mine to try not only my readers' but also my listeners' patience with this backwards or sideways looping narrative style I seem to have. I have always put it down to my reading of Thomas Mann's work as a student, not, I confess, always in the original German. His sentences at times almost fill whole pages. (Henry James's later prose has a similarly convoluted and labyrinthian style.) I have come to see it, however, not so much as a stylistic fault as a valid, if somewhat idiosyncratic, device, the use of which I have felt all the more relaxed about since a discussion with my well-read and intellectual friend Sally, a university lecturer in the Canary Islands, whose opinion I respect greatly. We were strolling along the tree-lined Ramblas Avenue in Santa

Cruz de Tenerife, where we both lived at the time. It was a hot Sunday afternoon and we were talking about life and loves and everything else under the sun. We got round to discussing books and language and to my surprise Sally confessed that she, too, found herself indulging in 'the loop' as I shall call it, that it was supposed to be a common trait of eccentrics, something neither of us minded being branded as in the least. Why then should it worry me that young Zamzam is starting to develop this same style in her English writing? Perhaps it is because reading such prose tends to require a higher degree of concentration and a certain amount of tolerance, and when grammar errors crop up, as they inevitably do in the writing of non-native speakers, they jar all the more and the EFL teacher reaches wearily for the red pen.

Anyway, the reason for this warm glow of well-being, as you may have guessed, was an unexpected and much longed-for pay rise from our Emirati employers. All of a sudden that rather extravagant trip to Thailand this summer I've been toying with the idea of seems the only really sensible thing to do – nowhere on this earth to date, after all, has the same calming yet energising effect on me as my beloved Siam with its serene temples, incomparable food, and childlike people. Arriving that first time from India with my partner Rick, in the early eighties (how we wished it had been the roaring forties or even earlier before the internal combustion engine had taken hold), it was like arriving in paradise, with its gilded, glistening temple roofs, the gentle acceptance of visitors in its holiest places, its abundance of good things at ground level for everyone – edible delights of every shape and hue, strange fruits and vegetables, plump live fish in buckets beside smiling vendors, skewered seafood and baby bananas smoking on tiny roadside braziers, barrow loads of vivid purple orchids, peculiar sights, sounds and smells everywhere, a real onslaught to the senses but a welcome onslaught, manna for the soul. In comparison, for me, this land is a barren and dismal place; the mosques are mainly for the male members of society and their doors are certainly not open to non-Muslims in search of solace; middle-aged Emiratis cruise by in air-conditioned vehicles with their sinister tinted windows, assuming unaccompanied fair-skinned women to be East European sex workers out touting for business; small children in lifts turn away from Westerners in distress or dissolve into tears of terror, while stout women past childbearing age trudge dolefully along the dusty streets draped in dreadful black heat-absorbing garments, whilst the men wear crisp sun-reflecting white. Oman is only just a stone's throw away and shares both the religion and many of the customs of the UAE, yet the atmosphere is so very different and so much healthier. It's not surprising that many a teacher ends up opting for a vastly reduced salary and a far humbler abode there for the sake of living in a land where there's colour and audible laughter, where infants reflect a smile from a stranger and children marvel at rather than fear sights and sounds that are unfamiliar.

Still, the imminent pay rise makes all these things seem at least bearable for the time being, and the batch of paperbacks and videos I picked out at the college jumble sale in aid of the tsunami victims yesterday – now colourfully displayed on the IKEA ironing board and the floor beneath – will hopefully transport me to other shores in the mind's eye and as the loudspeaker starts broadcasting the local *muezzin*'s call to prayer (I referred to the chanting in class as singing the other day… 'It's not *singing*!' one of my smugly devout, *niqab*-sporting girls informed me with a derisive curl of the lip – I'm fairly sure the sneer was there, though, of course, only her eyes were visible). I shall blot the sound out with some music of my own. Now, what shall it be? Perhaps I'll play that Bangkok bootleg CD of the maturing Spanish crooner Julio Iglesias. I don't think I've heard his voice since slaving away as a waitress at *Le Bistro* on the roasting Red Sea coast all those years ago. Surprisingly, it still sounds pretty good.

Chapter 2

Compensations of Gulag Life

That sinking Sunday feeling has been creeping up on me all day long, deftly removing some of the sparkle from the sun's rays - only here in the UAE it's that Friday feeling, the national weekend currently being Thursday and Friday. There are several hours left, in fact, before bedtime and, having polished off Carrie Fisher's *Postcards from the Edge* this morning over breakfast, and seen the protagonist, Suzanne, finally claw herself back from the edge and onto firmish ground, there's the starting of a new book to anticipate – Fay Weldon's *Wicked Women* perhaps, Ronald Wright's *Time Among the Maya*, Hunter S Thompson's *Curse of Lono*? (Poor Hunter, he recently put an end to it all with a bullet. I don't think he'd have tolerated my wishy-washy, liberal politics, but I have admired him hugely since an eccentric, young French-Canadian called Jean gave me his dog-eared copy of *Fear and Loathing in Las Vegas* when we were on the road in Israel in the late seventies, assuring me he was one of the best writers of all time – along with Nietzsche of course, he added – and he may well have been right.) Other potential reading matter beckoning from the bedroom bookshelves are De Bono's *Children Solve Problems*, John Updike's *Golf Dreams* and a Steinbeck I have somehow never got round to reading, *The Wayward Bus*. There are probably a hundred or more other choice publications on shelves around the flat to choose from… so much delicious literature to look forward to. I sometimes wish we had a whole lifetime to just read, another to travel, another to study, one to have children and so on, but each moment now is tinged with regret at the fast-fading light and with it the approach of the working week.

It's not that I hate my job; in fact, there are aspects of it that really suit me quite well. Take the physical environment, for example. The campus itself, and actually the whole complex of tertiary colleges here in Sharjah, known as University City, is astonishingly beautiful. It's nothing short of a wondrous blooming of the desert, a pleasingly symmetrical arrangement of buildings, boldly Moorish in design, bordered on all sides by neat rows of vibrantly coloured flowers and shrubs, trees in blossom, and majestic fruit-laden date palms. Our workstations in the health science department, where I have mostly worked since my arrival, are set up rather like little mouse houses; each cubicle is surrounded by three high partitions and contains shelving, lockable cabinets and drawers, along with our own PC and telephone with unlimited internet use and free national landline calls. All that's missing really is a roof with a chimney and a little painted door. I've covered the walls of my mouse house with the most heavenly pictures (deluxe, glossy postcards, mostly, that I've collected expressly for this purpose in my travel breaks). There are sumptuous tropical fruits, breathtakingly beautiful landscapes, magnificent predatory animals – wild cats predominating – outrageously flamboyant sunflowers, spectacular waterfalls, lush primordial jungles, gorgeous Greek donkeys, and beaming African children. No space at this workstation for boring old bumf – The Higher Diploma Level 4 Course Matrix, System Achievement Indicators, ICDL Training Schedule, and Testing Times. No one really looks at charts and documentation on office walls anyway; they're only ever put there to make the place look more serious and academic. What I need is colour and exotic scenes to lift me high above the mundane and provoke flights of fantasy.

Like my colleague Jay B, whom I first met at the Emirati Embassy in London for our video conferencing job interviews, a fellow Sagittarian and kind lender of remarkable talking books that have transformed my tedious daily commutes to and from work into veritable adventures – macabre, voyeuristic journeys into other realms and eras. Jay has similar tendencies with regard to workstation decor and outdid the whole college one year with an impressive array of hothouse plants, the year we resided in the brand-new circular building, on the floor above the state-of-the-art library (or ILC as it is called – Independent Learning Centre – why give something a *simple* name when it could be given a fancy-sounding acronym?). It was to this workstation that Farid, our affable Palestinian dictator, once paid a surprise afternoon visit during the Muslim holy month of Ramadan, when all devout Mohammedans fast from dawn until dusk, and caught the bold Jay B tucking into a large bar of Nestlé's chocolate. (We non-Muslims are allowed to eat at work during the day in Ramadan, but only in designated rooms, where we can't be observed by Muslim students and staff.) It's a wonder she wasn't given her marching orders on the spot. I suspect by the time of this incident, Jay B had proven her worth at the college with her superior organisational skills and level-headed professionalism in times of academic crisis, which in our college were not that infrequent.

This preoccupation with colour since starting work here, some might say, is verging on the obsessive. I sometimes think of a character in Toni Morrison's outstanding, Pulitzer Prize-winning novel, *Beloved*. Baby Suggs, an aging emancipated slave living in Cincinnati, develops a similar obsession with colours on her deathbed and goes through phases where she only sees and deals with one particular colour at a time. I prefer to mix my colours, but like her I need them, perhaps to counteract all the black we are surrounded by here in the women's college with our students' deathly dark, head-to-toe polyester garments. Thankfully, I have at least a modicum of freedom in this job to bring some colour into my classroom. No expense is spared when I create my student worksheets; thanks to our state-of-the-art photocopiers, they end up liberally sprinkled with colourful images, headings appear in varying shades – cerulean, citrine, cerise – while boxes and circles are similarly shaded in until the desired effect is achieved. If ever I am found in my mouse house after hours or way before classes begin, the chances are I will be playing around, not only with words but with colour combinations, seeking out tantalising images to complement the nitty-gritty grammar point or key vocabulary that constitute the teaching points of the day.

As for actual lesson content, there seems to be a growing reluctance at this college to allow teachers any real choice about what and how they teach. Then, of course, there are always the fundamental Islamic or 'fundie' types to contend with – students, that is, who seem to be against colour, humour and fun in principle. For these, to my mind, unfortunate types, music, cinema, and art, in general, aren't considered suitable pursuits for decent, Allah-fearing beings. However carefully the set texts and accompanying videos are chosen, when the time comes to bring a scene to life on the TV screen there are those who rise instantly to their feet and troop silently to the door, the same ones no doubt who put '*strongly disagree*' for each of the forty-odd items on the biannual surveys, conducted to obtain student views of teaching staff, diminishing our popularity ratings significantly and making us feel – on off days at least – that we should probably pack it all in and do something we're better at or better appreciated for. It's not really the girls that I hold responsible, it's the elements in society that attempt to brainwash them. We're not quite at the point yet where we have cameras in classrooms trained on teachers to ensure that we use the correct hand signal for each type of grammatical error made (such schools do exist, I have been assured) but we seem to be moving in that direction. As an antidote to disturbing thoughts of Big Brother watching us, I shall endeavour to focus on the *good* things around me and stop beating myself up about why one student felt I didn't *respect* her, and about *which* two of my girls had insisted that I hadn't given them enough graph practice when they know quite well that I run a democratic classroom and that it's the class who decide how we divide our time when preparing for exams. So, keep your pecker up, *don't* let the bastards grind you down and all that. In the overall scheme of things, such details are of little consequence – as my dear Croatian friend, Dunia, who works in our library, always says – focus on the *positive*!

I've just made a quick trip to see what's going on in the kitchen and found a fine-looking spicy bean and herb casserole bubbling away on the cooker beside a new and interesting-looking bottle of Umbrian drizzling oil – well, that's something else to look forward to. As my old pal Neil once said, somewhere around my 40th birthday when I went to visit him in Hamburg – 'you've always got to have something to look forward to in life'. I was going through a bit of a rough patch at the time and he was trying to bolster me up. He reported something his grandmother had once told him at a moment of crisis in his own life. She had said that 'God never gives us a heavier burden than we are capable of carrying'. Well, perhaps, as my brother Richard would say, he *might*, but there is always a spiritual lesson to be learned from it – our suffering is never in vain.

I also spied, on the draining board, some particularly fine-looking deep green rocket – it's one of the biggest bargains in this part of the world and, if you pick your time, you can get huge bundles of fresh, giant, crunchy leaves for a single dirham – currently around 16p – so naturally, being big fans, we eat masses of it. The Indian guys in the shops around here call it *gigir* – with the emphasis on the second syllable. Until recently I had wondered why my careful articulation of the word, with the correct emphasis, provoked a certain restrained hilarity amongst them. It seemed to be more somehow than simple amusement at a foreigner attempting to pronounce a word in their dialect. I had been working late the other day and had stopped off to pick up a few things from Spinneys on the way home. Spinneys is our preferred local supermarket; we like it because there is a far wider variety of imported European goods than any other supermarket in town, and, to our glee, these include an increasing number of items from our old favourite back home, Waitrose. Added to this, the staff are generally very friendly and courteous and actually understand the concept of customer service, if not the somewhat outdated idea that 'the customer is always right'. Anyway, I made my way over to the fruit and vegetable section, requesting our usual two bunches of *gigir*. I was served by a rather thickset, imposing-looking male assistant from Kerala, who tends to be on the surly side, particularly in the evenings, by which time no doubt his feet are giving him gyp. He looked at me for a moment, then decided to finally put me in the picture with regard to *gigir*. He informed me, in a soft confidential tone, that *gigir* was the stuff to 'make men *strong*' and in a flash, I understood that the twinkle that had been noticed in my eye each time I bought a bundle or two had been taken for a merry twinkle of anticipation of the effects of this magic herb on my husband. I laughed, along with several other Indian co-workers, who had suddenly materialised to listen in to our exchange, and probably blushed in mild embarrassment. Still, if it caused them all a moment or two of levity in their hard, loveless current lives, all the better. So many of these sub-continental guest workers, we must remember, leave wives and families behind to come and work here for meagre salaries, only returning once a year if they're lucky, every two years more commonly. There, but for the grace of God, go we.

To the amusement of our good friends and neighbours, Jean and David, much of our food, on being served, finds itself nestling on a little bed of rocket – toasted goat's cheese with browned pine nuts, for example, char-grilled squid with chilli and coriander or strips of lightly cooked fillet steak marinated in Thai spices. We don't eat food like this every day, but it doesn't take much excuse to do so. I should be careful, though; I have a terrible reputation in my family for filling my postcards home with food references. It seems to me to be such a natural thing to do, describing a superlative meal, just as you might describe a gem of a painting, a striking sculpture or an awe-inspiring panorama; I don't see the difference and I forget that for many people food isn't so much a source of wonder and pleasure as a necessity of life, fuel for the works, rather a nuisance even. My mother is a fabulous cook, though she'd modestly laugh and pass this off as nonsense; she might cook a truly splendid hot pot or cottage pie with vegetables straight from the garden, cooked to a tee, and my stepfather, being a food-is-fuel type, on enquiry, would state, with mild puzzlement as to why the question was being asked in the first place, that the food was 'fine' – never marvellous or delicious, but 'fine', which to my ear sounds as though there's nothing *wrong* with it, there are no foreign bodies, no burnt or slimy bits. It seems so rude, though I'm quite sure he doesn't mean to be. I taught my favourite class of young ones the term 'foreign bodies' the other day. I expect they'll misuse or overuse it, but still. I didn't tell them this, but I can never hear the expression without thinking of poor Jamal.

When we first arrived in the UAE, before we bought vehicles of our own, my new bosom friend Maria and I used to share a taxi home after work with a Lebanese colleague, Jamal, who also had a flat in Kalooti Towers. We were rather envious of him as his flat overlooked the lagoon, although the windows had an odd horizontal bar that ran right across the room and ruined the view when you were seated. As Maria and I had arrived last of all the newbies, we'd ended up with what we considered rather a raw deal. Our flats were on the lower floors overlooking a building site, where poor Indian construction workers lived in desperately cramped conditions in tiny makeshift huts. Seeing them emerge from their substandard, sweaty quarters each morning, stretching, coughing and performing their ablutions in full view of the flats around, we later counted our blessings and felt vaguely ashamed at having complained about our accommodation.

We had heard that Jamal, a small, short-sighted, endearingly earnest bachelor of indeterminate age, was having a spot of trouble with his supervisor, but we didn't realise just how serious it had got. On that particular afternoon, we had been waiting a good fifteen minutes or so for Jamal in the car park outside our college building in our taxi driver Moydeen's old Toyota Corolla (an inferior model, mostly used for taxi transport in developing countries). Like most taxis in the UAE, this one smelled faintly of curry and sweat, an odour the vanilla air freshener, dangling above the dashboard along with some bits of religious paraphernalia, did little to dispel. Our car, however, had the uncommon advantage of containing functioning seat belts, a much-appreciated addition when being driven at high speed on these treacherous Emirati roads. In the end, I trudged back into the college and approached his workstation, finding there not *our* Jamal, but the other Lebanese doctor of the same name. 'Is Jamal still here?' I politely enquired. 'Do you mean *Doctor* Jamal?' the podgy pompous man responded with an unpleasant humourless smile, and at my bemused affirmation, was told coldly that he was with Tim Smith, our Director of Studies. I returned to the car and reported back to the others. Things didn't sound good. Time dragged on and finally 'our Jamal' came plodding out to the car, our similarly proportioned boss, Tim Smith himself, following close behind him, bearing – a little comically if the situation hadn't been so charged with emotion – a heavy-looking cardboard box of assorted books, files and office equipment, the entire contents in fact of our poor colleague's workstation. This turned out to be the first of a spate of ruthless sackings, all of which we were assured were '*highly regrettable but totally unavoidable*' and in 'everyone's best interests' – the regime of terror had begun and, though we joked about it, it was hard to dispel the feeling that at any moment you too would get that tap on the shoulder, the call to the director's office and you would be handed your ticket home, wherever that might be, and given so much time to get out of the country.

It was particularly sad in Jamal's case, we felt, as he seemed to be such a dedicated teacher, and, though we hardly knew him well, a decent enough and kind individual. It was the beginning of Ramadan and there was a hushed atmosphere of reverence and purity in the college that is hard to define. It might perhaps be compared to Christmas from the point of view of boisterous young children being told that Santa Claus is on his way, his sleigh laden with glittering gifts of every description, but will only visit well-behaved and deserving souls. This, if I got it right, was Jamal's first job since he'd gained his doctorate, and his parents had made the journey to Sharjah from Lebanon expressly to join their only son, of whom they were evidently extremely proud, for this very special time in the Islamic calendar. A few days earlier, Maria and I had felt quite honoured to have been invited to join Jamal's family for the Iftar meal, the breaking of the day-long fast at sundown, when all manner of special dishes are brought out and there is an atmosphere of anticipation, deep respect and thankfulness to Allah for his blessings. There's also an awareness of the sufferings of the poor, who receive food and donations at this time. It's the same throughout the Muslim world. Unfortunately, that fateful night Maria had a streaming cold, so her dinner was carried down to her on a tray. I did my best to be cheery and conversational, but the fact was that we were in the midst of a family catastrophe and everyone reacted in their own way. The father, a trim, snowy-haired dapper gentleman of advancing years, who spoke virtually no English but fortunately knew a little French, did his best to entertain this stranger in their midst, while the mother, anxious, plump and motherly, fought back tears, not always successfully, and kept declaring that Allah, who knew all, would make things right in the end, that He knew her son had done no wrong, while Jamal himself offered his guest dish after dish, carefully listing their ingredients, explaining how they were made; he retained his composure, but was evidently grappling desperately with the situation and seeing the whole direction of his life changing before him in a way he had no control over.

What, you may ask, had the poor man possibly done to bring about such a harsh decision? Probably, we suspected, not a lot. He had simply got on the wrong side of a supervisor – foolish, but easily done – had got a bit steamed up, and, unforgivably at SWC, had let it be known. Next thing he knew he had been summoned to the director Farid's office to answer for himself. Jamal had not held back; he had articulated his grievances in full, surprisingly quite unaware that he was in the presence of a cold, calculating, fiercely ambitious despot. He ended in a flourish: 'And what is *more*, there are woggits in the food in our cafeteria, yes, there are *woggits!* I found one in my food last week and *so* did Carrie Evans! Woggits! It's disgusting!' He had meant maggots. I had told Jamal a few days earlier that I thought I'd seen a maggot in my white rice one lunchtime. Unfortunately, I had been unable to prove it as the Indian lady who then managed the cafeteria, a scrawny, aggressive and humourless individual, after listening to me impatiently, her left eye twitching disconcertingly, had picked the offending object off my plate and squashed it between her thumb and forefinger, declaring that it was 'Rice, madam, just *rice!*' The matter was closed.

Wednesday 20 April 2005

Earlier today I was gazing at the African animal calendar on the wall of our kitchen when I realised we had not written in the date of our wedding anniversary. We've only been married five years and yet have both forgotten the date, not realising until days after the event, more than once. It was only because one of my classes reminded me last year that we were able to salute the occasion at all. I'm fairly hopeless about dates in general, and would be hard-pressed to tell you what year I left home, when I graduated and when the birthdays of my immediate family members are. Fortunately, Simon has hit upon a rather fine way to remember the date of our highly impromptu and altogether very successful wedding reception on the terrace overlooking the creek at Dubai Creek Golf and Yacht Club – 'the social event of the year' our Irish friend, the lovable libertine Gerry Griffin, assured us. All we have to do, Simon explained, is to look out for four-wheel-drive vehicles and sooner or later one will come along with the date in question written clearly on the side for all to see. If you inspect the side of a Nissan Patrol, one of the pricier yet more popular of the various four-wheel drives dominating the roads in the UAE, you will see written its cubic capacity – 4500cc. We were married on 4/5/2000.

Thursday 5/5/5

What a satisfyingly rounded date that is – almost devilish! The day has been quite satisfying in its way too. I started by completing Anne Mustoe's account of her 12,000-mile bike ride around the world – well, 11,500-mile really, but someone took the liberty of rounding it up to 12,000 on the cover. It's not that the slight inaccuracy bothered me, it's just that I felt it a little odd that the admirable cycling lady author herself should have approved it, after learning about her heroic refusal on a number of occasions to lessen her physical suffering and 'cheat' in any way; by accepting a ride from a friendly truck driver, for example, on a particularly nasty and treacherous stretch of road, or by taking a train across a difficult and dangerous bit of desert terrain. It was a terrific feat and I am filled with admiration – she was three years older than me (she was fifty-five) and, by her own calculations, rather overweight at the outset of her journey. It took her 439 days and cost around £6,000 – that was in the early nineties. I told Simon of her safe arrival home over breakfast this morning and we toyed with the idea of following in her wheel tracks when we finish up here, but after completing his much-loathed weekly chores – sweeping and mopping half the flat, including the main balcony, while I tackled the other half including the bathrooms – he quickly made it clear that he was really joking, whereas I had taken the suggestion in deadly earnest and had even composed a polite note to Ms Mustoe in my head requesting precise route details.

One of the things that struck me as a little strange, reading her book, was that the one place she had felt lonely and a complete outsider had been in Thailand, the place where I felt at home right from the start and always have done on the countless occasions I've returned. That was another satisfying thing about the day – I booked my flight to Bangkok, two days after I finish working here for the academic year. So now I know I shall be dipping my toes into the cool, clear water of the River Kwai, tasting spicy squid on a stick and *tom yam gung* (spicy prawn) soup, having foot massages and early morning boat rides up the *klongs* (navigable waterways), and experiencing moments of peace and serenity in my favourite temples – my reward after a long, hard year at the chalkface.

Oh, we all dream about not having to work, of getting out of 'the system' and away from this conventional, materialistic, xenophobic society we live in, but the strange fact is that some of the greatest pleasure for me these days comes from things that happen at or are related to work. One of the things I can't bear at this time of year is the inevitable marking of dozen upon dozen of graph descriptions, many of them mangled and convoluted to such a degree that I sometimes have to exercise extreme restraint not to fling them out of the window. It was with something akin to joy last night when I marked the efforts of my current favourite class of seven and found that six of their graph descriptions were actually half decent and, of those six, two were positively polished – and written under exam conditions. It did my heart good, especially as we'd whisked through the basics of graph descriptions in record time and I had been rather dreading the results of the latest round of mock exams. Teachers have been known to be hauled up before our premier for a thorough dressing down and to answer for themselves after their students have received poor exam results.

'It's a well-known fact that we all need three males a day, and the first one should be the largest' (from a student essay on nutrition), 'the girls loved the piano recital and gave the pianist a standing ovulation' (from a student essay on music), 'downstairs in our house are the kitchen and the *majlis*, and upstairs there are sex bedrooms' (student essay describing her home). This is the kind of startling student error that brightens up the dreariest pile of exam essays and makes a mind-numbingly boring marking bee bearable, if not, at moments, positively enjoyable. I am compiling a list of such errors which I keep on my PC desktop, but often you have to read them in context and bear in mind the hours of drudgery one has endured before coming across such gems to get the full effect.

I let on to the class of seven the other day that I was writing a memoir about my career as an English teacher, including my experiences teaching in the UAE, and they all promised they would buy the book the moment it came out, particularly if they knew that they would be in it. I told them that I couldn't promise anything, but the fact is they're as lovely a class as you could hope to teach anywhere and each one quite a character in their own right. I sometimes tell the students their wishes are my command and, in this case, I see no reason not to indulge them, though everyone knows the risks of being immortalised in print – you may or may not like what you read and once the words have been committed to print, that's it, there's no going back.

Well, here we go – I think I have to begin with Noura, a colourful, cheerful, generously proportioned young lady, not a classical beauty, yet always neat and tidy and immaculately made-up. She tends to race through anything she has to say as though there were a giant stopwatch ticking away at the front of the class and a significant penalty for hesitation of any description. She is quick to laugh at herself, however, and there's no doubt that she possesses humility and respects age and experience. I see her going far in the world of work, taking on extra responsibility without batting an eyelid and coping admirably, juggling family and career with aplomb when the time comes. Next, comes

Maryam, now mother of two, yet as delicate-looking and diminutive as Noura is robust. She has a stern streak, however, and a capacity for defiance if she suspects unfairness of any sort, a trait that makes one watch one's p's and q's. It was Maryam who informed everyone recently, leaving us to draw our own conclusions, that the devil had a really soft spot for music and dancing and offered to back this up with quotes from the Koran if we doubted her word – which we didn't. Despite her earnestness and serious approach to life, she enjoys a joke and will become quite bashful and coy when teased, which she too handles well, as she instinctively knows that laughter is an essential ingredient in life and especially in a language class, where one is so often required to take risks and reveal far more than one does in life science or haematology lessons, for example. With her strong sense of justice and love of a good debate, I could see Maryam as a trade union leader, had she been born in the West, or a lawyer, perhaps, fighting for female rights. As it is, she'll run a tight ship as a health information manager and woe betide you if you break the code of confidentiality or misclassify your documents! Her children, I feel sure, will be polite and well behaved and will know their Koran well. Zamzam has already been mentioned in my musings for the phenomenal length of some of her sentences, which she is now trying valiantly to rein in, with varying degrees of success. Her writing, however, continues to be well above average for a student at her level and a source of joy to her teachers. Quiet, bright-eyed, a little intense and an absolute sponge when it comes to information, Zamzam never misses a thing – each grammar tip or choice new item of vocabulary is instantly recorded and highlighted and – wonder of wonders – put into practice, usually correctly, in each subsequent piece of writing assigned. She has positively blossomed before my very eyes in English and to see her confidence in her own abilities grow accordingly is a reward in itself – it's most 'gratifying' as our colleague Duncan would say. The name Zamzam, I learn, means 'source of water in a parched and arid land' – a befitting name for a true flower of the desert. Zamzam will not necessarily go for high-profile positions in the workplace, but if she does, her modesty will provoke admiration rather than envy. One can be sure that whatever she does she will do it to the best of her ability; she will go beyond the call of duty and be an asset to whatever institution she happens to work in. Khawla is a deep one, one of life's thinkers, and a gentle, humble soul. The smoky black kohl eye-liner has become more pronounced as the year has progressed, but the dramatic look belies her retiring nature. The complexities of English grammar and spelling try her patience to the limits, but she rarely lets it show and for the most part works stoically, only admitting to domestic troubles when questioned (her family's maid ran off, giving no notice, making life very hard for everyone for several weeks), yet, as always, Khawla is impeccably mannered and quick to smile. We will miss her next year, as she's moving to Abu Dhabi, but perhaps we'll be lucky enough to get the odd letter...

Thursday 26 May 2005

Another week has passed – though Simon assures me there is no such thing as time. He's just been reading Julian Barbour's book *The End of Time*. The shocking pink neon lights outside catch my eye tonight and make me think of that expensive Jaeger suit in the Wafi Centre I was momentarily tempted by earlier today (I settled for a jar of Marks and Spencer's blueberry preserve instead). Strains of music reach me from the other end of the flat – 'She Bangs the Drum' from the Stone Roses' first album – about as good as it gets, I reckon musically, truly sublime. It's hard not to get up and pogo or waft around barefoot on the soft, rust-hued rug in my bedroom, or better still the large and magnificent Afghan one we just bought that now graces our lounge. I have recently come to think of it as the beetley carpet, as young cockroaches tend to come out these days just after we've eaten, lured from their cramped beetle holes out onto the soft, tightly woven threads of our carpet by the enticing aromas of lemon pepper chicken kebabs or Anthony Tobin's Saucy Kidneys from the *Ready Steady Cook* book that Maria gave me for my birthday. You don't notice them at first, as the intricate patterns of the black, tan, and dark spicey orange carpet provide the perfect camouflage for the little critters. But let your gaze rest at floor level for a few seconds and you will see movement. We must call Moideen, our ever-vigilant and vaguely menacing building caretaker, to do some fumigating whilst we are out at work.

But I digress. The time has come to give my attention to the other half of the class of seven. I think the two Ayeshas come next. Ayesha Mohammed would have been a natural 'flower child' had she lived in the sixties in San Francisco or Amsterdam. She radiates love and peace and sunshine, favouring floral handbags, shoes and *shaylas*, a tad scatty and not the world's greatest time-keeper, but a diligent student all the same and a cheerful stoical soul, especially when one considers that Ayesha struggles with asthma and has had an amazing run of family misfortune this semester. Ayesha Salim is a very different kettle of fish – a real Asian beauty, though I doubt she realises it. She has the most remarkable silky-smooth complexion and dusky colouring, which she likens to chocolate and jokingly relates to the amount of the substance she consumes (a common class trait). Her natural expression, in the English class at least, is one of slightly anxious earnestness; she has grounds for anxiety as the language does not come naturally to her, but she works closely with the studious and introverted Hind and the liaison seems to be mutually beneficial. Hind is another one who would have fitted in well with the flower children of Haight-Ashbury. She would have appreciated the ideology of the bohemians and tripped blissfully and tranquilly through the 'Summer of Love'; she has an other-worldly quality about her and writes the most incredible poetry – it was no surprise that she won the Mosaic poetry competition with her poem 'Environmental Inspiration', but she has to guard against the temptation to withdraw totally from the crude outer world when it doesn't live up to her expectations. Sometimes, when things seem irrelevant and burdensome and mysterious pains take over her earthly body, she just collapses onto the table before her and when people try to bring her back from wherever she's roaming in her mind she lifts heavy pearly eyelids and blinks long dew-studded eyelashes, bemused by and disinterested in the affairs of mere mortals. I think the only hope for Hind in this hidebound society is to marry an unconventional and equally spaced-out arty-type, a graphic designer or musician perhaps, who appreciates the finer things in life, understands the complexity of human emotions, tolerates ambiguity and eccentricity, but can nevertheless afford the little luxuries that distract one from the harsh realities of desert existence and allow for a time-out from intolerable routine. I hope she finds him.

Chapter 3

Antics, Attachments and Antipathy at Primary School

Owing to my father's peripatetic lifestyle throughout my childhood, a lifestyle in which he cruised from job to job with apparent ease and enjoyment, selling family homes and overseeing the packing and unpacking of our belongings from copious tea chests each time, I attended a series of primary schools in Liverpool, London, and the Midlands, each with its own peculiar odour, character, culture and set of memories. All I really remember from my first school in Prescot, Lancashire, was eating custard cream biscuits and drinking from little glass bottles of milk through a straw at breaktime, sitting at tiny, brightly coloured tables, and cutting out shapes with special children's scissors, sticking them onto larger squares of paper that ended up decorating the classroom walls. We had to go out into the schoolyard to get the milk from the crates, and in winter the cream would form a thick layer of about an inch and a half on top, which tasted delicious but was really best for breakfast on top of Weetabix with sugar. The teachers were kind and I suffered no trauma in my first school.

My next school, in Kew, south-west London, was more forbidding – St Luke's was a sooty, old Victorian building on a busy main road, with a cramped playground surrounded by high, red-brick walls and from which several steps led up into an ill-lit vestibule and cloakroom. The cloakroom always smelled of damp clothes and disinfectant and long, dark, high-ceilinged corridors led off from it. Perhaps the school's budget only allowed for forty-watt light bulbs, or perhaps the lack of natural light just gave the place an air of gloom and confinement. In any case, it was not a place I hurried to in the morning – I invariably dawdled, scraping the toes of my Clarks' brown lace-ups along the uneven pavements, kicking up piles of crackly leaves or stopping to pick crab apples in autumn, interrupting my journey in spring to scoop up cherry blossom from the pavement, talk to dogs or sniff the newly creosoted wooden fences. I was often late for school and to my shame I confess that I was dreadful about arriving in time for lectures as a student too; even today I have a terrible job getting myself to meetings in time at work. There's no excuse for this, but it's not hard to see where it all began.

The one and only time in my life that I was spanked by my father, the issue was getting up for school – or to be more precise, not getting up for school. It was a particularly cold winter's morning and the flat my parents were temporarily renting was dismal, draughty, and poorly heated. I had made a dash from my own narrow bed to the luxurious warmth of my parents' double bed, apparently unnoticed by either of my parents, who were hurriedly getting dressed and probably assumed that I was doing the same. On spotting a lump beneath the bedcovers in their room, it was my father who gave the order for me to get up and get dressed 'quick sharp', but whether it was his vaguely threatening tone that awakened my innate streak of perversity or simply that the warm patch my father had vacated in the bed was just too good to forfeit so readily or a combination of the two, I will never know. The countdown came and with it the promised spanking, but I was by all accounts a bold and defiant child, and instead of then getting on with the beastly job of getting dressed, I am told, I put my hands on my hips, looked my father in the eye and told him *it hadn't hurt*. Not surprisingly, the second time it *did* hurt and I suppose in the end I did get dressed, no doubt stomping off to school in an even blacker funk than usual.

Once we had moved into our far nicer semi-detached house in Chelwood Gardens, with its French windows, its rowan, peach, and almond trees in the garden, the sundial, and the stone birdbath, I would quite often come to a halt in the alley less than halfway to school and arrive back at our front door, claiming that the fog was too thick to see where I was going (which it sometimes was) or with some feeble excuse about having a sore throat or a tummy ache. On one occasion I was late for school yet again and to avert the blame, I invented quite a detailed story about having been stopped by a 'strange man' in a car near the railway bridge, who had offered me sweets, which had the police round to our house in the evening and led to a very serious talk on my father's knee. I don't recall confessing to the fib, although I suppose I must have, as I remember the final conclusion reached between the stern uniformed copper and my parents was that it had all been 'a storm in a teacup', an expression I had not heard before that day and one which I found particularly bizarre and appealing. I don't suppose I really hated St Luke's, but I don't remember enjoying it much either. The strongest memory I have of that school is of the awful disappointment at not being allowed to play the triangle in the school orchestra – I don't actually think I was allowed to play any instrument at all, and I so much wanted to – perhaps it was a punishment for my repeated late-coming.

Tiring of his work in the City at the Fatstock Marketing Corporation, or possibly just tired of wearing an uncomfortable bowler hat and formal dark suit to work each day, my father moved to another management position, with Marsh and Baxter in the Midlands. Our lovely home with its delightful garden, where I had my very own flowerbed, in which I grew radishes and pansies, was sold. Another house was duly bought at the top of a long hill, opposite the very posh Mount Hotel with its imposing gates and extensive grounds, in a smallish town near Wolverhampton called Tettenhall Wood. Whilst waiting for the final exchange to take place, we lived – camped out rather – in a bleak and draughty cottage in the middle of the countryside that belonged to a business associate of my father. My younger brother Richard was then still in nappies, which to my mother's dismay would freeze on the line drying in the garden. Most of our toys and precious things were packed up in tea chests and it was so cold that winter that even a roaring coal fire in the evening failed to create a homely atmosphere and keep us warm. My brother caught a nasty bug of some sort that led to him being given a fearsome, never-to-be-forgotten injection in his bottom by an unsympathetic doctor called Dr Tweddle, who carried a sinister black bag, full, I was quite sure, of gruesome torture implements. The syringe was one of those cold shiny metal ones and it gave the poor toddler a nasty bruise that changed colour several times before it finally disappeared.

Although it was only for a few weeks, I was bundled off to school in the village of Kinver, where, rather oddly, games, painting, and creative activities of various sorts seemed to take precedence over basic arithmetic, reading and writing. One such activity involved creating a miniature garden out of a round biscuit tin, with real soil, tiny coloured paper flowers, and a handbag mirror for a pond. Enchanted to be allowed to play most of the day instead of actually doing any work, I threw myself into the task and ended up winning a prize for the best effort. A lot of smiling and singing went on at this little school and I'd happily have stayed on indefinitely if it hadn't been for the rather scary journey home, which involved taking a bus all on my own on dark winter afternoons. I once overshot my bus stop and had to walk back quite a distance beside tall hedges with occasional cars whooshing by inches away from me as there was no pavement. I don't think my mother was exceptional in allowing her five-year-old child such independence – today I suppose it would be called negligence, but then it was nothing out of the ordinary.

Our move to the exciting new centrally heated house on the hill in Tettenhall Wood was welcome, to say the least. The local primary school, conveniently, was just at the bottom of our road and it was really the only one I attended for any length of time about which I have a distinctly positive set of memories. It was a newer, better-lit building than the London school, with spacious classrooms and a recently fitted gym with ropes, which I became very adept at climbing, almost undoubtedly on account of the exceedingly pleasant sensation I found the action produced in the nether regions as I neared the top. The teacher was not unaware of my skill in this area and would sometimes ask me to demonstrate the floor-to-ceiling manoeuvre with the whole class looking solemnly on. In the schoolyard, there was a similarly appealing, multi-coloured climbing apparatus, which we were allowed to play on in the break unsupervised (and without the benefit of mats to cushion our falls). Another favourite was communal skipping, where two girls turned a long rope and you had to join in one by one until there were several of you all jumping in unison. It became a huge responsibility to get your timing right so as not to mess things up for the others. Oranges and Lemons was a popular game in those days too, the best bit being when the executioners started chanting menacingly as they anticipated their next victim. The former game required quite a bit of skill and the latter none at all, but both had an element of danger and excitement, as did taunting poor Mrs Bone, a wild and volatile middle-aged woman whose overgrown garden backed onto our playground. Such outrageous behaviour would never have happened had our schoolyard been supervised during breaks, as I'm sure most are these days. I have no recollection of any teacher ever being present during playtime – it was our domain; we made the rules and it was very much a case of survival of the fittest.

I suppose I must have been quite a popular, outgoing, little girl at that time, as I had a lot of friends at school, all quite different and distinct in character: to begin with there was Tina Bampfield, a young hedonist if ever there was one, with her house full of frills and lace and countless plump cats; and Susan Winder, an open, down-to-earth lass, whose family took holidays in Rhyl, North Wales, and whose household was as spartan as Tina's was chichi, but whose older sisters had a record player on which they played Acker Bilk's hit 'Stranger on the Shore' and, even more significantly, whose bare living room contained a television, long, long before our house did. It was my greatest dream at that time to have our own television, so I'd be able to join in the animated discussions about what had been on the next day at school. Then there was Jennifer, who, like Susan, lived in a council house and came from quite a large family. She resembled a pixie, with short, light brown, spitefully straight hair, green eyes, a smattering of freckles, and a devil-may-care attitude to life. But there was a dark side to Jennifer. She appeared to have a strange, secret, masochistic streak and would regularly whisper to me in the playground about having been held down and beaten by her father. I don't think there could have been very much truth in these stories, as Jennifer appeared to be quite a happy child and I never remember seeing any evidence of these supposed beatings, but she told me about the episodes in such a way as to make them sound exciting and quite delectable. I knew I hadn't enjoyed my own spanking that winter's morning back in Kew, but these earnest revelations made me think I should perhaps keep an open mind on the subject. We used to play a chasing game in the breaks with the boys, called *Kiss, Kick or Torture*, and unless I was caught by sweet-smelling Peter Jordan with his soft, downy cheeks, or man about town, Mervyn, with his cheeky grin and shiny blue-black hair, I'd choose torture and remember the brief thrill of pain as my boy captor screwed up his face and put all his strength into giving a really punishing Chinese burn.

My 'best friend' though was Sally Anne Lowe, a minx like me, who had tufty short auburn hair and mesmerising, hazel, almond-shaped eyes. Her parents, a quiet, corpulent, affectionate couple, were quite a bit older than mine and had had a rather imposing house built for themselves on a huge plot of land halfway down Compton Hill. I believe her father had done very well with some sort of scrap metal business and she had a brother and sister who were grown up and married, which to me at the time seemed quite bizarre. It was, however, Sally Anne's grandmother who inspired the most awe and envy in me as a child, as she had her very own sweet shop in a neighbouring Midland town. I couldn't think of anything I'd rather have had at that age than my own sweet shop. One of my best Christmas presents ever as a small child had been a toy sweet shop with tiny jars of real sweets, and my very earliest and happiest memories nearly all revolve around sweets in some way: Granny Jackson arriving from Hollingworth on the bus bearing Dolly Mixture and Red Lips in conical paper bags twisted at the top or pink and white sugar mice with little string tails, for which I used to build houses out of red and green triangular wooden bricks, my father helping us to make liquorice water by smashing black, brittle, coal-like lumps of the stuff into little pieces, which would be tipped into a bottle of water and shaken and shaken until they finally dissolved, producing the most delicious drink in the world. I also clearly remember standing on a chair at the counter of the wooden-floored sweet shop on the main road in Prescot, watching Liquorice Allsorts tumble from the glass jar and plop into the brass scales, and perhaps, if I was lucky, being handed a favourite aniseed one covered in tiny blue or pink balls by the shop girl, Annie, who also used to save me old *Robin* comics. Staying with Granny B (B for Baildon, the village where she lived in Yorkshire) and being given acid drops dusted with icing sugar from the round metal tin she always kept close at hand or staying at the Red House, where Mum grew up, hunting for chocolate Easter eggs in my other grandmother's large semi-wild garden. It was at the Red House that I would clamber up onto the wide marble worktop and go through the tins on the top shelf of Granny's larder, tasting all manner of interesting sweet things – glacé cherries, marzipan, large juicy Muscatel raisins with seeds in and, my favourite of all, green, diamond-shaped pieces of angelica. I was never caught at my thievery, but I doubt there would have been much fuss even if I had. My maternal grandmother, Laura, was kind, tolerant, and fun-loving and would no doubt have shown me a tin I had missed with something equally delicious in it to taste. Late one evening, years later when she lived with us in North Wales, she came across me and my pal Charlotte about to tuck into one of her famous iced coffee and walnut cakes in the pantry. 'Hello, girls, what are *you* up to?' she boomed (her faulty hearing-aid was often on the blink and on these occasions led her to speak unnaturally loudly). '*Do* have some of my coffee cake, won't you? You could take it upstairs in case you get hungry in the night.'

If ever I found myself in possession of money – copper pennies, halfpennies, even farthings – found at the back of the kitchen drawer, in the dusty gutter, or possibly given as a reward for performing some household task, it would instantly be converted into sweets. Black Jacks, which were a favourite and a bargain at four a penny, sherbet fountains with liquorice straws or, if I was feeling flush, a slab of crumbling pink and white coconut ice. In their tall glass jars beckoned sugary pear drops, pineapple chunks, aniseed twists, cough candy (anything medicinal tasting was particularly satisfying), chewing nuts, liquorice cuttings, Pontefract cakes – the choice could be overwhelming. My possibly inherited penchant for liquorice (made, I recently learned, from an extract taken from the Glycyrrhiza glabra plant) lasted well into adulthood. Friends who knew of my weakness, instead of discouraging me, would exacerbate matters. They'd return from summer holidays bearing gifts of liquorice, sometimes odd varieties from countries like Denmark, Sweden, or the Netherlands, salted, caramel or blueberry flavoured. Over the years, dentists profited greatly from this youthful liquorice addiction. It also got me into hot water with my mother the time the Prince of Wales, shortly after his investiture, came to Llandudno to speak about the preservation of the Welsh countryside. Charlotte and I, as usual, had managed to get ourselves a back seat in the pavilion on the pier, where the prince, then aged around twenty, was scheduled to give his talk. The venue was packed as all the schools in the area had been invited. At the end of the talk, Charles made a beeline for me and Charlotte, undoubtedly as my friend was the only girl of mixed race, apart from her older sisters, who may not have been present that day. My accomplice and I had been alleviating our boredom by eating a bag of mint-flavoured liquorice cuttings and imagining what outrageous things we'd say to Big Ears, as we called him, should we have the opportunity. Well, girls, the prince beamed down at us, what are *you* doing here this afternoon? We had to come here to listen to you, we replied, beaming back at him with hideous, stained black teeth. My mother was horrified when she heard the story later that day and I got a royal roasting.

Returning to my childhood friend Sally Anne and her granny's sweet shop, it was really all a terrible let-down and I never got to profit in any significant way from my connection with the favoured granddaughter. Once or twice a month Sally Anne was taken to visit the grandmother and was allowed to choose for herself a largish bag of assorted sweets, for which naturally she didn't have to pay a thing. I really don't think she could have made the best decisions in this wondrous and highly coveted position, as the drawer she reserved at home for her sweet supplies was a rather colourless and unappealing mess; I feel sure I would have done a lot better. As you may have guessed, it was the rather stale and sticky remains of the month's supplies that I was allowed to have whenever fresh stocks arrived from Granny Lowe's sweet shop. I couldn't help but feel a bit cheated, yet I never complained or even suggested that she let me try some of the fresher items, just as I never protested when turned out into the garden while Sally Anne had her weekly elocution lesson – I'm sure I would have preferred to stay in the playroom, which contained a mountain of toys that positively dwarfed us six-year-old girls, but again, I was not given the choice and meekly complied, sitting under the weeping willow tree making daisy chains, or riding my bike up and down the grassy lawns, swerving to avoid the mean-looking nettle beds that grew thickly at the lower end of the garden.

When we weren't exploring the neighbourhood on our bikes, we'd be building tree houses or dens of some sort in the garden, playing leapfrog with the boys, or satisfying our sadistic tendencies by playing Surgeons and Nurses using items from the cutlery drawer or my father's tool shed as operating implements, employing any small children or sometimes domestic animals we could find as patients. One of our naughtier experiments involved smoking a packet of ten Woodbine cigarettes, which we bought from the sweet shop down the hill from our house in Mount Road, assuring the shopkeeper that they were for my father. We took them furtively down to the bottom of our garden, where mid-operation we were spotted from a public footpath by a couple of elderly ladies out walking. We were terrified they would make their way to my front door and report us, so we escaped through the fence into Mrs England's large, immaculately kept garden next door and from there across the paddock, risking attracting the attention of various unfriendly horses and cattle, to the relative safely of the empty old house beyond. On another occasion, the day after quite a large party of some sort given at our house by my parents, Sally Anne and I decided to taste each of the drinks left in the bar in the little conservatory that overlooked the garden. I'm not sure how far afield my parents had gone, how long we spent at this tasting session, and what happened to Sally Anne at the end of it – I just remember coming round in my own bed and my father's concerned face peering down at me. I suppose I'd been found more or less unconscious beside the bar, and imagine my parents must have been so shocked to find us there and then relieved that we hadn't come to more harm, they didn't actually get angry about it. You'd have thought that drinks might have been kept under lock and key after that little incident, but they weren't, and I continued to help myself to a little taste now and again, though nothing on the scale of that summer's afternoon, and I don't suppose it did me too much harm.

One morning, soon after the passing out affair, I came down to breakfast to find my father sitting at the table looking rather subdued, with his leg in plaster. It was some years before I got to hear the real story of how this had come about. My parents had had guests round for dinner, and after the meal, a fair bit of drinking had taken place and my father had recounted how, in his youth, he had taken ballet lessons and had even considered a career on the stage. This was, of course, all complete fantasy.

In order to demonstrate his balletic skills, he had attempted to perform a *grand jeté*, surging across the room to build up momentum for his leap, then failing to judge the point at which he should slow down, and had gone crashing down the steps into the conservatory, breaking his Achilles tendon in the process. My father was in any case brewing up for another job change. He'd been managing a Marsh and Baxter's meat processing plant and used to tell us children with glee how the pigs would arrive at one end of the factory and all that went out at the other end, apart from all sorts of delicious pork products, were the poor pigs' trotters. He attended an interview in Liverpool, believing a change of air would do us all good. He was offered the job and accepted, but instead of moving to the Wirral, as we'd all expected, we found to our great surprise quite late in the day that we were to move to North Wales, as it turned out the job was managing an ice-cream factory in the coastal resort of Llandudno, fifty-odd miles west of Liverpool. My brother and I had mixed feelings about the move. We loved the house we lived in with its marvellously slippery parquet hall floor, the long sloping garden with its majestic old willow tree and swing, the shed at the bottom of the garden with its rich earthy aroma, where we hid things and had secret meetings after dark. Added to this was the thrill of catching sight from my parents' bedroom window of the dark and impossibly handsome next-door neighbours' son, Ian Fallon, playing with their adorable bouncy boxer, Candy, on their perfectly manicured lawn. The prospect of living by the sea, however, with unlimited ice cream all year round did go some way towards assuaging our sorrow.

It was only when the removal men started loading our furniture into their enormous van that it started to hit home what we were leaving behind. I'd been happy at school, and had several good friends, including a 'boyfriend', Peter Jordan, who claimed he loved me and treated me with great respect. We'd sit in his back garden after school and his mother would bring us large glasses of cold milk, which would give Peter an endearing little white moustache. I was presented with a small leather-bound address book as a leaving present with his address on Compton Hill written in such perfect handwriting, I can only think his mother must have spent a good ten minutes writing it for him. We wrote to each other regularly for a while and the following summer Peter and his parents came to Llandudno on holiday. Of course, we met up and walked to the end of the pier, trying to make conversation, but, sadly, the magic seemed to have gone and we both agreed that we should no longer 'wait for each other' – life had to go on.

Although my parents ended up buying a house in Conway, a little way above the town itself, on the rather beautiful Sychnant Pass, they were advised to send my brother and me to a primary school a few miles away in Llandudno Junction, as it was supposed to have a better academic record. My first day at Maelgwyn school was not a happy one. I was told to sit at an ancient wooden double desk at the front of the class next to a large, plump, rather remote boy called Dylan Williams, in Mr Lloyd-Williams' class. Lloydie, as he was known, was, I believe, a Welsh nationalist, who had no affection for the English and certainly made no effort to welcome a posh-sounding little English girl to his smallish class – perhaps he just thought I was one more kid to be prepared for exams, which meant more marking for him. Despite him knowing I didn't speak a word of Welsh (I don't think my parents had ever mentioned the fact that the Welsh had their own language; perhaps they hadn't even known themselves), I was still made that day to stand in front of the class with all the other girls to sing the Welsh national anthem, in a tongue that sounded very strange to me with all its nasal and guttural sounds. I was told I would have to learn Welsh, as there would be Welsh exams and that I had a lot of catching up to do. Several of my new classmates spoke quite good Welsh; some, I think, may even have spoken it at home, though the really Welsh children were sent to the Welsh school opposite, where all subjects were actually taught in Welsh. I think I found it all rather daunting, if not downright scary and, though I could have been imagining it, Lloydie seemed to take distinct pleasure in seeing my discomfiture. At break time that first day, I followed the other girls into the girls' yard, where they quickly ran off in twos and threes to form groups. The leader of the largest group was a sharp-looking, raven-haired girl with dark brown eyes and thin lips called Linda Robson. She clearly didn't want me in her gang and none of the other girls spoke to me or even approached me. What a contrast to my last school where boys and girls played more or less happily together and where I had not just one but several friends, both boys and girls, with whom I could joke, share confidences and have fun.

After a week or two, I formed an uneasy threesome with a freckled, red-haired girl called Marion and a neat, dark, well-behaved girl called Ellen. If these two were animals, Marion, with her wide, feline smile, would have been a tiger, while Ellen, with her calm, sedate manner, might have been a llama or possibly a doe. Three is never a good number for friends and things rarely went smoothly for our little trio either. One day Ellen went running to Lloydie in tears in the break and Marion and I were summoned to the classroom by Lloydie before the others returned. Not waiting to hear our side of things, our teacher turned on me, red in the face, and quite viciously shouted: 'These two girls were perfectly happy until *you* came along, Miss Evans! From now on, just leave them alone, will you!' What could I say? Nothing. I knew that whatever I said I wouldn't be believed. Some years later I was discussing Lloydie's class with another girl, who went on to share a class with me at the grammar school. She told me the most outlandish story about something she remembered me saying soon after my mid-term arrival. Apparently, I had told the class that in my old school if children were caught chewing gum in class they were made to 'wear' the gum on their noses for the rest of the day as a punishment. I find it very hard to believe that I said such a thing – there can't have been a grain of truth in it, but I'm equally sure that Rosie wouldn't have made it up. I can only think that I was desperate for some sort of attention in a world that had made it very clear that I didn't belong. There's a black and white class photo somewhere, taken soon after my arrival at Maelgwyn. Lloydie's warm-hearted, benign appearance in this photo belies his distinctly unkind treatment of me. I am standing right in front of him, my head inclined slightly to the side. My smile is an unnatural one (perhaps the nasty man was quietly pinching me in the side as we stood there posing) but at least I was trying to behave normally and even look happy – the effect is one of a gentle, slightly bewildered special needs child. I was only seven at the time.

Lloydie was not the only unpleasant member of staff at that school. The following year I had the misfortune to be in the prefab huts with the dreaded Dynamite for a form teacher. He might well have been related to Warbie, the Mephistophelian French master at the grammar school I was later to attend, as he was thin and wiry, always manically alert with unnaturally black hair and five o'clock stubble that steadily darkened as the day progressed. He was from Pwllheli, of Butlin's Holiday Camp fame, quite a drive away on the Llyn peninsula, and his subject was maths. He would give us regular mental arithmetic tests, for which we had to be pretty sharp with our times tables, which used to be printed on the back of all exercise books back then. We'd get almost-daily practice of the times tables, having to chant them rhythmically as Dynamite rapped out time with a bamboo switch on his desk. By this stage in our education, in the absence of calculators, it was expected that all twelve times tables be indelibly etched in our brains. I was fortunate in that my mother had taken the time, when we were living in the dark Kew flat, to help me practise my times tables and had taught me a very clever trick for remembering the difficult nine times table, which has stood me in good stead all my life. Luckily, I was quite good at arithmetic and used to do well in these tests, but that was not the case with poor Kenneth Scragg. He was an unfortunate-looking boy, to begin with, scrawny, ginger-haired, and freckled (freckles were not yet fashionable). He had a poorly repaired hare lip and a hunted, haunted look about him. No wonder. He was caned regularly in front of the class by this vile, sadistic teacher, who had a collection of weapons in an alcove behind his desk. I will never forget those canings – they were barbaric and dreadful to behold. From time to time, I wonder what became of Kenneth Scragg. I wonder if he went on to live a happy life, despite such rotten beginnings. I do so hope so. He was not the only one to suffer. Each day, my brother Richard, who was in Jam Pot's class in the adjoining classroom, was given the task of carrying a cup of tea into our class in the morning break. It was such an ordeal for him, as Dynamite could see the poor boy was very shy and nervous (it was a wonder the cup arrived with any tea in it at all as my brother's hand shook so badly while carrying it). Needless to say, Dynamite used to tease him without mercy until he blushed painfully and, his mission completed, hurriedly withdrew. I hated having to witness this daily charade, and would willingly have traded places with him.

These were our formative years and I was getting very mixed messages from my peers and teachers. It was obviously not always enough to do my best in class, to do my homework on time, sing in assembly without passing out, as some children entertainingly did, and generally try to be amusing and good company, as I had been brought up to do. I had the same sort of problems out of school. Along our bit of road on the mountain pass where we lived were a couple of families that had girls of around my age, but unfortunately yet again I became part of a threesome. This time my playmates were a mousy-haired, rather reserved individual called Valerie Walne and a slightly older girl, Pat Jellicoe, who was as sweet, gentle and warm as Val was otherwise. (My early impressions of Val turned out to be correct as, a few years later, when I was having some sort of a mini-breakdown during a storm in the North Sea on a school cruise, Val not only failed to come to my aide but went out of her way to avoid me. One doesn't easily forget such things.) When outings or special occasions were planned, I was not always included and was made to feel, by Val's parents at least, that there was something about me that was just not quite right or respectable. This was not exactly spelled out, but I was a sensitive child and quite definitely felt it. Val's parents were both scientists and ran a very tight ship at home. There was an allocated play room with minimal furniture and a nasty lino floor for children and a luxuriously carpeted and furnished private sitting room for adults next door, with a highly polished brass fireplace and a Lowry factory town print on the wall that I found downright sinister. In our big old rambling house, Overdale, a couple of doors down, there were no designated rooms for certain people – we children roamed about wherever we liked, and were even permitted to play records on the Decca stereogram in the lounge if we were extra careful. Mealtimes in the Walne household, Arfryn, were always at precise times and drinks were to be drunk by *kids*, as the Walnes called children (I used to loathe being called that), out of plastic cups, which tasted revoltingly of plastic. The fruit in the garden, of which there was an impressive abundance, was never to be picked without permission (which was almost never given). The only time I got to eat my fill of the fruit was when the Walnes were away on their annual camping holiday in France. At these times I was tasked with feeding the various small pets in their absence – rabbits, guinea pigs and mice, the last of which I later guessed were kept not as pets but for mutilating in Anne Walne's biology classes. On one occasion I took Charlotte round to Arfryn with me and to our delight we found the raspberry bushes behind the guinea pig run were simply laden with plump ripe berries. As a point of honour, we gorged ourselves until the bushes were practically bare and, in the process, became quite beside ourselves with hysteria. I suspect much of the fruit had fermented in the powerful August sun and the effect of eating it was not dissimilar to drinking a bottle of whisky each. Any fruit and vegetables that were not consumed fresh were expertly bottled by Anne Walne and her toxic mother Mrs Godwin – or Mrs Goblin as we called her – meticulously labelled and stored in the attic. There were enough provisions up there to keep the family going through years of siege.

The cheeky, confident, bold little girl was still somewhere there inside me and on more than one occasion I let slip something slightly outspoken, possibly daring even at the Walnes' house and the father Peter Walne was down on me like a ton of bricks. I remember once contradicting him about some trivial point of fact, whilst swinging nonchalantly on the bottom of the banister. His face transformed disconcertingly from an unhealthy greyish colour to livid crimson and he barked at me like a rabid rottweiler, leaving me too stunned to respond or even shed a tear. In retrospect, I realise it was probably my parents' laxer style of parenting and slightly hedonistic lifestyle the older Walnes disapproved of rather than me personally, but at that age it's not easy to be objective, analyse situations effectively and emerge philosophical. My parents themselves were not insensitive, but they were busy living their own very full lives. I probably appeared to be alright on the outside, but inside was a different story. I seemed to be losing some of my natural self-confidence and the early onset of adolescence was not helping.

One weekend I was on what today would be called a sleepover at Val's. We were romping around upstairs on the landing with her younger brother, Tony, instead of getting ready for bed as we should have been. My mother had not yet suggested I start wearing a bra, but my rapidly developing, by now quite pointed little pubescent breasts were clearly visible beneath my cotton vest, the type with tiny holes, a little like a juvenile version of the string vests my father wore. Tony, who had already developed a keen interest in female anatomy, assisted by a stash of *Playboy* magazines he'd 'borrowed' from his unsuspecting father and shown to my brother Richard, was getting rather over-excited and flirty in a very boyish sort of way, something I had done nothing to encourage. All of a sudden, Peter Walne came pounding up the stairs to see what the commotion was, and seeing me in my see-through, some might say seductive string vest, hit the roof and gave me such a ferocious bollocking I barely knew what had hit me. I still feel indignant and angry when I think of it today – we were, after all, only children having a bit of harmless fun.

I think perhaps my saving grace throughout this rather difficult period was my lively imagination, and ability to dream and fantasise, helped no doubt by the love of books that had been instilled in me from a very early age. I read avidly all through my childhood and teens; from the fairy tales of Hans Christian Andersen, Beatrix Potter, *Alice's Adventures in Wonderland* and Rupert Bear, read to me by my grandmother when I was knee-high, I moved on to tales about horses, fantasy classics, adventure stories and from there to Agatha Christie and James Bond. I was always fascinated by tales of foreign lands and the summer my father drove us all around Europe in an old green

Rover was simply magical. For as long as I can remember I had wanted to travel to far-off places and on occasion even used to walk home from primary school in the Junction all the way back to our house some way up the Sychnant Pass to save my bus fare (then one and a half old pence) for my travel fund. It wasn't so much about getting away, though that must have been part of it; it was more about arriving and exploring once I got there, wherever that might be.

Chapter 4

The Teenage Years

Whenever I think back to my school days, particularly those as an awkward adolescent, the song Lulu had a hit with in 1967 'To Sir with Love' plays in my head. To my mind, it's a beautiful song, a moving tribute to an exceptional teacher, played in the film by Sidney Poitier, who has a tough time gaining the respect of an unruly class of teenagers in an underfunded inner-city secondary modern school. In the end, not only does he gain his students' respect, but also their friendship and in some cases love. Sadly, in all my days at school, I can't think of one single teacher who I could honestly say influenced me in the way Lulu describes or helped me through the challenging years of adolescence. I've had many teachers in my life, some quite kindly, others totally unsuited to the profession, but while the kindly ones were by and large ineffectual and forgettable, the despotic ones tended to make a greater impression and remain more vividly imprinted on my brain. 'To Sir with Hate' might make a more fitting song in my case. If there's one thing that I'd like to be remembered for during my own teaching career it's not to have drummed the basic grammar rules of the English language into my students' heads, or enabled them to order a meal in English, but for helping them in some way on their own path of self-discovery. To have opened their eyes to something overlooked, to have pointed out a quality they didn't realise they possessed, to have made them laugh and relax into what they might initially have perceived as a boring old English lesson, to have planted positive memories into their minds to be retrieved and smiled at in times of strife or grief. To be remembered with love not hate.

When I stop to consider how little fondness I had for school as a child and particularly as a teenager, it seems quite odd really that I should have ended up a teacher myself, peddling the present perfect to non-native speakers of my mother tongue for a living. As a schoolgirl, I think it was the confinement and regimentation that I found hardest to deal with rather than the work itself. The name of the institution I attended from the age of eleven to eighteen was John Bright Grammar School; it was a stone's throw from my father's ice-cream factory in Llandudno, North Wales, and it was in fact the school I opted to attend myself rather than my mother's beloved old boarding school, St Elphin's. John Bright's may have had a decent reputation academically, but the encouragement of critical thinking, informed debate, and classroom discussion were, I'm sure, alien concepts to many of the teachers in those days and if 'the Beak' himself was a fatherly sort, learned, thoughtful and even-tempered, only caning pupils for the very worst offences, some of his staff, there is no doubt, were out-and-out tyrants and unbalanced to boot.

The two most memorable of these characters – dark, demonic, and menacing are the first adjectives that spring to mind – were Brookes and Warbie, by whom we were taught English and French respectively from the tender age of eleven or twelve. The former was a stocky, florid-complexioned man with thinning, gingerish hair and intense dark brown eyes that flashed with manic fervour as he paced the room reciting Macbeth's soliloquy or glazed over unsettlingly as he rubbed his hands in avaricious glee, playing Shakespeare's Shylock in *The Merchant of Venice*, a favourite role of his. Brookes was a keen pipe smoker, a habit which led to the punctuation of his speech with short goat-like coughs and gave his tweedy smoking jackets, in fact, his whole being, a powerful fragrance of sweet, stale tobacco, which at the time I didn't mind in the least, quite liked in fact. Perhaps it reminded me of my dear, rather portly father, whose own tobacco-tinged smell, however, was generally mingled with Old Spice after-shave, Cuticura talc for men, and some sort of hair product he used, possibly Brylcreem.

Brookes, just like Warbie, had reached middle age without marrying; rumours abounded as to how he'd been jilted in his youth by the love of his life and how this had unhinged him and later on brought on bouts of crippling depression, preceded by paroxysms of classroom rage, which might be triggered by something as minor as a stifled girlish giggle as he entered the room or the dull thud of a felt pencil case falling off a desk as he took morning 'attendance'. During these frightening and not-infrequent outbursts we awestruck, captive, pimply teenagers would be subjected to torrents of the foulest verbal abuse – 'You think you're the *crème de la crème*,' he'd sneer nastily, 'but you're not – you're the *scum* of the gutter!'… 'Pearls before *swine!*' and so on, interspersed by disturbing rhetorical questions and the inevitable goatish coughs.

One routine morning in the life of 3A, a fateful one though for the quiet and unassuming Richard Hopkins, who sat at the front of the class just in front of the teacher's desk, Brookes, then our form teacher, surged into the classroom with a blotchy, purplish countenance and the all too familiar 'panda eyes' as my best friend Charlotte and I called them. We later confidently attributed the dilated pupils, feverish hue, and hyperactivity to lunacy, but I am sorry to say that as far as I remember we never really bothered to check up on the phases of the moon at these times and so to this day our clever 'theory' has no empirical evidence to support it. Whether there was any truth too in the rumour that Brookes harboured some personal grudge against innocent Hoppy Poppy's father I couldn't honestly say, but the fact remains that it was on this small fellow redhead that Brookes chose to vent his pent-up feelings that particular day and the poor boy suddenly found his green-rimmed National Health glasses knocked from his face by our half-crazed English master and trampled on the dusty wooden floor before our very eyes.

The year 1968 must have been an inauspicious one for Brookes. Perhaps it was some perverse reaction to the vibes of peace and love emanating across the globe from San Francisco during the *Summer of Love*, though I distinctly remember receiving lavish praise for my essay, Hippy, in which I got my drugs a bit mixed up and talked of dissolute young people needing *fixes of acid*, and probably rolling joints of speed. Anyway, it was that same year, in the very same classroom that the ultimate drama was acted out before us, the key players being these two lonely men, who shared a smoky staff room year in year out, taught the same classes and no doubt experienced many of the same tedious problems with us irreverent schoolchildren. Yet despite the fact that they probably had much in common, we firmly believed that the two despots were arch enemies, that they loathed and despised each other, competing on a daily basis for tyranny over their classes, and that they never so much as exchanged a 'Good Morning', a 'Nice Weekend?' or even a 'Merry Christmas'.

Warbie was a very different kettle of fish to Brookes, a cold fish you might say, though at times his dark, frog-like eyes seemed to be laughing about some private joke, and he had a cruelly mischievous air. He could be a merciless tease and loved nothing more than to have an excuse to keep the whole class in detention, which was quiet torture for me as I had no way of letting my mother know I'd be late back, and I used to worry that *she* would worry, especially on dark, wet, winter nights. It was usually the boys he picked on, placing his long, white index finger, which he could bend upwards like a Balinese dancer, on their noses if he wanted them to read or respond to questions. The pallor of his gaunt face was accentuated by short, dark, slicked-back hair and well-cut, dark blue suits. He was not really tall, but his strangely bony head, his thinness, his very upright posture, and no doubt our mainly seated position certainly made him appear so. He always walked quickly and purposefully, with short, mincing steps, and as he approached 4A carrying a pile of thirty or so red French exercise books, he appeared to almost glide along on casters on the other side of the glass panes that made up the top half of the right-hand classroom wall. As he entered the room a deathly hush would fall, and on days when homework or a test was being returned – which was most days in fact – the tension was palpable. He reminded me of a character I'd read about in a Victorian novel as a child called Daddy Long Legs, a mysterious, creepy figure, only ever glimpsed, until the end of the story, as an elongated shadow on the wall of dimly lit Kafkaesque corridors.

Of all the events and misadventures that punctuated our days of tedium and terror at John Bright's, the highlight, I'm sure all would agree, had to be the board duster incident. On the day in question, Brookes was writing vigorously on the blackboard in our classroom above the old gym with a squeaky, steadily diminishing piece of chalk; the lesson's focus was one of his old hobby horses, punctuation; why he didn't simply dictate to us I can't imagine. The bell rang and, as the following class was French, everyone was anxious to put away their English books and get their French books out of the desk. Warbie always insisted on complete readiness for his lesson; failure to do so would result in varying degrees of discomfiture and humiliation, depending very much on who the culprit was. Three of the boys, quiet, studious Elly Belly (if ever a surname could be made into a ridiculous nickname by joker man Warbie, it was), diminutive, mischievous, curly-haired Peter Tscherewic, Cherry, and cocky, carefree Leelee, would be standing to attention at the front of the class, one poised expectantly to catch the board duster and clean the board if necessary, another to announce the date in French and the third to report on absences and returns from an absence so that interrogations could be conducted, again in French – quite an effective deterrent, I'll give him that, to would-be skivers.

The seconds ticked by, and still, Brookes kept on writing, intent on his task of filling the board with meticulously written notes on the correct use of the semi-colon and such things. No one dared say a word and if we darted sideways looks at each other or poked a classmate in the back I don't remember doing so. Then it happened; the door burst open, and in came the old-fashioned, wooden-handled board duster, hurtling across the front of the room and hitting Brookes squarely on the side of the head, with a ghastly, audible clunk. Warbie froze, horrified, in the doorway and Brookes, turning a familiar shade of puce and glaring with pure hatred at his sworn enemy, bent swiftly to pick up the offending object, hurled it back at Warbie, and lunged towards him, upon which, not surprisingly, Daddy Long Legs retreated in a flash to the corridor, from whence we heard strange sorts of scuffling noises and low-pitched, pig-like grunts, but we can only ever imagine what actually happened out there. A few minutes later a rather flustered and visibly chastened Warbie stepped gingerly into the room and proceeded to conduct his lesson. From that day on, or at least for some time afterwards, we had no real trouble from Warbie and, in fact, that was the last year we had Daddy Long Legs for French. I can't say I was altogether sorry, though later French teachers seemed a bit tame and inept by comparison. One thing is for sure, though – I wouldn't have missed the spectacle that day for the world. Charlotte, my bosom friend throughout these formative years, and I must have gone over and acted out this episode, along with dozens of others, a hundred times or more, squeezing the same amount of drama and hilarity out of it on every occasion – what bliss to have such memories.

Having said how much I detested educational institutions in general and how strange it was in many ways that I should end up teaching myself, it has to be said that all the fear and loathing of those schoolgirl days were mitigated and indeed transformed over the years into the most delicious mixture of blackish comedy and stifled hilarity, to be enjoyed to the full at weekends and during evening phone calls thanks to the most extraordinary aforementioned friendship. Charlotte Williams, or Charlie as she then liked to be called, my partner in crime and soul mate at John Bright's from about halfway through the first form right up until O levels, was in many ways my counterpart. In her own autobiographical work, which, not surprisingly, was highly acclaimed after its publication some years ago now, Charlotte made no mention of this monumental friendship, choosing instead to focus broadly on exploitation and prejudice, and more specifically on the struggles of her white Welsh mother in London as a young woman and later on in North Wales after the departure back to South America of her black Guyanese father. Most poignantly, however, the book dealt with her own inner search for identity in a homeland where our milkman once said, eyeing our weekend guest with faintly lecherous fascination: 'Does she speak English?' It can't have been easy, yet I feel compelled here to say here that I am still undergoing my own private struggle to come to terms with

Charlotte's omission and from time to time remind myself of her bemused and gentle protestation that some relationships are simply too special to be put into words.

We once went to one of my parents' New Year's Eve fancy-dress parties dressed in bowler hats and old suits of my father's as a very credible Laurel and Hardy, and in fact, in real life, we must have seemed to others a bit like the comical Hollywood pair – both physically and in character, we were like chalk and cheese, Charlotte large, dark-haired, athletic, highly articulate and definitely noticeable, me skinny, blonde, balletic rather than sporty and some might say a bit of a retiring wallflower type, but we shared, amongst other things, a highly developed sense of humour, an equally strong sense of occasion, a vivid imagination, and of course, we were both incurable romantics – we complemented each other beautifully, but it was not a lesbian attachment, as Mal, who was to become her husband, once suspected, or perhaps pretended to. We shared a capacity to find endless humour in human foibles and mannerisms – our own not excluded. We joked and joshed our way through each term, ever on the lookout for mimic-worthy targets, spending each minute of each school break, if not cramming for tests, living out our fantasies and, as though that weren't enough, we'd go on to spend hour upon hour on the phone each evening; our parents were amazingly tolerant about paying the bills. We talked into the phone until our ears were red and sore, analysing and injecting humour into the day's events, staying up half the night at weekends at each other's houses, playing Consequences in bed on strips of folded paper, mainly pairing ourselves off with our tennis heroes, Newcombe and Roche, if not our silver screen idols, Paul Newman and Steve McQueen, putting ridiculously romantic or riotously risqué language in their mouths and usually marrying ourselves off to our favourites in 'happily ever after' scenarios. We both became ardent fans of the American pop group the Monkees and would buy up all the magazines we could afford with pictures of them in to put in our scrapbooks. During these Monkee Mad days we'd indulge in guided erotic fantasies – favourite songs by the band would be played on my little red Dansette record player in my pokey bedroom, and while one of us lay on the bed with eyes closed the other would paint the most exquisite, delicate and delicious love scene featuring whichever of us was lying supine and one of our favourite Monkees, Davy Jones or Peter Tork (even very occasionally waggish, fuzzy-haired Micky Dolenz or the rather dull, woolly-hatted drummer, Mike Nesmith, for variety's sake), ending invariably in passionate clinches on freshly mown lawns or tropical beaches with the sun setting gloriously in the background.

At school we would daringly pass scraps of paper to and fro in class during lessons with Monkee news, cryptic observations, often about fellow classmates, and faintly obscene limericks about joke-worthy teachers. On one occasion, having finished a French test early, I had just penned a saucy little rhyme about the Beak himself – something to do with him investing in a waterproof plastic coating for his already extremely shiny bald pate. I was just reaching forwards to place the folded paper by Charlie's right elbow when Warbie, ever self-consciously theatrical, wheeled around unexpectedly, causing the secret missive to leap out of my hand, tumble to the ground, and roll slightly out of arm's reach in the aisle between the girls' and the boys' desks. We still had five minutes or so to go before the end of the test – painful ones for me as Warbie had spotted and made a beeline for the offending object and was slowly pacing the aisles reading the less than complimentary verse, apparently several times over. The faint flicker of a smile that played around the corners of Warbie's thin, cruel lips, if I noticed it at all, did little to assuage my growing consternation and when, at the end of the test, the author of the note was asked to own up, I simply shot to my feet, red in the face and burning with embarrassment, almost shouting out in my guilt and semi-terror, that it was *me*, which of course Warbie knew perfectly well. There was a great show of shocked surprise that the 'damsel' should stoop to such a disgraceful act, but what with Warbie's reportedly strained relations with the Beak and the fact that, being one of the more assiduous students of his subject, I believe he was probably quite fond of me, no more was ever said about the incident. I wonder though what might have happened if one of the duffers at French had been caught writing a rude verse about Warbie. It hardly bears thinking about.

In our lunch breaks, if we weren't re-enacting scenes from *Animal Farm* with corrupted dialogue in the long grass at the far end of the playing fields, larking about playing 'telephone dare' in the little telephone kiosks in the antiquated department store uptown, or cavorting up and down the prom, narrowly dodging or failing to dodge freak waves and getting soaked on extra stormy autumn days, we'd amuse ourselves acting out the famous board duster scene or other incidents from The Life of Brookes. Back at school, we'd lie in wait for him behind a wall outside the third form block. Sooner or later, our protagonist would emerge from the main building. This was often to be the highlight of our day – witnessing his daily stroll across the yard to the canteen thirty-odd yards away. Out he would stride, always alone, smoking his pipe, arms swinging and held at a slight angle away from the body, penguin fashion, then, in exactly the same spot each day, he would kick a small imaginary stone out of the way, cough a goaty cough and look at his watch, all neatly synchronised so that he would arrive at the canteen door without once breaking his stride. Did he ever have any inkling, I wonder, that he was being spied on by these evil teenage girls from their crouching positions behind the wall on the other side of the yard? Could he have imagined for one minute how we would double up, writhing in ecstatic spasms of hilarity, at the very sight of him performing these very mundane actions? Will he ever read these pages from his smoky earthly lair, in his chalk-, student-, and board-duster-free heaven, or from among the spirits of the damned in his shadowy underworld? What on earth would he make of them? I think he might be amused.

In case he does, and even if he does not read my memoir, I feel here that I should perhaps counter some of my less than complimentary remarks above by saying that for all his eccentricity, cynicism, and periodic bad humour, Brookes was undoubtedly a very dedicated and indeed a good teacher in a number of ways. He went out of his way to encourage us to read good literature soon after our arrival at the school, to the point of bringing a collection of his own favourite paperbacks to class and distributing them amongst us, with no obligation to report back or complete written tasks, as far as I remember. Some of the novels I read at that time had a lasting effect on me; Graham Greene's *A Gun for Sale*, for example, made me realise that good writing didn't necessarily require big words and fancy language – on the contrary, the very force of Greene's language came from its directness, its lack of superfluous adjectives and lengthy subordinate clauses. I was blown away by it. Who knows, it might even have been the original stimulus that led to a lifetime fascination with gangsters, criminality, and the underworld. James Joyce's *Dubliners* introduced me to the complexities and beauty of human relationships, while Gerald Durrell's *My Family and Other Animals* produced in me an unquenchable urge to experience the call of the evening cicadas and warm, dappled shade of Corfu's olive groves for myself, which I did at the very first opportunity. To this day, too, I am grateful to Brookes for his encouraging remarks on my early attempts at creative writing and literary criticism. I've kept all those old blue

English school books with their comments in distinctive large red, loopy handwriting. I wonder how many of my own students over the years have kept the books of work they did for me and if the comments I wrote in them had any lasting impact.

There was, of course, a human side to Brookes. I seem to remember him telling us himself, on more than one occasion, that he was very fond of young children and small birds, although of course, this may have been mere fabrication. Every so often I'd knock at the male staff room door to hand in a late piece of work, blaming a migraine – which was usually true – and witnessed an undoubtedly kind, sensitive, even fatherly side to him (that could have been the powerful tobacco aroma, mind you), a side quite at odds with the tormented monster we glimpsed in his mad manic moments. He was not without a sense of humour and, what is more, he had the ability, an essential ability to my mind, to laugh at himself. The occasional mistake or omission on the blackboard would prompt an exclamation of 'Silly Brookes!' and he would strike himself repeatedly on the forehead with his fist and dart fiendish looks at us sideways from under his beetling brows, though, of course, no one in his right mind would have dared to laugh out loud at such moments!

I happened to be good at English and French, and so was never singled out, as many were, for criticism, ridicule, and public derision by one or the other of the tyrants. I was, however, part of the smallish sixth form group who were told, to their horror on returning from the Christmas holiday, that they had to re-sit the English exam on account of the fact that the exam papers had been written in biro as opposed to fountain pen. Never having been *told* that the use of fountain pen had all of a sudden become compulsory for English exams, we felt ourselves to be wholly innocent and quite unjustly accused. In Brookes' poor addled mind, however, our use of biros constituted an act of unpardonable defiance, which clearly demonstrated that we had no respect for or interest in the subject, and on top of this he believed that it constituted a grave insult to him personally, hence a particularly vile, spittle-strewing tirade, reminding us that we were *not* the crème de la crème, etc., etc., and that we would have to get down to some serious swotting for this new exam if we wanted to continue studying English with him.

I decided that I did not and indeed this seemed like a very good excuse for me to give up formal English study altogether. As it was, in the absence of any Asiatic or Romance language courses at our school, besides French, I was doing a crash course in the only other language offered (Welsh didn't count) and that was German – seven years' work, both 'O', and 'A' level crammed into two; I reckoned I had enough on my plate and was only too happy to opt out of English. My parents were quite liberal, very much concerned that I should be happy whatever I did in life, so didn't object. I think Mum probably still thought at that time that I would find myself a nice, comfortably off husband and wouldn't have to worry too much about having to make a living myself, while Dad seemed to think that a year or two at the Sorbonne, after perhaps receiving a modest degree from a British university, would be all I needed to land a good job, as a high-flying, tri-lingual PA of some sort, in Brussels perhaps. As for myself, I didn't feel I really needed much guidance in my reading of literature (my great-uncle Lionel did a pretty good unofficial job here anyway). Pope's *The Rape of the Lock* really didn't seem to me to merit the close scrutiny it was being given in our English class and I simply wasn't enjoying Shakespeare's *Antony and Cleopatra* at all. The decision was made and with it came the end of my dealings with dear, old, batty Brookes. We had already seen the bony blue back of Warbie, as he only taught us up until the fourth form. So that was the end of our days with the despots and, as my best friend, Charlotte, moved to another town at the end of the fifth form, it was really the end of an era.

We had a motley bunch of modern language teachers during our last two years at grammar school. First, there was the tall, humourless, anaemic-looking man with the double-barrelled name and the gorgeous younger wife, after whom the sixth form boys I'm sure lusted endlessly. He took over command of our translations and literary commentaries and though undoubtedly well qualified, well organised and all the rest, he was cold, aloof, and critical and so not remembered, by me at least, with any affection. He was later joined by a very pretty, petite, and competent young blonde woman, who had a curious way of rolling her eyes back into their sockets as she was reflecting, and an egg-shaped, bespectacled young man with greasy hair, sensual lips, and a habit of pushing up his glasses and laughing in a despairing sort of way at our – or probably mostly my – feeble attempts at translating from the very bizarre and abstruse detective novel by the Swiss writer Friedrich Dürrenmatt – *Der Richter und sein Henker* – that had somehow found its way onto our A level reading list. With the tyrants out of my life and my best friend no longer there with whom to create our special brand of magic, my last two years at school were comparatively dull and lonely. The day after I sat my last A level exam, I was on a plane to Switzerland for a working holiday in a restaurant in a remote mountain resort in the southern canton of Valais – my independent travels had begun.

Chapter 5

From Oxford to Paris via Istanbul

Gai Paris! Quelle ville! Quelle chance! Graduating, as I did, in the mid-seventies, I think you might be hard pushed to think of a better place on this planet in which to embark upon adult life, especially if, like me, you were something of a romantic to begin with, were known for your epicurean tendencies and had a strong leaning towards the arts. It was here, in any case, in the quiet, leafy and extremely bourgeois suburb of *La Varenne Saint-Hilaire* (a good forty-minute journey by high-speed RER train then metro to the official *centre point* of the city, just in front of *Notre Dame* cathedral) that I came to share a spacious, ground floor apartment, unmemorable except perhaps for its bottle green and canary yellow kitchen and meticulously carpeted (for the sake of sound-proofing) lounge walls, with a certain Alain Tou Te Heng, *mon premier amour*.

We'd met a year or so previously in Oxford, at the beginning of my third and final year at what was then Oxford Polytechnic, now, rather more grandly, Oxford Brookes University. I'd just returned from a summer of wandering and wonderful, carefree abandon, sleeping out under the stars in the bewitching olive groves and dancing barefoot in the sand on the moonlit beaches of the Cyclades. My hair was bleached almost white by the Hellenic sun and I was as brown as a berry, browner than I'd ever been before or have been since. The fact that I am now paying heavily for all those years of ardent sun worship is neither here nor there – if I had that part of my life to live again, I doubt I'd have done things any other way, coconut oil and all. I was feeling fit, confident and at peace with myself, blissfully unaware up until this point of what had been going on in my absence in the quaint, terraced student household in Osney Mead, of which I was officially lessee.

Alain was there in the small, dingy living room when I made my grand entry via the backyard and the pokey, stone-floored kitchen, easing myself in through the door, bulging army-surplus rucksack on my back, woven hemp hippy bag over my shoulder, containing the inevitable bottle of ouzo and carton of duty-free Camel cigarettes along with assorted, battered mementos from my travels. He was sitting at the table writing something or other – quite possibly a poem – and appeared very cool and self-possessed, not exactly hostile but evidently unimpressed at my announcement that I was the lessee of the house, and then nonplussed at hearing that I would be needing to reclaim his room in a week or so along with the rooms of all the other characters I'd just learned now lived at 19 West Street. There was something intriguing and exotic about this dark, reticent stranger before me – I don't think I guessed at first that he was half Chinese, though the French accent was almost certainly detected and, as part of my degree was French, I suppose the thought must have crossed my mind that having a French native speaker under my roof could have its advantages. A week or so later I learned that someone I'd promised a room to at the beginning of the college term would not be needing it after all and as Alain was up to date with his rent and offered to pay cash in advance for another month I accepted. By the time the autumn weather had set in, we were already spending most of our free time together and our lives were becoming increasingly entwined.

As for the others living in the house that September, a motley crew would be a polite way to describe them. First, there was Mario, the stocky and impressively hirsute, nomadic Mexican, whose battered zebra-striped camper van sat most of the time up against the kerb, right outside our very front door. He had a contented, laissez-faire, worldly air about him, smelled unashamedly of sweat and patchouli oil and his natural expression was one of tolerant amusement. Then there was Camillo, the pale, earnest, well-educated young Italian, a man of artistic temperament. In another age I might have guessed that he was suffering from consumption, but in fact he was probably just fashionably thin, half-starved even, as his finances were clearly poor, and pale because, unlike us foolhardy Brits in those days, he knew better than to strip off, coat himself with Ambre Solaire and lie supine on a bath towel in our scruffy back garden each time the sun showed its face. Though evidently a serious type, Camillo always seemed to be about when things livened up at weekends in West Street, when giro cheques were cashed, weekly wage packets were torn open and brown ten-shilling notes hastily exchanged for chillum fodder. (A chillum, for those who were wondering, is a clay pipe of sorts, a vessel favoured by the French and undoubtedly others at that time for smoking marijuana.) Last and in every way least were the two wild, pill-popping Cockney chefs, one of whom had been romantically entangled with my beautiful and likeable, if wayward, and ultimately sadly untrustworthy young friend, Yasmin Watts. It was to Yasmin I had handed over my keys as I departed for Greece earlier that summer, inviting her to stay in my room and make herself at home until she was able to save up the money to join me in Mikio's olive grove in Sidari, on the north-west coast of Corfu. I now wonder if she'd ever had any real intention of leaving Oxford that summer. She'd continued working for the eccentric Bodymeads in the health food shop in Prince Edward Street, where we'd met, had somehow got in with a bit of a bad lot, developed a taste for vodka and amphetamines and, in order to fuel her new habit and fast lifestyle, had filled the other rooms in the house with odd bods she met in pubs, clubs and at 'happenings' around town, collecting rent from each of them and swiftly pocketing the money herself.

When I arrived back in Osney Mead to take up the household reins once more, the characters just described, minus Yasmin, were all comfortably installed in West Street, under the false impression that they had found a cheap and more or less permanent abode in this unpretentious yet pleasant street, not that far from the railway station and only fifteen minutes or so's walk to the city centre. It had two or three excellent pubs nearby – the one I remember most fondly being the Bricklayer's Arms, which was just around the corner from the house, opposite a small tributary of the Thames. On some days, if you were lucky, you might encounter some of its fine resident swans, but perhaps the less said about these swans the better. On one occasion, a year or so before the arrival of the motley crew, another slightly dodgy house resident, a certain Dave Ivory, then an undergraduate at Magdalen College, attempted to lasso a particularly aggressive female bird, with the intention of roasting it for one of our famous student gourmet dinners. Fortunately for the indignant pen, he failed and almost lost his right arm during the confrontation. One of the attractions of this pub, apart from the extremely amiable and tolerant landlord and landlady, was the fact that the landlady's elderly dad, Mr D, who helped out behind the bar at weekends, had little idea of the correct measures for certain drinks. One of my favourite tipples at this time was Warninks Advocaat, hardly a student drink as I had pointed out to me by sneering pseudo-proletarians more than once at student parties, but nevertheless a comforting sort of drink, particularly in winter. Many a time I opted for buying a miniature bottle of the excellent yellow concoction to sip on walks home from other parts of the city on winter evenings, rather than buying a bus ticket. For some unknown reason, dear old Mr D tended to choose a *ballon* style wine glass for advocaat and, I suppose not wanting to appear stingy, would invariably fill it almost to the brim. It was only towards the end of my time at West Street that this erroneous practice was spotted by his daughter and the use of slender, measly liqueur glasses encouraged instead. Luckily, by this time I had discovered mead, Cherry B, Ponys and other such bottled sweetness that my youthful palate seemed to crave. Another big plus for impoverished students and fringe youth living in this area was the practice of an elderly grocer, who had a dimly lit but friendly little shop in the terrace that ran parallel to ours, of letting people have things on tick. Not only this but he also had a wooden shed in the overgrown garden that backed onto ours that he used to store, amongst other things, Strongbow cider. He rarely locked this hut, it seemed, and though I never actually stole from it myself, I confess I did on occasion drink cider that I was told by certain household members had come from 'the cider tree' at the bottom of our garden. My conscience cringes at the memory.

Mario and Camillo appeared fairly unperturbed at being given notice. Mario could always live outside in his Ford Transit, which in fact he did continue to do for quite some time, appearing at regular intervals for water, the odd bath and company when he felt in need. At some point he became acquainted and quickly enamoured with my extremely 'alternative' friend Cathy, whom I'd also met working at the health food restaurant. Cathy was an alluring, wanton hippy nymph, highly artistic and creative in a number of ways, but with a common weakness for drugs. She had short, wispy, baby-blonde hair, which she'd once dyed black when travelling in Morocco, so as to blend in with the crowd and avoid being hassled. I have an amusing dog-eared Polaroid photograph of Mario and Cathy, taken I assume by myself, though I have no recollection of ever owning a Polaroid camera. They are gazing up into the lens from beneath the feather duvet, wide-eyed and surprisingly innocent-looking, considering the rather compromising position they'd been discovered in. They'd only met the evening before but had smoked a joint together then slipped away upstairs and had made a nest for themselves in the single bed that stood in the alcove outside the draughty, antiquated bathroom. Mario disappeared soon after the photo was taken and the last I heard of Cathy she was living on a barge on the River Cherwell, just outside Oxford. The barge was sinking and I suspect Cathy may have been too, as she was on a path of self-destruction that I found puzzling and very sad to witness. I was always very wary of drugs myself. Hearing so much about them, however, as one did in the psychedelic sixties and seventies when I was growing up, I was naturally curious. As a student, I experimented very occasionally and very cautiously, though I often watched on with great interest as those around me consumed large amounts of whatever pharmaceutical was on offer. My few experiences with drugs over the years tended to be rather unpleasant, if not downright terrifying.

One such experience remains indelibly etched in my memory. I'd returned from Blackwell's bookshop the week before college began to find the West Street inhabitants sitting on cushions on the living room floor ceremonially drinking tea with J J Cale playing on the record player at high volume. Knowing full well this was no ordinary tea, but one of Mario's special brews, I would have been quite happy to have done without. A cup was poured for me, however, the last in the pot, therefore the strongest, and not wanting to appear churlish, I accepted and drank it down. Being of light build and at that time prepared to more or less starve myself for the pleasure of seeing bones protrude from my youthful frame, I suppose the quantity of Moroccan black, or whatever it was that had been used on that occasion, was way, way too much. I have vague recollections of drifting in and out of consciousness and each time I opened my eyes I would find myself in a different room with a different set of people and, most bizarrely, it seemed at the time, with a different language being spoken. The languages would in fact probably have been French, Spanish and Italian, all Romance languages and all familiar to me. What is more, I knew most of the players in this surreal comedy, yet it was all too much for my poor addled brain. I lost all concept of who and even what I was and ended up sitting on the cold, cork-tiled bathroom floor, stuck in some sort of time warp, a perplexing nightmarish Alice in Wonderland-type bubble, believing I'd done some awful permanent damage to myself – whoever or whatever I was, I really didn't know. Why on earth would people do this to themselves voluntarily? I later put it all down to part of the unique experience of student life – the best days, my dear late father had assured me, I would have in my life. Today, I'm not so sure of the wisdom of his words.

Unlike Mario and Camillo, one of the resident chefs took his marching orders very badly and, fanciful though it now seems, looking back, actually held some sort of flick knife to my throat, looking very much as though he was about to use it. He had an extremely young girlfriend living with him in the smallest of the five bedrooms, the one that later got transformed into a satanic grotto by the disturbed yet highly personable, clairvoyant juvenile occultist Bertrand de Quincy, direct descendant, so he claimed, of the Marquis de Sade no less. But I digress. I had noticed right from the start that this girl was strangely subdued and had bruises on her arms, so when she chose to confide in me and tell me she was thinking of returning to live with her parents, I naturally encouraged her to do so – the sooner the better. When the boyfriend got back from his evening shift, having slaved away for hours in front of a blazing grill, to find his malleable, young bedmate gone, he was more than a little peeved and wasted no time in coming straight into my bedroom to tell me so. He guessed correctly that I'd had a hand in her decision to desert him, but, to my enormous relief, thought twice before drawing blood with his evil-looking weapon and took himself off for good a day or so after the incident, as did the other chef, an equally sly, street-wise villain, who got short shrift from me despite his silvery tongue and brazen, flashing smile. Yasmin was gone when I arrived back from Greece, along with several of my favourite clothes and LPs and didn't show her face again. I sometimes wonder what became of her; she could well have become a gangster's moll. Were the drugs to blame for her character change and ensuing perfidy? Quite possibly, though she might equally well have been born with a serious character flaw – the age-old question of nature versus nurture. I know of people whose trust in humanity has been marred by such betrayals, but I don't think it changed the way I saw people or made me distrust people's motives. I had the benefit of having a mother who tried to bring me up to look for the best in people. I don't think I ever heard her say a bad word about anyone – except possibly my father's secretary, Hazel, who knitted little matinee jackets for my baby brother when I was eleven, then ran off to Jamaica with my father during his mid-life crisis.

I'd never met anyone remotely like Alain before. I'd listen spellbound as he talked in his native language (excellent listening practice for me) about his childhood and adolescence, growing up as one of five children with industrious, working-class parents, living in a fairly affluent, south-eastern suburb of Paris. Being of mixed race, he had suffered a fair bit of bullying at school and had teamed up with two other boys, also *métis*, Sunny and Eric, both half Vietnamese, half French; they became known as *les trois Chinois*. Before they took their school-leaving exams they had started dabbling in hard drugs, but being of well above average intelligence, all three of them graduated along with all their conscientious, line-toeing peers and left school with respectable qualifications. Sunny became an accountant and Eric, very surprisingly, joined the army. I met and liked both of the other two *Chinois*; apart from their good looks they had charm, style and were quick to laugh. Sunny lived with us for a while in our Parisian suburb, cooking the most fantastic exotic meals, doing most of our housework while we were out working and even taking it upon himself to do bits of DIY around the flat. We returned home one afternoon from the local open-air market, where we had a stall, to find a bizarre-looking object lying on the kitchen worktop. What I first took to be some sort of Asian wind instrument turned out to be a dozen frogs' legs strung up on a bamboo rack ready for roasting for our dinner that night. Sunny lived up to his name and was always good-humoured, yet led his Parisian life with the horrific knowledge that two of his young siblings were being held in prison in Vietnam and that the prison guards were demanding a large sum of money to help them escape and not break their legs. I gave him all the savings I had at that time as did Alain, though we never heard for sure if they'd been released. I think it was this quiet revelation of Sunny's the day he told us what his family was going through that made me start to really count my blessings each night as I fell asleep – a practice I have continued until this day.

Alain was a mere nineteen-year-old when we met in 1973 and at 5'6" was exactly the same height as me (meaning we could and sometimes did wear each other's jeans and jumpers). There's no doubt he had lived rather more than I had. Since leaving school with a *bac* certificate in the sciences, he had worked as a freelance photographer at Megève, a fashionable French skiing resort, played the guitar in a band, had had a sugar mama in Paris and a number of *aventures* with girls more his own age – he was quite an accomplished lover. He had exquisite, smooth, pale skin and dark, Asiatic, almond-shaped eyes that would draw me into another world until I lost all sense of place and time and was willingly mesmerised, luxuriating in a haze of Gitanes and Eau Sauvage, caressed by the tendrils of his white Afghan coat when he came in from the cold and kissed me. I fell steadily and deeply in love – I was twenty and had just lost my father, who, as I'm sure many had predicted, had gone out in a blaze of wine, women and song on his beloved island of Ibiza. Perhaps my father's premature departure had left a vacuum in my heart that Alain filled – who knows. He bought me a litre of advocaat and the Allman Brother's double album, *Eat A Peach*, for my twenty-first birthday and, as we fell asleep that night in each other's arms between my purple brushed-cotton sheets, I felt loved and content.

It was Alain who, in due course, after I'd completed my first degree, led me to his native Paris, but perhaps more importantly for this story, it was here that I gave my very first paid English lesson. My student was the most agreeable and kindest of beings imaginable, dear Madame Postelle, mother of pretty, elusive, peripatetic Mireille, a friend (and almost undoubted fellow dope-head) of *mon petit* Alain. But before we enter the home of Madame Postelle, I must delve a little further back into the recesses of my memory to the months that led up to this fortuitous encounter.

We had arrived just before Christmas 1975 at the tall, locked iron gates of 4, *Rue Parmentier, La Varenne Saint-Hilaire*, on the outskirts of Paris, the chicest of capitals, cold, ragged, and virtually penniless after six months travelling around Europe, Turkey and North Africa, Alain morose and thoroughly disgruntled at the various deprivations we had suffered en route, and me in desperate need of a dentist on account of a raging ulcer in a lower left molar, which wads of cotton wool soaked in neat Turkish alcohol had done increasingly little to alleviate. Both of us were modishly lean and bronzed and still itching from the bedbug bites we'd acquired in the sleazy dive that called itself a 'hotel', just up the road from the renowned Istanbul pudding shop, hang-out of hippies and Magic Bus passengers en route to or returning from India, in the vicinity of the equally famous Blue Mosque, which dominates the city skyline from the south.

We were accepted unquestioningly, however, into the Tou Te Heng household with a remarkable degree of indulgence and stoicism by Alain's long-suffering parents, the slightly stout but handsome, and always immaculately-groomed Denise and the smaller, equally reserved, birdlike and enigmatic *Papi*. As a young man in the late nineteen forties, I learned, *Papi* had stepped off a ship from his native China with no more than the clothes on his back and knowledge of the craft of leather work, had fallen for a serious, blue-eyed beauty, then serving in a Marseille boulangerie, and, though speaking barely half a dozen words of her language, had succeeded in persuading her that they should combine their fortunes, marry and start a family.

Twenty-five years or so on from this brave decision, *Maman et Papi* owned a three-storey villa with a double garage and walled garden in the highly respectable suburb of Paris *La Varenne Saint-Hilaire*, had their own successful wholesale leather business, in the narrow, medieval street *Rue du Temple* (a stone's throw from that site of unutterable suffering and bloodshed during the French Revolution, *Place de la Republique*), had five children, five grandchildren and so much undeclared cash from their ongoing enterprise, they kept bundles of used hundred-franc notes hidden around the house and felt compelled to throw, at the very least once a month throughout the summer, extravagant family garden parties, and slightly less often in the winter elaborately planned banquets, where vast amounts of expensive food and wine were consumed at long trestle tables in the garage cum pantry cum laundry that made up the ground floor of the house. The lounge, which occupied most of the first floor along with the well-equipped kitchen, was reserved for extra special occasions, such as Christmas. Strange though it might seem, *Papi* never really did get to grips with the French language, though to his credit he made a concerted effort during my second year in Paris, when he would have been around sixty (although with his greying wispy beard, he always seemed much older) to study the Western alphabet, writing out simple sentences in a lined exercise book in a steady and flowing hand, which he would proffer shyly to us for approval and correction.

As for me, *la petite anglaise* in their midst, having survived for three years as an impoverished student living mainly on cauliflower stalks (salvaged on the way home from college after the open-air market had packed up), sultanas, faggots and Ambrosia creamed rice pudding, usually eaten cold straight from the tin, these parties were a revelation to me as to how much simple pleasure could be had from eating and drinking, though as time went on and I saw Alain repeatedly drawn into – or probably more often provoke – heated family arguments, I came to appreciate these long drawn-out meals rather less (I think the actual record was a full twelve hours one Christmas at *Rue Parmentier*. I seem to remember settling down at the table in *Mami et Papi's* front room with its heavy, ornate Chinese furniture to *aperitifs* and *amuse-gueules* soon after noon and I swear we were among the first to leave that night when the clock struck midnight). Champagne, Mami's drink *de choix*, of which she always had a bottle chilling in the *frigo*, flowed freely on these occasions and bottles of vintage wine were brought up from the cellar at regular intervals to accompany the caviar, *pâté de foie gras*, oysters, *coquilles St Jaques* and other outstanding Chino Franco delicacies: rabbit with sherry and lotus flowers, beef with aged soy sauce and perfumed black mushrooms, aromatic peppercorn-studded *choucroute* – the French version of sauerkraut – with half a dozen or more cuts of ham and charcuterie nestling among the sublime wine-permeated slivers of white cabbage. If I was not yet a foodie when I first set foot in Paris, I was to steadily become one over the next three years.

The various Tou Te Heng family members regarded me in turn with barely disguised disdain, suspicion, amusement, curiosity, solicitous concern and affectionate indulgence. They really weren't quite sure what to make of this polite, educated yet fairly inarticulate '*Mademoiselle d'Angleterre*', so carried on for the most part as though I wasn't there at all, which in fact was quite a relief, as my French, it had to be admitted, wasn't really up to fast-paced often somewhat aggressive debates that went on under the Tou Te Heng roof. Besides, I simply didn't feel I had a great deal to add to their dialectics on French politics, economics, unemployment, religion, the price of horse steak and other such worldly and impersonal topics. I had been brought up to believe that most of these subjects were not to be discussed at the table. Our table talk at home had mostly consisted of amusing anecdotes, snippets of news, holiday plans and family history. I was not about to start revealing such personal information – my lack of confidence and fluency in French wouldn't have allowed it – even assuming anyone might be interested, which I rather doubt they would have been.

The main thing of course, as far as the family was concerned, was for me and Alain to become gainfully employed and, after our irresponsible flirtation with Bohemia and the Kerouacinspired on-the-road lifestyle, to grow up, settle down and join *la petite bourgeoisie*. After a brief and fairly disastrous stint as a night-time attendant pumping gas in a service station the other side of the city, Alain managed to secure a rather more suitable and comfortable post for himself in the electronics dept of a duty-free shop at Charles de Gaulle airport. It was many years later that I discovered an extra perk of the job had been a fairly liberal supply of cocaine and probably other illegal substances that were shared out during working hours by fellow employees with similar predilections.

Meanwhile I had spent week upon week that perishing cold January and half of February scouring the papers over endless cups of *café au lait* in the tiny overheated kitchen chez *Maman et Papi*, or over glasses of heady, steaming *Grog* – mulled wine laced with Martinique rum – at the bar of smoky brasseries in the city, hunting for possible jobs for myself, descending the narrow spiral stairs to the *sous-sol* in search of a public telephone, braving wafts of pungent air from the unisex hole-in-the-ground *toilettes*, tripping off hopefully for interviews, most of which turned out to be a complete waste of time, as my newly acquired French and German degree meant no more to them than my pearly white teeth, new black velvet jacket and impeccable manners – what they were really looking for were hard-nosed, experienced receptionists to balance the books and keep out the riff raff in seedy *Pigalle* hotels or tartily dressed '*hostesses*', professional good time girls, who knew how to apply war paint and were willing to remove their clothes at the end of the evening, though none of this, of course, was ever explicitly stated in the advert or even mentioned in the interview.

One such interview, I vaguely remember, took place inside a type of caravan in a small secluded yard just off *Rue Royale*, not far from the famous club *Maxim's*, where, I would inform my groups later on during my guided tours, Maurice Chevalier had dined in the film *Gigi*, and the *Place de la Concorde*, displaying its grandiose Egyptian gift to the French people, the obelisk, sister to Cleopatra's Needle in London. Initially, I was told that a 'model' was required for a magazine in which the story was told using photographs and speech bubbles, rather like a cartoon strip, only longer. The job did not entail the removal of one's clothing, I was assured. I daresay I shouldn't have even stayed in the caravan long enough to be told this, but it had taken me so long to find the place and the money they were offering was so much higher than anything I'd been offered up until this point (four times as much, in fact) that it was in a kind of a hushed aside that I said I didn't think my boyfriend would approve of my doing this sort of work. At the very mention of boyfriend, the interviewers shot each other a conspiratorial glance and fixed me with an unnerving stare. An even larger sum was mentioned – if the two of us were willing to be photographed *together*…

I think it was perhaps the report of this last interview that got Alain thinking about other possible ways of making money, where we could work side by side, and he could keep a protective eye on me. Alain had a suave and rather enigmatic older brother, Patrice, to whom he undoubtedly looked up, not least on account of his gambling prowess and his extremely glamorous partner Katrine, with whom he had a petulant yet rather enchanting daughter of around three called Dorothée. Patrice had made something of a killing selling leatherware from his parents' wholesale leather goods shop in the open-air markets surrounding Paris. Perhaps we might similarly set ourselves up in business too. The fact that we would have to negotiate reams of red tape to obtain the necessary papers to operate as such vendors ourselves, and of course somehow acquire a fairly substantial sum of money to buy stock and a vehicle, didn't seem to deter Alain in the least. To my slight surprise, *Maman et Papi* turned out to be all too willing to offer their financial support to this second male black sheep of the family (the three daughters were by comparison all exceedingly virtuous, *sérieuses*, law-abiding citizens), investing quite a chunk of their hard-earned capital in this new enterprise, despite the fact that they had officially disclaimed him in his teens for fear of losing their sanity over his fondness for hard drugs. In the end, however, I think it was his belief in himself, his facility with figures and finance in general, that enabled Tou Te Heng Jnr to take this bold step into *le monde des affaires* and set up as a '*commerçant de maroquinerie*', a leather goods merchant.

While '*le business*' was still under discussion, however, above-board employment for Mlle Caroline remained a daily topic of conversation at the Tou Te Heng dinner table. Curiously, *Maman* rarely addressed me directly on these occasions, though my French was really quite adequate for the task, but communicated through Alain, as though she and I had no language in common whatsoever or perhaps as though I were a small child with very limited comprehension of the issue under discussion. On one occasion she even asked through our interpreter if I had had enough to eat, upon which I piped up '*Ah mais oui, merci, vraiment je suis bien pleine!*', provoking a raucous response as I had inadvertently informed the gathering that I was not in fact simply 'full' but heavily pregnant. It wasn't long after this that I made a similar gaffe *à table* in announcing, at a tender enquiry from *Mami* as to whether I was warm enough, that the cool air coming in from the open window didn't bother me at all, as I was feeling *bien chaude*, 'in a state of extreme sexual arousal'. I'm not actually sure which of these two gaffes took place first, though of course it would all seem rather more logical if the latter had preceded the former.

Total immersion in the lingo, all the same, must have done my tentative textbook French a power of good, although the majority of Alain's friends would have spoken a brand of

Parisian argot that was – I was sensible enough to realise – not to be used indiscriminately. Although Alain was often critical of my French once we arrived on his territory, quite cruelly so on occasion, and if at first the pace of the talk generally made it hard if not impossible for me to add my own comments before the conversation veered off in a totally new direction, I generally got the gist of things, or thought I did, and picked up some interesting new words and idioms here and there along the way. One such expression that I would hear constantly from Alain's cronies or *copains* was '*la bonne femme*', literally translated as 'the good woman' and what I took to be a jokingly formal expression of respect when referring usually to their mothers. Despite the cool image these *mecs* exuded, I should add here, with their hip long hair and leather jackets, their abundant supply of best Moroccan Rocky Black or Lebanese Red Leb hash and their air of having everything sussed, they almost all still lived at home with their parents, were fed and clothed by them, even had their blue jeans ironed by *la bonne femme*, such was the norm among the bourgeoisie of *La Varenne* in the 1970s and no doubt still today.

After submitting endless paperwork, Alain had finally succeeded in getting a licence to trade on the open-air markets – anywhere in France, but not within Paris itself. After a brief flirtation with brightly coloured wooden clogs, he turned to leatherware, which we bought at his parents' wholesale shop in *Rue de Temple*, just up the road from the Georges Pompidou Centre. Against everyone's advice, we had expanded quickly and were struggling with a ridiculously large double pitch and eight metres of rather good quality stock laid out on two trestle tables, only partially protected from the elements by two giant umbrellas, which were a devil to erect and dismantle. It was a tough job, requiring very early morning starts in all weathers, endless patience with the general public and more than a little stamina. The constant loading and unloading of heavy boxes of wares meant I had more or less permanent backache during that period, an ache that quantities of powerful homemade sangria consumed in the evenings only partially alleviated.

It was in the early days of our leather business that I found myself one particularly vile, wet and windy February lunchtime cursing under my breath in my best Parisian argot as I studied a sodden banana box, used for packing belts, that the umbrella had failed to protect. We were at a virtually deserted open-air market somewhere on the southern outskirts of Paris, a good hour and a half's drive from home. The morning had been a fiasco. Arriving at the crack of dawn, we'd followed the arrogant market manager, or *placier*, around the market along with a crowd of eager fellow vendors, like so many rats scampering after the Pied Piper of Hamlin. Despite managing to catch his eye and giving him what I hoped was a winning smile, we were given a poor pitch at the far edge of the market beneath a crumbling wall, and had sold virtually nothing. Hopeful of being given a better spot on subsequent occasions, we'd given the *placier* a larger bribe than we normally did, so what with these expenses, plus petrol money, we were seriously out of pocket. Twice the umbrellas had blown over in freak gusts of wind, tipping calf leather wallets into puddles and knocking the *portes monnaies* (ladies' purses) into the *pochettes* (a type of male handbag with a convenient if faintly absurd little wrist strap. No self-respecting Englishman would have been seen dead with one of these *pochettes*, but in France at that time they seemed to be an essential piece of male kit and we sold them by the dozen). With our ever-expanding stock, it now took us a good hour to set up the stall and the same to dismantle it and pack up again. I think we were both wondering that day if we were mad to be trying to make a living in this way.

It was just as we'd called it a day and Alain had growled '*Embalons!*' (let's pack up), that a well-dressed, mature lady walked purposefully up to our stand and started looking, perhaps not surprisingly, at our two most elegant and expensive handbags – our latest additions to the stock, which we had almost not bought on account of their fancy price tag, even wholesale. As I was generally better than Alain at making sales, I took charge and learned that she was looking for birthday presents for her twin daughters. I simply couldn't believe our luck. It was quite evident that this was a serious customer and if she bought the two bags she was looking at, this one sale would cancel out the day's losses and we'd even end up making a modest profit. It didn't take much to convince her that her daughters would be delighted with these high-quality, hand-crafted items. A chequebook was produced and she was about to start writing out a cheque when she looked up and asked me if we did in fact accept cheques. Normally, we were not at all keen on them, so, despite every appearance of her being of good character, I thought I'd better check with the boss, whose head at that moment was under the table reaching for an empty box in which to pack the *pochettes*. '*Est-ce que la bonne femme peut nous faire un cheque?*' I enquired, smiling apologetically at this most valued of customers, at which Alain jolted and practically knocked himself out on the underside of the table in his haste to extricate himself. His expression was one of pure incredulity, quickly darkening to anger, which both puzzled and alarmed me. I actually thought he might hit me, but instead he swiftly took over the sale, assuring the customer she could indeed write us this cheque, and banishing me to packing duty until the transaction was completed. It was made quite clear to me on the drive home that this '*bonne femme*' expression was derogatory and not ever to be used with customers – or anyone for that matter – again. I had guessed as much. It was only that evening, though, when I looked the words up in the dictionary that I got the full flavour of the phrase – it had been used since

Shakespearean times and could perhaps best be translated as 'the old shrew'.

Returning to my first private student, dear Madame Postelle, though evidently far from well off and with nothing of the elegance of our customer at the windswept market that day, she did share with her the qualities of sensitivity, gentility and kindness, the latter to my mind the queen of human emotions. I can't imagine she had any real use for English – I don't believe she had any dealings with foreigners whatsoever, either at her office job or in her personal life. I think perhaps she must have simply taken pity on me – had obviously heard that a young man from Mireille's rather dubious circle of friends had returned from his sojourn across the channel with a quiet and retiring English rose, who seemed to be having difficulty finding herself suitable employment. Her request for some private English lessons was made, I am sure, more out of a desire to help than to be helped in any way.

There's nothing very much to report about the lessons themselves. I feel ashamed when I think how little preparation I did – I don't actually remember doing any at all – and my knowledge of the intricacies of second language acquisition in those days was slim to say the least. My whole approach as far as I remember was based on the soon-to-be-abandoned grammar-translation method I myself had been subjected to not so many months earlier in tedious undergrad tutorials with the affable but uninspiring ex-army type Dr Collins at Oxford Poly and before that at grammar school with the aforementioned tyrant Warbie – the very method that had so ill-equipped me for communication with my French contemporaries and had led to so many great gaffes during those first blustery months amongst the French natives. I knew no other way and I suppose had the courage of my convictions at that point that this was the way to run a professional English lesson.

Tea, biscuits and chat – mainly in French – fortunately broke up the two-hour session, though what we found to talk about once we switched to the easier medium of French, I can't for the life of me remember. Today I would have asked her about her life, her early ambitions, her marriage, her children, so many things, but at that age it would have seemed, I suppose, too forward, impertinent even, to delve into the private life of a woman who was rather older than my mother. Perhaps too, with the self-absorption of youth, I wasn't even particularly interested in what made Mme Postelle tick. I know I found the whole business of getting to and giving these weekly lessons a tremendous effort, being paid was always faintly embarrassing and I couldn't say I really enjoyed the sessions at all, but I was grateful for the money, touched by her kindness, recognising the sacrifice that was being made on her part. I still have stored away somewhere the farewell letter she wrote when one of us, I believe she, brought the arrangement to a close. Mme Postelle is one of those dear souls who live on in my heart. The world is a better place for them.

Though I did no more teaching in Paris during my remaining time there, finding more dynamic and physically arduous ways to earn a living, it was while still living there that my younger brother Richard, ever concerned for my welfare, convinced me that, with my passion for travel and fascination with far-off cultures, a TEFL qualification (teaching English as a foreign language) might be the very thing to see me on my way. Being something of a Francophile himself and a great lover of the arts, he had spent the year between the sixth form and university in Paris too, residing in *Rue Mouffetard* – one of the oldest and most atmospheric streets in the city. He had found himself a rather fascinating job in the theatre coffee bar at International House, a highly reputable English language school in *Rue Mazarine*, a short walk away from the River *Seine* and *La Bourse* – the nation's mint – on the fashionable Left Bank. Having observed and talked to many of the teachers at this establishment, Richard had come to the conclusion that teaching English as a foreign language could be quite an interesting way to earn a living. When he pointed this out to me over a *kir* (a delicious mixture of blackcurrant liqueur and Muscadet) in the buskers' haunt *Le Mazet*, not far from *Place Saint-Michel* in *Rue Saint-André Des Arts*, adding that a TEFL qualification was more or less a passport to teaching jobs around the globe, given that I was about ready to move on to fresh pastures anyway, this seemed like a pretty good suggestion. So, when I finally managed to extricate myself from my much-loved Parisian life, it was to the Bell school in Cambridge that I ventured to get myself – at some considerable cost, I felt at the time – the tools of the TEFL trade.

Chapter 6

From Cambridge to Crete via Brittany

I'd heard a fair bit about the joys of student life in general and the charms of Cambridge student life in particular from my father, who, despite reports from Bradford grammar school, of which he used to be inordinately proud, spiced as they were with juicy comments alluding to his outrageous shirking and incomparable tomfoolery, had won himself a scholarship to Peterhouse, Cambridge, allegedly the oldest college at the university, to read history. I had never been warned, however, of the city's cruel, icy winds and generally inclement weather in winter, which is exactly when I ended up doing my one-month initial TEFL course there. Arriving at the train station on a frosty November morning, I barely noticed the weight of my hefty backpack, still dusty and possibly still ant-infested from lying around in Greek olive groves, as I strode out and began my search for cheap accommodation. I succeeded in renting an attic room in an old townhouse in Garlic Row from an ill-humoured, lecherous and decidedly seedy-looking landlord, whose mercenary instincts would have been evident to a half-witted badger. My fellow tenants were a bit of an odd bunch, composed mostly of foreign students taking advantage of the many language schools that flourished, at least in part, on account of the city's reputation as a hallowed centre of learning. First of all, there was Eswary, a demure and rather beautiful young Piscean girl from Malaysia, who attended a sixth form college and with whom I shared a room; I was impressed at her maturity and knowledge of astrology and birth charts, which I learned were taken very seriously in educated circles in her country. Then there was a desperately good-looking but decadent and roguish young Iranian, Sami, plus a couple of ever-jocular Latino gents in their early thirties, Carlos and Paulo; they behaved a bit like a comedy duo, teasing and tormenting each other constantly with such gross insults as '*cabron*' (loosely translated as bastard or son of a bitch). Carlos, I quickly learned, was a film producer from Venezuela and, as he was in the UK principally to improve his English, he leapt at the chance of free English lessons on the course I was taking, so he became not only my housemate but also one of my first guinea pig students, along with his quieter, introspective comrade, who was taken on from time to time during those bitterly cold weeks as my amiable, easy-going, no-strings-attached bed-warmer. We Garlic Row inmates would congregate cheerfully in the evenings in the tiniest, draughtiest, grimiest kitchen imaginable with its orange and grey lino tiles, ill-fitting back door and outdated equipment, which included an ancient gas cooker with an eye-level grill. I have no recollection of any actual meals being cooked there, so I must, I suppose, have lived, as I did in my student days, on charred buttered toast, Cornish pasties, Brain's frozen faggots, those superb culinary delicacies, inexplicably spurned by many yet second to none as wholesome, meaty comfort food on chilly fenland evenings, and bowls of steaming Ambrosia creamed sago or tapioca.

The main tutor on the course, Sandy, was to my mind a highly original character, a bouncy, vivacious, rolling snowball sort of a woman, heavily pregnant with the second child of her estranged Japanese husband, yet with more positive, pent-up energy it seemed than all of us passive, mild-mannered students put together. She bombarded us with Japanese during the course – in daily greetings, role plays and so on – the intention being to give us a taste of what we would ourselves be subjecting our own beginner-level English students to in the fullness of time, should we pass the course and succeed in getting a job at the end of it. I remember she insisted on calling me Evans San throughout the four-week course, and would often refer, not unkindly I have to say, to my outrageous and unseasonal suntan, as, almost up until the very start of the course, I had been soaking up the blessed rays in warmer climes. Those were the days when I would sunbathe at each and every opportunity, anointed with whatever oil was to hand, with a fervour verging on fanatical. This was, of course, long before my poor fair skin started to rebel and I was told in no uncertain terms by dermatologists that this reckless behaviour would have to stop. I had heard earlier in the year that the south-western corner of the Greek island of Crete fell into a different climatic zone to the rest of the country, to the rest of Europe in fact, and that it often enjoyed quite warm sunny weather right through the European winter. It was for this reason that I had lingered far longer than I should have done in the erstwhile hippy haven of Palaiochora, long after the summer crowds had departed, as did once the youthful Joni Mitchell, hanging out with a beguiling, eternal traveller type she had fallen in love with, my namesake Carey, about whom the song was written. Right up until mid-November I had been wafting barefoot through the olive groves in my faded cut-off jeans and tie-dye T-shirt, living on Greek salads and garlicky green beans, drinking copious amounts of ouzo and resinated wine, living out my days hedonistically, reading Carlos Castaneda and Hermann Hesse, discussing the meaning of life, pairing off with whoever took my fancy under the full moon – under the waxing or waning moon, for that matter – doing my best to concentrate on the joys of here and now. So, as you can imagine, it had been quite a wrench leaving this place, idyllic as it was in many ways, to attend the course I'd somewhat dutifully signed up for, unbeknownst to me, in one of the bleakest, or if not certainly the windiest, parts of the UK. A very real sacrifice had been made.

Needless to say, I had done no preparation whatsoever for the course, which makes me a complete hypocrite when I proffered my advice recently to my (very much younger) brother William, who had decided at the ripe old age of forty-something to embark on a career in TEFL. I emphasised how imperative it was to do some serious pre-course reading (on the challenging English tense system, for example) and suggested he organise some classroom observations in a reputable school before embarking on his TEFL course, something that simply hadn't occurred to me to do before my own.

My memories of that month in Cambridge in 1978 are a bit fuzzy, I have to admit. (I shall have to liaise with Jude, my kind, generous and multi-talented thespian friend, whom I was fortunate enough to meet on the course and who has remained a close and devoted friend ever since.) It always fascinates me how two people who experience the same situation at the same time will later recall things in such a different way. I remember the Bell school as being a little way out of town, having to take a bus at the crack of dawn and arriving, despite my efforts, late for my first class in the unprepossessing, prefab hut that had been allocated for our course. Our hut was hidden away amongst the bushes behind the rather beautiful old building where the main school was housed. I arrived drenched from a mind-numbing, icy downpour, timed by the weatherman to start the very moment the bus came to a halt. The heating in the hut was turned up extra high, as though to compensate for the fact that a place had not been found for us in the Bell school proper, and Sandy's welcome was similarly warm if a tad theatrical and in a language unknown to me at that point, which turned out to be Japanese. As my damp clothes gently steamed in the clammy hothouse atmosphere, I glanced around at my fellow students, the majority of whom were female, some cheerful, ruddy and matronly, others earnest, undernourished and academic-looking. Few, I remember thinking, would ever become real friends. As for the men, I wasn't so sure – one of them, a bespectacled and rather dashing-looking young man of mixed race, caught my eye and we exchanged a brief smile. I later learned he was of Indian ancestry, was called Dilip and had plans to work for the *Times of India*. Towards the end of the course, we went out for a drink together and the following day, thinking I was possibly in need of enlightenment, he lent me a small library of ultra-feminist literature, which, to my eternal shame, I only ever skimmed through and sadly never had the chance to return. Strange how female emancipation was a hot topic during this decade, yet I don't recall being drawn into much intellectual discussion about our progress with my peers. Without lifting a finger to advance the cause, I casually reaped some of the benefits – in the form of the freely available contraceptive pill, for instance, and the more relaxed attitudes towards cohabitation before marriage. I have no doubt that Dilip would have made the most of his time on earth and would have worked in some capacity for the well-being of others, whether through teaching or some other worthy, altruistic profession – he appeared to have the maturity I lacked at that time, a sense of purpose and an inner glow that distinguished him from most other men I'd met up until this point in my life. Should I have made more effort to cultivate this liaison? Quite probably. My teaching career might have taken off a lot sooner than it did with Dilip in the wings, but I was on my own winding path of self-discovery and it's only with hindsight that we see these things.

As for my recollections of the actual content of my initial TEFL course, I recall regular rather inconclusive discussions each morning about grammar, 'aspect' and the complex English tense system, along with a whole series of mini role-plays, which often involved passports, customs inspections and shop purchases – or huffy exits from imaginary shops due to the exorbitant prices of imaginary goods. Observed lessons, which formed an essential part of the course and were graded, started off with a tiny five-minute slot and gradually increased to a full horrendous hour. These longer observed lessons tended to provoke a huge amount of stress, even last-minute, full-scale hysterics, especially as highly detailed accompanying lesson plans were required. On top of this, not only was one observed by an experienced Bell EFL teacher, if not our tutor Sandy herself, but also by the whole gang of peers, most of whom already seemed to me to have had a large amount of classroom teaching experience, whilst I had none whatsoever. It later transpired, however, that having undergone a regular teacher training course, whether at primary or secondary level, could actually be counterproductive, as there was a risk that one might not be able to make the vital adjustments necessary in order to become an effective EFL teacher, which we were rapidly learning was a very different thing altogether to any other type of teacher.

My first short observed teaching slot revolved around the teaching of the minimal pair – 'i' (as in the word ship) and the long 'i' (as in the word sheep). My class of elementary-level guinea pig students for this first observed lesson happened to include the aforementioned Latin American characters from my intimate little household, the charming but worryingly garrulous film producer, Carlos, and my quiet but rather intense new companion, Paulo. Carlos, ever the keen student, had got himself a seat right at the front of the class and was wearing, for some unknown reason, the most ridiculous schoolboy-type cap – perhaps he thought it would improve his performance. One of the keywords we soon discovered on the course was 'elicit' – instead of *telling* the class things, grammar rules for example, or discussing the target language the idea was to *elicit* it from the class with clever prompts, pictorial flash cards and gestures. It was during the preliminary stage of eliciting words that contained the minimal pairs that things started to get out of hand. Having successfully elicited a list of words containing the short 'i' sound (fit, kit, split, etc.), I now called for words containing the long 'i'. Model student that he was, Carlos' hand shot up and on receiving the nod he succeeded in enunciating a beautiful string of appropriate words: 'feed, bead, seed and need'. 'Excellent, Carlos.' I beamed encouragingly... 'Now, give me a sentence to demonstrate how we use the word need.' A penetrating and rascally look flitted across the thirty-five-year-old schoolboy's face. 'Carolina,' he said, the fervour of his emotions plain for all to see, 'I *need* you... *now*!' His declaration was so dramatic and unexpected that I did what I had dreaded doing all through my schooldays but thought I had finally grown out of: I blushed furiously from the neck upwards until I could feel the burning glow warming the four corners of the room. I remember little about the rest of this lesson or about the subsequent lessons for that matter, except for my final long observed lesson, which I orchestrated in the throes of a nasty cold bug. A prolonged, tear-inducing coughing fit hindered the smooth operation of the cassette player and I found myself rushing to the window and flinging it open for fresh air. Once my coughing had subsided, I was quietly instructed to abandon the lesson and take my seat. 'I think we have the general idea' I was told kindly.

One of my fellow trainees stands out in my mind as she was probably a little older than the rest of us and very obviously considered herself a true academic – a Cambridge University academic at that. She approached the course in an extremely cool and analytical way – my approach by contrast was what I can only call experiential, intuitive and rather naïve. Not only did 'the academic', whom I shall call for now Tabatha, become a personal friend of our trainer, Sandy, but she actually went on some sort of mini-holiday with her mid-course, which I think some of us found rather strange at the time, as they really did make a very odd couple indeed – Sandy we suspected was something of a bohemian at heart, an opportunist who made things up masterfully as she went along; there was no doubt that she was an exceptionally gifted and dynamic teacher. She seemed to live on her nerves, to believe in things turning up when you needed them. She rather implied during the course, in an airy, offhand manner, that she was virtually penniless after the demise of her marriage, but whether that was strictly true or whether it was just a temporary state of affairs we never got to hear. Above all, she was someone who simply exuded enthusiasm for her work and zest for life. I'm not sure I realised it at the time, but her approach to life, her *joie de vivre*, made quite a deep impression on me. Tabatha, on the other hand, appeared to lead a life ruled by discipline, caution and restraint; she took herself rather too seriously, yet one got the overall impression that she had never been further than the end of Brighton pier with her mother. (That was once said about me, too – by Jude, as it happened – but as she got to know me better, she added… 'and I couldn't have been more wrong!') Whilst most of us trainees cobbled together lesson plans in our bedsits sometime around midnight after the pubs had closed, Tabatha almost certainly raced home after the class ended and got stuck into her grammar reference books before typing up detailed and meticulous lesson plans, backed up by up-to-the-minute research gleaned from the latest publications on language acquisition theory. The ironic thing was that Tabatha was, I believe, the only one to fail the course. I think it became clear to us all, in fact, during one of her longer observed lessons that she was simply not cut out for this type of teaching – she had included a rather complex dialogue in this lesson, which was on the language function *making suggestions*. In this dialogue the students had to negotiate a meeting at a local pub called the Pig and Whistle. It was an unfortunate choice of pub name as, to begin with, some of the students were unable to pronounce Pig and Whistle, and Tabatha became positively draconian on her insistence on the correct pronunciation, the result being a farcical performance with much embarrassment and no obvious learning benefit. On hearing that she had failed the course – we all learned rapidly through the grapevine – Tabatha had made an immediate appeal to the authorities. We suspected that, despite her temporary role as weekend buddy to our esteemed tutor, she did her utmost to discredit her in the end, no doubt criticising her unorthodox and apparently unplanned, organic approach to the development of our course, but I never did hear the outcome – I suspect her appeal failed miserably.

Perhaps my most vivid and enduring memory of that month on the windy plains of Cambridge, however, was an occasion towards the end of the course, when I was invited to visit Sandy in her modestly furnished temporary lodgings one evening after dark (as I gather all twelve trainees were around this time) to discuss my progress and I suppose for her to get the measure of me as an individual to see if she really felt I was ready to hack it at the chalkface as an EFL teacher. The interview took place in a cramped and very steamy Victorian bathroom, where Sandy was up to her elbows in bubbles bathing her two-year-old son. Little beads of sweat were gathering on her brow and upper lip, yet she seemed perfectly capable of tending to this olive-skinned, squirming, gorgeous boy and simultaneously discussing my ability to teach the present perfect tense and get to grips with the passive, as though such bizarre multi-tasking were the most natural thing in the world. The evening was enjoyable if positively surreal – I don't remember making notes of any kind or any serious discussion of my future as an EFL teacher, but I will never forget the Turkish hammam-like atmosphere, the beatific infant, the laughter and the fun we had whilst supposedly working. Looking back, I think I learned one of life's important lessons from Sandy – that if you have imagination and enthusiasm, not to mention stamina, however difficult your circumstances, you will generally find a way to pull things off workwise, and in all likelihood enjoy the process to boot.

I passed the course but, unlike the majority of my fellow newbies to the TEFL world, did not rush to take up a position with the first school that would hire me – instead I returned home for Christmas, where I made an effort, as usual, to get on with my stepfather and step-siblings, with whom sadly I seemed to have increasingly little in common as the years went by – they being mostly devout, church-going types, whilst my brother Richard and I were rather eclectic in our religious beliefs. To my surprise, there was a letter waiting for me when I got home, from Plume, the drummer of a Parisian rock band called Diesel, inviting me to join them at a château on the coast of Brittany, where they planned to make some sort of promotional video. I'd met the band earlier that year, queueing outside a telephone box in the centre of London. They were having some difficulty using the phone, so I helped them and ended up joining the jolly party heading westwards in their battered camper van. The fivesome were on their way to Reading Rock, a music festival headlining Thin Lizzy, Alex Harvey and Uriah Heep. As my mother lived in nearby Wokingham, that's where we aimed for but, as we got hopelessly lost trying to get across the city in the rush hour, we arrived at my parents' house quite late in the evening. My stepfather was not at all keen on the idea of this long-haired troupe camping on his newly mown lawn, so Mum kindly turned out into the dark and drove to a suitable camping spot in some nearby woods with the van tailing us. Mum's breakfast invitation was readily accepted. That's one of the things I love about Mum: like her own mother, she relished meeting younger people and learning about their lives. She was always willing to put up friends, friends of friends, and even on occasion total strangers. I once had a flight back to the UAE cancelled because of snow on the runway and I told her on the phone of a distraught young mother beside me with two young children; her immediate response was to bring them back from Heathrow with me in the taxi – she'd make up the spare beds and try to find a rubber sheet for the toddler. I was rather surprised when the tallest, quietest member of the band, the drummer, Plume, came forwards just before they departed next morning offering me a scrap of paper with his address in Paris and asking me for mine. I got the feeling that he had taken a bit of a shine to me.

I accepted the invitation and duly joined the band at a picturesque château on a desolate promontory just outside Tréguier, but I must say the experience wasn't a whole lot of fun, partly as it was perishing cold, despite our efforts to build roaring log fires in the great hall, partly as the magic mushroom omelette I was given for breakfast one day made me feel alienated, empty and forlorn, and partly as it became increasingly obvious to me that a relationship with Plume was not to be. It seemed to take the poor fellow a little longer than me to reach this conclusion, as I was later taken to meet his parents back in Paris, who treated me with such warmth and solicitousness I really wonder what they had been told about me and our plans. There was even some talk about the parents lending us the deposit to rent a flat together in the Bastille area and other band members started referring to us as a couple. I tried to let him down gently, but suspect he was quite badly hurt as he declined future invitations to parties when I later became one of the three graces (more of which anon) and I never saw my gentle, curly-haired, bespectacled drummer again.

I stayed on in Paris, after the psilocybin mushroom-fuelled séjour in Brittany, picking up some tour guide work, which I'd done previously and quite enjoyed, supplementing my income with bouts of bottling (passing round the hat) for buskers, that I'd got to know at *Le Mazet* bar in the Latin Quarter, when my brother Richard worked around the corner at International House. Funny how during that phase of my life I preferred to occupy my time in this way, rather than putting my qualifications to use and applying for teaching jobs, trying to 'get ahead'. I enjoyed the sense of anonymity mingling with the well-dressed, powerfully perfumed Parisian crowds on the metro or sauntering along the sun-dappled, tree-lined boulevards on the Left Bank; I felt at ease living for a while outside 'the system', doing what I felt like when I woke up each day, lingering over the paper as I dipped fresh brioches bought from the boulangerie below into my breakfast bowl of *café au lait*, stopping to smell the roses and, at all costs, avoiding responsibility.

I shared a flat with two excellent French women, Marina, a delicate, porcelain-complexioned astute Armenian beauty I'd met one evening that January at a Diesel gig, and Agnes, an equally striking-looking, extrovert, effervescent pure *Parisienne*, with a mop of reddish curls, an infectious laugh and strong links to the music and entertainment business. It was Marina who had rightly assessed at the gig that I was in a bit of a dilemma, to put it mildly, about what to do next with my life, given the Plume debacle and my lack of friends in Paris, and had decided that the best possible thing would be for me to come home with her to *Levallois Perret* (a sedate, densely-populated, tourist-free neighbourhood, bordering on the ultra-chic *seizième arrondissement*, a few kilometres north of the *Arc de Triomphe*) and stay until I came up with a plan of action. Agnes, I recall, was initially a bit put out at Marina's announcement that I had come to live with them and would henceforth be sleeping on the sofa-bed in their living room. As unalike in looks, outlooks, backgrounds and temperament as any three young women could possibly have been, we nevertheless in a short space of time formed a close bond and came to be known by our entourage as '*les trois graces*'.

We had regular dinner parties during which I was teased unmercifully, yet not really unkindly, about my English accent and idiosyncratic way of expressing myself. I always did – still do in fact – confuse the words '*cheville*' and '*chenille*', meaning, I believe, ankle and caterpillar respectively. You can imagine the sort of idiotic statements that could be made by confusing them. I continued to tell people I was feeling horny and that I was pregnant, when what I'd meant to say was that I was warm enough and replete, but unlike the times in *La Varenne* with Alain and his friends, I felt that here in *Levallois Perret* I was among my own friends and when people laughed, as they often did, at the way I spoke their language, I felt they were laughing with me rather than at me and I gradually learned to just go for it and muddle through when telling stories. I have Marina and Agnes to thank for that – they gave my confidence a much-needed boost. I was not exactly down and out when we met, but possibly not that far off, and I shall be eternally grateful for the kindness they both showed me back then. Angels, the pair of them.

Quite possibly due to my experiences living in Paris as one of the three graces, I later deduced that I fell very much into the category of 'experiential language learner' as opposed to an 'analytical' one. This inclination to dive in and 'have a go' at communicating, despite lack of vocabulary or knowledge of grammar, can be extremely irritating to other language learners of the analytic persuasion. I soon found this out on the MA TEFL course I later did at Reading University, where twenty of us were subjected to lessons in elementary Zulu in order to raise awareness of different language-learning styles. I found myself, during that first basic Zulu learning experience, at a table with an assortment of highly analytical types, who were far more interested in 'cracking the code' than in having a bit of fun attempting to communicate – albeit at a very basic level – in a totally unknown language. You could easily spot the other experiential types in the stuffy, rather overcrowded room that summer's afternoon by the grins on their faces amidst the clusters of frowning, head-scratchers. Sorry, I am obviously biased – there are clear pros and cons with either learning style.

Ever the sun worshipper, it wasn't long before the azure skies of Greece beckoned once more and I found myself forsaking the land of *baguettes*, *boeuf bourguignon* and *Beaujolais* and heading south to meet my Finnish friend, Aila, in the Venetian port of Chania, on the north coast of Crete. It had always been my intention to put the knowledge gleaned at the Bell school, Cambridge, to good use at some point and indeed, eighteen months or so after completing the course, I attempted to do just that, asking everyone who crossed my path if they knew of anyone who needed a qualified English language teacher and generally putting out feelers around town. Within a couple of days, I got into conversation with a young American traveller, who was getting itchy feet and was looking for someone to take over his English classes in a small private language school, a *frontistirio* on the outskirts of town. The following afternoon, I made my way along a dusty, almost deserted road running due south from the port, through a largely residential area to a small, nondescript single-storey building that matched the address I had been given. Sure enough, there was a small plaque on the front wall on which was engraved in blue cursive writing the name of the establishment – The English Language School. If the thought crossed my mind at that moment that this could be the very first important step in a long and rewarding future career in EFL, I have no recollection of it. I simply stepped inside from the still quite powerful late afternoon sun and, assuming the frazzled-looking, slightly bulbous-eyed lady behind the desk in the extraordinarily untidy office was the owner, Mrs Leptidou-Aretaki, announced myself as the prospective new teacher, sent by the itinerant American, Gerry. I was greeted warmly and invited to sit on a wooden chair, while she shooed a few children out of the room and spoke hastily to a parent, who was staring at me with undisguised curiosity. There was quite a din going on from the room opposite, which increased steadily in volume until a shrieking female voice could be heard overriding the rest, berating the class and no doubt threatening them with dire consequences unless they piped down that instant. I have always had a naturally soft voice and I knew from the end-of-course report at the Bell school that I would have to work hard at 'establishing a more positive teaching presence' if I were to become an effective EFL teacher. If I didn't have a strong sense of foreboding at that moment, and I don't think I did, then I certainly should have.

The interview proceeded quite satisfactorily – my education and qualifications all seemed in order. The fact that I had never taught an actual class of foreign language students before, besides those cashing in on the free lessons offered on the course, didn't seem to be an issue. If I was willing to give it a go, then so was Loula, desperate as she was to replace the accursed American deserter. Of course, I would not be paid the full rate (I was paid something insultingly low, I recall) until Loula – as I was invited to call my new boss – sighted the original documents, degree certificate included. My dear mother, after much rummaging amongst boxes and bags that had been mouldering away in the garage since my student days, finally managed to locate the requested items. Failing to run to earth an envelope large enough for the degree certificate, she gaily snipped off the edges – rather unevenly – with the bacon scissors and posted it off along with my TEFL certificate and only partially complimentary end-of-course report ('she has a friendly, pleasant personality… with more guidance and experience it is to be hoped that she will develop into an effective EFL teacher'), both of which arrived several weeks later.

It was just as well that I didn't have to pay for accommodation out of my meagre teaching salary; it wouldn't have been enough to pay for a stable. To begin with, I continued to live at Yani's Guest House in the port, where I had been working as a part-time receptionist. After I started teaching, I continued to put in some hours for Yani at the weekends and so maintained my accommodation deal. Not only that but, as I was later to discover the wretched man had designs on me, I was actually given a semi-decent private room with a view over the port – a big improvement on the basic dormitory I had initially inhabited at the back of the building, with its shared bathroom that periodically flooded and had us dashing around the dorm to lift articles left on the floor to the safety of bed level. My new upgraded accommodation contained a rickety iron bed and a small round wooden table and chair at which I would mark the mountains of homework that I brought back with me from the *frontistirio* each day, sometimes falling asleep over the table fully dressed, waking disorientated in the early hours with a horrible crick in my neck.

Later on, thanks to my Finnish friend, Aila, her jaunty but rather arrogant butcher boyfriend, Alecco, agreed to let me use the small beach house belonging to his family, a few kilometres outside town. The wonderful thing about this slightly dilapidated dwelling was its peaceful, isolated location, the magnificent views from the front patio of the majestic Cretan mountains – snow-capped for much of the year – and, not least, its proximity to a quiet, sandy beach, bordered by huge, spectacular sand dunes from which pampas grass grew, making the scene on sunny days quite heavenly. On such days I would often indulge in what I called a 'sea swoop'. After donning my swimming gear, I would climb to the top of the highest sand dune, digging my toes into the cool dry sand and breathing in the pure salty air. Then came the exhilarating swoop downwards and seawards as fast as I could possibly manage without spinning out of control and somersaulting forwards into a hopeless heap. At the end of the swoop, of course, lay the glittering Mediterranean Sea – never warm along this north coast, even at the height of the summer, and distinctly icy towards the end of the year, which was when I performed my sea swoops. As far as I am aware no one ever witnessed me in action on these occasions. It was a solitary ritual, and indeed just about the only time I came into contact with others during those challenging months in Chania was in the classroom with the rabble, with ever angst-ridden Loula when our paths occasionally crossed or with the other teacher she employed – a mild-mannered, plumpish Greek lady, not without charm, whom I suspect was paid as poorly as I was if not worse. I also had the occasional visit from Alecco, a typical Greek man of the seventies, I suspect – chauvinistic, egotistical and sex mad.

I was quite proud of what I felt to be my independence in Chania, although, of course, I wasn't really, living as I did in Alecco's house, and was not aware at the time that I was lonely. Looking back on my youthful self, however, I realise I must have been lonely – very lonely, in fact. How much more fun it would have been to go sea swooping with a companion, to have rustled up simple dishes together in the evening and eaten them on the patio, reminiscing, dreaming, philosophising and discussing the books we were reading. I used to think of myself as a loner – and to others it may well have seemed so. I have never been one for doing things in groups, especially girlie groups. I have little interest in their conversation topics, which tend to get watered down so. I have always preferred in general to see my friends individually, and to this day, if I don't have good company, I'd much rather be alone. As for boyfriends, I felt, in the end, I had been betrayed by my first love, Alain. He changed when we left Oxford; he was a depressing sort of travel companion and in some ways a rather unsatisfactory partner in our Parisian life – he was not always respectful in company and, though he claimed he still loved me, he dabbled in drugs behind my back and I suspect was not faithful to me on the few occasions I returned to the UK to visit my family. A book I read around that time – Germaine Greer's *The Female Eunuch* – opened my eyes to how things might have been and, along with meeting an interesting, rather intellectual post-grad student, James Dunkerly, on an Oxford visit, I worked up the courage to up sticks and leave. If I'd read this book or the ones Dilip had lent me when still a student I quite probably wouldn't have stayed with Alain as long as I did, and might instead have gone to the Bolivian altiplano on a research trip with the far more eligible James and taught English to rosy-cheeked Bolivian children, possibly even having one or two of my own.

As for my initial attempts to manage a classroom full of scabby-kneed, eight-year-old Greek boys and timid, whispering girls, they left a lot to be desired. As part of the course in Cambridge, we had been required to produce a set of twenty multi-functional flash cards. I had chosen the theme of leisure time, so my laminated cards had pictures of mostly white, middle-class families, cropped from magazines, having jolly picnics in the English countryside, gambolling with dogs on the Yorkshire moors or sunbathing on golden Cornish beaches under cloudless skies, watching TV in gleaming, comfortably furnished lounges and so on. Although I was in my mid-twenties by now, had been to Egypt, to several European countries and had lived in Paris for almost three years, I don't think I was as culturally sensitive as I might have been. I don't recall any of my flash cards having people of different ethnic backgrounds – perhaps it was harder to find such pictures in magazines in the UK at that time and, of course, this was well before the advent of home PCs with internet access to just about any image one might require. To my dismay, the flash cards didn't seem to have the magical effect I had envisaged. The boys in particular seemed to find some of the cards utterly hilarious, rendering them quite incapable of making the statements I was desperately trying to elicit. I think perhaps the problem was that I had half expected the flash cards to do the teaching for me. My efforts to set up tasks using the flash cards for the most part failed miserably. I came across these dreadful cards the other day in one of my many boxes of letters and memorabilia and the very sight of them brought back some of the anguish and frustration that I experienced trying to use them in that first teaching job. My teaching certificate had stated that to become effective in my chosen profession I needed guidance, yet here in Crete there was no such thing to be had – I was left to my own devices and would simply have to gain much-needed experience through trial and error.

The published materials available at Loula's school were not plentiful and those I was told I might use were mostly a bit outdated and overwhelmingly British. The dialogues appeared stilted and the pictures not altogether convincing. Still, I did my best to do justice to publications such as the old Longman favourite *Composition Through Pictures*, trying, as I had been taught, to elicit language that I then put up on the blackboard using squeaky white chalk, smearing my face with it from time to time, which didn't help my standing in my captive audience's eyes. The children were expected to note down useful vocabulary in preparation for an essay to be written over the weekend. The good ones, usually the girls, after all this laborious preparation, produced some quite reasonable work in endearingly neat and careful handwriting, but with the boys, at least with the majority of them, it was a very different story. The only comparison I can make with regard to their grubby offerings is with the diabolical, inkblot-covered exercise books and scraps of mangled paper handed in by the *Beano*'s Bash Street Kids. It was quite hard to believe that these were really their best efforts, not some warped joke intended to outrage and antagonise their green, newly appointed English teacher. Not only did I have to grade these compositions of widely varying quality but I had also been asked to give each pupil in each class a grade of some sort each day, as this was what the parents apparently required. The demand was excessive and I really don't know how I coped.

Reading through Loula's letter of reference just now I was a little shocked to see that I only worked for her for three months. It felt like very much longer, but then I was only twenty-four when I started teaching that September, twenty-five when I departed in December, and time seemed to go so much more slowly in those earlier decades. The incidents that stay in my mind most vividly from my time at the Cretan chalkface are mostly ones that caused negative emotions – anger, exasperation, embarrassment, despair and so on – all of which, in my first proper teaching job, I experienced more or less daily. Being an avid sunbather at that time and not teaching until late afternoon when regular school was over, I would have plenty of time for oiling up, toasting myself on each side several times, showering (only cold water in my primitive home), consuming a modest afternoon meal and dressing in something clean for work. I possessed a very limited wardrobe at that time, travelling as I then did with only a rucksack. I had a white V-necked T-shirt of which I was especially fond, the Mickey Mouse one given to me by my dear Parisian friend Marina. I had admired it on her more than once and touchingly she had insisted that I take it with me when I left on my Greek adventure. It showed up my impressive tan rather well, I thought, and it was this very T-shirt I was wearing the evening I was asked to take my colleague Eleni's class for a one-off lesson, while she attended a family occasion of some sort. The class contained some older boys, including two particularly boisterous, strapping, hirsute teenagers, positively bursting with testosterone. As soon as I stepped into the classroom, I regretted having put on the Mickey Mouse T-shirt. Apart from being rather casual for teaching, the v of the V-neck was rather low, and as my jeans were quite tight, the boys' attention from the moment I stepped into the room was most certainly not on phrasal verbs. Having absolutely no idea how to gain control of the situation, I attempted to focus my gaze on the keener language learners in the front desks, desperately willing the brutes at the back to knuckle down and concentrate on the task at hand, but whenever I glanced up my eyes would meet theirs and my embarrassment at witnessing their outrageous, brazen leers was extreme.

Another evening around the same time, as the summer drew to an end, some far younger children – boys of course, always the boys – managed to get the better of me. As my class was the only one running in the school that evening, I had been given the keys to lock up and Loula's home phone number should I need it, though I had no idea why I might. At the beginning of the lesson the classroom was rather fuller than usual, I seem to recall, and there was devilry in the air, which was garlic-perfumed as the housewives in the surrounding dwellings were concocting the evening meal. My board drawings at that time were rudimentary, if not faintly absurd, but I persevered as I felt they added another dimension to the lesson and as well as injecting some – not always intentional – humour; just as well I had been well trained to tolerate being laughed at during childhood, my father being a merciless tease. I must have spent a little longer than usual on this occasion embellishing some multi-coloured, chalk artwork, and as I turned around to face the class, I got the feeling that a good handful of the boys had disappeared. The expressions on the faces of the remainers strongly suggested what was dawning on me with growing alarm – that some of the blighters had jumped through the window at the back of the class and scarpered. Four empty seats just below the back window confirmed this. My big dilemma now was whether to inform Loula the following day about what had happened, revealing my lack of authority over the children and their lack of respect for me, or to simply give the missing boys their daily grade and keep shtum about the incident, hoping that news of their audacity would fail to get back to her. In the end, I kept quiet about it, as I did about another evening when a particularly troublesome boy asked if he could go to the toilet and succeeded in switching off the main power switch, plunging us all into darkness and leaving me with no alternative but to send the class home early.

Whenever I hear or use the word dilemma, I am reminded of a favourite activity of mine from an American book of discussion tasks for intermediate students of English. In this exercise, the class are told about an attractive young career woman called Sophie, who has three suitors all keen to marry her. The class is divided up into small groups who then discuss the pros and cons of marrying each suitor and decide which one would be the best bet, or if she should simply concentrate on her career and refuse to get serious about any of them. The name of the activity was Sophie's Dilemma. Depending on the age and maturity of the class, a lot of fun could be had coming up with unexpected, even faintly shocking suggestions. One particular class of mine, many years later in Croatia, excelled at this activity. I would always check at the beginning of the class that everyone knew what the word dilemma meant. When I asked this as an open question to one of my first classes with young adults in Thailand, an eager young man piped up: 'Yes, yes, Miss Carrie, I know! I know! He's from Tibet!' A quick slot on pronunciation then ensued using the IPA (international phonetic alphabet) demonstrating the difference between dilemma and Dalai Lama. Sadly, no such materials existed in Loula's school, and even if they had, none of my classes were mature enough to handle such potentially risqué topics.

The end of the year was drawing nearer and Loula had already asked me if I would like to spend Christmas with her and her small family, an invitation that today I would be quite touched by and inclined to accept. I think it was actually this invitation, which took me rather by surprise, that prompted me into a serious review of the situation I'd got myself into in Chania, living alone in a cold and very sparsely furnished tiny villa in a somewhat remote location, which, with the scarcity of buses, meant hitch-hiking into town and back each day, often with slightly lecherous Greek men, working in a difficult job for which I felt ill-equipped and for which I was earning a mere pittance (my sole luxury during that time was a weekly copy of *Time* magazine, which I devoured from cover to cover, determined to get my money's worth; its coverage and graphic photos of the Jonestown horrors in the Guyanese jungle haunt me to this day). The one-month TEFL course I had done in Cambridge was geared far more towards teaching adults than towards young learners. It was only very much later in my teaching career, working in a mountain top state secondary school in Tenerife in the Canary Islands, that I came to the conclusion that I simply didn't like teaching children at all. By then I had gained quite a lot of experience in the EFL classroom, having worked in half a dozen countries in Europe, the Middle East, the Far East and New Zealand, my board work had improved enormously, and I had developed a fairly eclectic teaching approach that suited me and for the most part worked and kept me gainfully employed in reputable institutions. I could afford to pick and choose my work. At that time in my mid-twenties in Crete, however, I was badly in need of experience. I should probably have grinned and borne it and carried on at least for a whole academic year, but a little experience at Loula's *frontistirio* had gone a long way; enough is enough, I told myself.

I decided to hand in my notice, which I did the following day, in all probability with some hastily dreamed up reason linked to family – an ailing parent, a hospitalised sibling perhaps, I forget just what I came up with. Loula accepted my undoubtedly unwelcome decision with good grace. She was evidently upset, however, to be losing not only a dedicated albeit inexperienced young teacher, who would not be easy to replace in a hurry, but also perhaps a slightly exotic guest for Christmas. I have no recollection of feeling any real remorse about delivering this unpalatable news to my ever harassed, yet amicable Greek boss, just relief to be extricating myself from a situation I no longer wished to be in and a town that no longer held much charm for me. I could, in fact, have stayed on for Christmas at least – indeed, it would have been the kind and courteous thing to do – but my mind was already elsewhere. I intended to follow the sun in search of new adventures. I had heard Israel was the place to go once the weather turned chilly in Europe. My French ex, Alain, always swore he would never set foot in the country, but I had no such scruples at that time and the thought of picking citrus fruit in the winter sun, mingling and exchanging stories with international travellers, experiencing a new culture, a new continent was more than a little appealing. *Antio Kriti!* I shall be back someday.

Chapter 7

From Tiberius to the Tropics

On board a smallish El Al aircraft bound from Athens to Tel Aviv, I got into conversation with a pale young Fin called Heiki, who was embarking on his first lone trip around the globe and was keen to hobnob and share information with a fellow traveller. As he was Scandinavian, his English was, not surprisingly, impressive and we chatted away like old friends over airline trays of welcome free food, exhilarated to be footloose and fancy-free above the clouds with new countries and experiences before us. Tippling a sweetish but rather delicious Israeli wine after the meal, I was intrigued to learn that a film was being made in the south of the country, near Eilat, on the edge of the Sinai desert, starring an old heart-throb of mine, Tony Curtis. According to Heiki, people who had experience dealing with horses were needed and would be well paid for their services. The idea of grooming and exercising horses in the Sinai, even washing down sweaty, restless animals after filming, with the possibility of running into Tony himself, as opposed to flogging the future perfect to smirking Greek youths for mere peanuts, was immensely appealing and as soon as I landed in Tel Aviv,

I made my way straight to the bus station to buy a ticket southbound. Heiki had no interest in horses and was eager to experience kibbutz life, so we bid each other a fond if hasty farewell on a dusty pavement and went our separate ways.

'Are you Jewish?' I was asked, particularly by older men, in the streets of Tel Aviv, at roasted peanut and pumpkin seed stalls, on buses, in the post office, at supermarket checkouts, wherever I went in this new, exotic, yet vaguely unnerving country. Open and approachable though I am, perhaps increasingly so as I grow older, I remember being quite taken aback by the directness and intensity of feeling that was apparent behind this very personal question. People's disappointment, when I replied that I was not, was evident and in a way touching; it was as though these quite possibly distressed and displaced individuals were desperately seeking out others who, like them, harboured appalling memories and sought comfort in the company of similarly traumatised individuals. The other thing that struck me as decidedly odd that first day in Israel, as I made my way across town in a crowded bus to the main bus station for the coach down south, was finding myself pushing past young soldiers clutching M16 rifles, and seeing faintly hostile young women also in army uniform, military service being compulsory for them for two years, while for men it is three. One was never allowed to forget that the country was surrounded by enemies – remaining alert and poised for possible attack was crucial. It was partly this knowledge I think that, later on in my Israeli interlude, tormented my hitherto unthreatened being and brought me excruciatingly close to complete physical and emotional breakdown.

The journey down to Eilat through the Negev desert was longer and dustier than I had expected. The rocks are of granite, far harder and darker in colour than the Sinai sandstone further south, which makes the landscape quite forbidding in aspect. The overall effect, once we had descended into the heart of this other-worldly terrain, was of suddenly finding oneself transported to the moon. It was certainly weirder than anything I had encountered before and I found it hard to believe that people had actually chosen to live here, either in isolated settlements or leading a nomadic existence, since the time of the Nabateans as early as 500 BC. These remarkable people, I later learned, became so skilled at water conservation that they succeeded, in a land with minimal rainfall, in building a thriving wine business, exporting vast quantities of what became known as Gaza wine to Europe. Another important source of income came from spice trade caravans that crossed their territory and from pilgrims passing southwards through their city of Shivta en route to Santa Caterina in the heart of the Sinai. Such was the wealth of the Nabateans that they could afford to import fish and crocodiles to supplement their diet. The only inhabitants I saw on that first southbound trip were occasional wiry, weather-beaten Bedouins, clad in long white *thawbs*, still semi-nomadic, gazing stoically into the middle distance with their small herds of goats.

A couple of stops were made en route to Eilat at bus and gas stations, where I experienced for the first time the joys of Israeli falafel. Always freshly made, light, crispy and aromatic with a subtle blend of spices, encased in warm pitta bread, complete with tahini sauce, hummus, salad, sliced gherkins and pickled hot green peppers. *Al hakefak*! No other falafel eaten before or since my stay in Israel have come even close to matching them. I found the food in Israel, in general, to be utterly delectable – any local supermarket or deli would sell a wide range of mouth-watering, freshly made salads, many including caramelised roasted vegetables and particularly well-prepared aubergine, which in my experience can be bland and oily or succulent and *taim* – delicious – depending on who has cooked it. I will never forget either the first time I tasted *baba ghanouche*, or *mutabel* as it is called in some Arab countries. It is made from baked aubergines, which are skinned and blended with garlic and mayonnaise to make the most divine concoction imaginable. We used to make huge vats of it for functions at the Nophit Hostel in Eilat, where I ended up working for the best part of half a year. I could have lived on the stuff, and in fact more or less did, which is almost certainly how I came to gain so much weight at that time. The other irresistible calorie bomb was the *shamenet metukah* – a rich, creamy, satiating food I discovered in the dairy section during my first exploration of the main supermarket in Eilat. For some time, I was under the impression that it was a type of extra creamy yogurt, when in reality, I later discovered, it was sweetened sour cream. As I ate at least one tub a day for months on end it is perhaps no wonder that I filled out somewhat during my time living in the Gulf of Aqaba, particularly during rare periods of rest, when the excess calories were less likely to be burned off by physical activity.

On a healthier culinary note, as an employee later on at far and away the best eating joint in town, *Le Bistro*, owned and run by the dignified and engaging Ram Cooper, a Moroccan Jew, who had learned the tricks of the trade working at the Ritz in Paris, I enjoyed some of the freshest and finest seafood I have ever had the good fortune to consume. Once a week a tall, silent Norwegian called Axel would slip furtively through the back door of *Le Bistro* and into the restaurant, bearing a large, old, battered, brown leather suitcase. The first time this happened I was intrigued, especially as he entered unexpectedly, unannounced and with a certain swagger, then bent down to open his case right there between the tables, which we were in the process of laying for lunch. From inside the murky depths of the case emerged a whole colony of desperate, clambering, grey crayfish. For the last hour or so of their lives the poor creatures were given the run of the premises while the chef, Yousif, and his young female assistant – his niece we were led to believe, although there was no doubt in our minds that the couple were an item and very much in love – boiled up a huge pot of water, laughing at my exclamations of horror at the prospect of such cold-blooded mass execution. Customers who ordered crayfish were given a selection of steel implements with which to extract the pink flesh from the various bits of the body. It was surprising how many of them didn't know how to use this specialised cutlery nor did they seem to realise that the choicest bits were in the main claws. Thus, quite often when crayfish was ordered, the claws remained intact when we whipped the plates from the table. The minute we got back to the kitchen my fellow waitress Laura and I would pounce on the claw crackers and get to work in earnest, devouring the succulent morsels with glee, laughing at the ignoramuses sitting outside in the restaurant, waiting patiently for us to take them the dessert menu.

Once a week, too, Ram's disarmingly beautiful blonde wife, Etti, would materialise in the kitchen and concoct the most remarkable lamb couscous. I had eaten couscous from time to time in the Arab quarter of *Barbes*, when I lived in Paris, but nothing quite compared to this. We worked extremely hard waitressing for Ram; his standards were high and silver service requires great skill and finesse if done properly. We waited on tables at lunch and dinner seven days a week for very modest wages, but the great perk of the job was that we were allowed to eat more or less whatever we wanted when on duty, with the exception of fresh oysters, which we'd occasionally help ourselves to in any case when a fresh batch was delivered. We were treated at least as well as Ram's son, Danny, who waited on tables with us and whom we always regarded as a bit simple-minded. He was sharp enough when it came to totting up the shared tips, however, and unless we watched him like a hawk, he would pocket whatever he thought he could get away with. Alcohol too was permitted in moderation, especially when customers bought drinks for us, which they often did, provided we could perform our duties with charm and grace, which thankfully we always seemed to manage to do.

After hours there would often be invitations to join Israeli gents or parties of revellers and bacchanals, such as the French crowd from *Club Méditerranée*, if not Ram Cooper himself, heading down the coast to one of the various hotels' sparkly yet sophisticated nightclubs, the best one at that time being at Coral Beach. This was 1978, the era of disco mania; the Bee Gees' *Saturday Night Fever* was top of the charts that year along with Chic, Gloria Gaynor, Donna Summer and – my favourite at that time – the original rap number, 'Rapper's Delight', by the Sugarhill Gang, which to this very day can transport me back in an instant to those heady nights in our glittery tops, grooving away into the early hours on the dance floor, strobe lights flashing and disco balls spinning, blue curaçao cocktails on the bar and sultry looks from dark and debonair Israeli men. Fortunately, we were not required to report for duty until around noon each day, so we were able to get our beauty sleep and sleep off the after-effects of an evening's drinking, although, of course, it was not the drinking that was the main attraction of these Eilat hot spots – it was the music and dancing. Along, I must confess, with the men.

All sorts of celebrities had dined at *Le Bistro* over the years, the photographic evidence covering one of the walls of the smallish dining area – Princess Margaret with her current beau, film stars, jet setters and chart-topping singers of various nationalities. One evening there was a bit of a stir as it had become known that Julio Iglesias was in town and had made a booking at the Bistro. I knew and liked his music, which I had only become familiar with during my time working for Ram, but had no idea what the Spanish crooner looked like nor really how big a star he was. I didn't wait on his table that night – I believe Ram himself did – but at the end of the evening there was a certain buzz around the bar and I learned that we had all been invited to a beach party that weekend by Julio himself. I'm afraid to say that, though I did attend and have a hazy memory of a beach bar, lavish food and drinks laid on, a medium-sized crowd of beautiful, bronzed, well-dressed people milling around, I never really did work out which one was Julio himself. Given a second chance I might possibly have found out, sidled up to the man, told him how much I loved his music and flirted a little, hoping for a whispered word or two in return to store away in my memory casket. Many years later, when I lived in the UAE, I saw his charismatic son, Enrique, perform in an elaborately orchestrated open-air show in Dubai and read up on the lifelong rivalry between the father and son. I came to the conclusion that Julio probably wasn't a particularly nice individual at all and that I had been better off keeping my distance that day on the shores of the Red Sea.

Although not exactly generous with wages, Ram was, however, extremely generous when my mother came out for a week's visit. I was given paid leave and told I could bring my mother to eat at the Bistro whenever I liked. Mum and I spent most of our time, in fact, out of town on a fabulous jaunt, travelling down the Red Sea coast by local bus to the Bedouin fishing village of Dahab, stopping off en route at the wondrous under-water aquarium near Raffi Nelson's beach, overlooked by the notorious Mandy Rice-Davies' restaurant, *Mandy's*. There was a dramatic moment in Dahab when Mum was swept off her feet by a freak wave whilst bathing before breakfast and thrown inelegantly onto a coral bed. The lurid bruising that resulted served to remind her on her return to grey old England of her carefree, sundrenched days in distant Dahab. On the evening I did take Mum to dine at *Le Bistro*, Ram waited on us himself as though we were royalty. We had a sumptuous and unforgettable meal that included prawn cocktails, pepper steak and an excellent full-bodied French Cabernet Sauvignon. *Merci beaucoup*, Ram!

Well, after that lengthy digression, back to the nitty-gritty of trying to make a living by following the sun and one's instincts, keeping an ear to the ground and being ready to jump in if and when opportunities presented themselves. Arriving in Eilat early that January 1979 and discovering that Tony Curtis and the film crew had just moved out, I was naturally disappointed but only considered it, as I recall, a minor setback. The hostel I had ended up staying in on my first night in Eilat was called the Nophit, modest enough in terms of comfort and facilities but situated in a remarkable elevated position to the south of the town, overlooking the glistening waters of the Gulf of Aqaba and the granite mountains of Jordan and Saudi Arabia beyond. As the sun set each night, the mountains would steadily change colour – from orange to amber to red then through every shade of purple imaginable until they returned once more to lifeless grey. The whole show took no longer than fifteen minutes, but each moment was pure magic; it is one of the most enduring images I have of that often harsh and at that time largely barren land.

The Nophit hostel had a function room attached at which various Jewish celebrations took place, *bar mitzvahs* and *brit milahs* or circumcision ceremonies being the main ones, but also weddings, birthday parties and so on. As it turned out, a young English woman had just left her kitchen job there all of a sudden and in rather mysterious circumstances. I later heard that she had simply collapsed from exhaustion, which was exactly what happened to me a few months down the line, and I wouldn't mind betting that we were just two of many other young female travellers who were similarly exploited then cast aside, when no longer functioning satisfactorily, by the owner, the despicable Joski Ben David, who looked a little like Colonel Sanders but without the cheery smile. In any case, if I fancied stepping into her shoes as a general kitchen hand, washing up and assisting the Russian cook, Itsik, the job was mine, I was told that first evening, so without too much reflection I gratefully took it. An added bonus was that the job included board and lodging and I was given a small room, somewhat spartan but my own room nevertheless, with a bird's eye view of the sparkling Red Sea, bordered by the majestic Jordanian mountains.

I ended up spending eighteen months in Israel, with a short break in the UK to see family somewhere in the middle. When I returned to Eilat from the UK I seriously wondered if I had done the right thing coming back – the flat I was renting had been burgled; only a few bits of costume jewellery and a cassette player had been taken but the thought of someone rifling through my possessions in my absence was most unpleasant. Karula, the lovely young red-headed German woman who lived in the flat opposite us, had been raped by someone she had considered a friend, and there had been a murder on the floor above us – our block was not known as Sing Sing for nothing. I was told by locals that the crime rate in Eilat was unusually high as when the prisons were full in the north of the country, convicts were sent down to Eilat, where they were put on probation. It would not be an exaggeration to say my dealings with the police in Eilat over the burglary were quite ridiculous and downright strange. After I reported the break-in, my flat was given a cursory inspection and my personal letters taken, supposedly for fingerprinting. I had a great deal of difficulty getting these letters back and indeed I was treated so disrespectfully during the inquiry it was as though I was suspected of having committed some crime myself. My only crime, I suspect, was consorting with Israeli Arabs and possibly making a trip to Gaza with my Bedouin boyfriend, Marhy, and an interesting friend of his, Harboosh, a large, hirsute and intense-looking individual, who made a mean *shakshuka* (a wonderful dish involving eggs, tomatoes, peppers, garlic and smoked paprika) and may have had questionable political leanings; odd though it may seem, on leaving the country to visit my family I was picked out of the crowd and searched, while my rucksack was taken apart, frame and all. I was also picked up by plainclothes police late at night in Eilat when returning to the Nophit, after spending an innocent evening in a bar in town run by a compatriot, Bill, a retired boxer who despised the damp British climate and liked to live life on the edge. A certain amount of furtive drug dealing did go on in this bar, but that was not the reason I was there. It had a great jukebox and was a good place to meet friends. At first, I refused to get into the jeep as instructed as I simply didn't trust these shady-looking men. They had to walkie-talkie back to the station for a police vehicle, which I finally reluctantly got into. I was told I was suspected of buying drugs, so at the station, I was strip-searched by a hard-nosed policewoman, who of course found nothing, and as I left the station the humourless, pock-marked chief standing inches away from me snarled nastily that I should count myself lucky I was a woman because if I'd been a man they would have 'done me over well and good'. He and his henchmen were little better, I'm quite sure, than the so-called criminals they were being paid to track down.

Despite these unfortunate events, my time in Israel was interesting in many ways – I worked in several jobs, from catering and gardening to ironing and window cleaning, meeting some remarkable people along the way. On my first day of work at the Nophit, I was approached by a tall, jovial young man with a thatch of black hair and enormous eyes with thick eyelashes on both top and bottom lids. His name was Avi and he reminded me of a startled ostrich. He had a part-time job in the kitchens with me and was invaluable in giving me the low-down on my colleagues – who to trust, who to look out for and so on. It was Avi who accompanied me down the coast to Coral Beach early on in my stay in Eilat and persuaded me to take my first camel ride. There's a photograph of me somewhere beaming down from atop the understandably sullen beast, wearing an overly large green army jacket that Avi had insisted I wear to protect me from the blistering midday sun. One weekend I learned from Itsik that Avi had been admitted to hospital for minor knee surgery. He had reacted adversely to the anaesthetic and had not regained consciousness. I was heartbroken; Avi had just completed his military service and was simply bursting with excitement at the prospect of travelling outside Israel. He was intent on reaching London and I had promised him that if I was in the country, I'd meet him there and we'd go to Buckingham Palace. Also very close to my heart were the thoroughly likeable, hospitable, hard-working Syrian relatives of my Arab boyfriend and Nophit colleague, Marhy. One of Marhy's brothers was an English teacher at a school in Nazareth. I was assured that if/when I married his younger brother, he would introduce me to the principal and I would almost certainly be given work. The marriage was not to be, but we travelled all over the country together, from the Golan Heights in the north, where we were given food and shelter by a gentle Druze family, to the monastery of Santa Katarina and Mount Sinai in the heart of the Sinai desert, which I climbed in wooden Dr Scholl sandals, as they were the only footwear I possessed. Whilst recovering from a mini-breakdown, mainly due to overwork at the Nophit, I made a lone trip down to Sharm-el-Sheikh at the southernmost tip of the Sinai (now part of Egypt), where I was fortunate enough to go snorkelling and see some of the most spectacular coral and sea life on the planet.

I lived not only in the desert town of Eilat during my time in the Levant, but also, later on, in a verdant valley filled with flowers and fruit trees in Kafr Kanna (where Jesus, so the Bible tells us, turned the water into wine at the wedding feast), in Tiberius, on the banks of the Sea of Galilee, where we'd catch fresh fish in the evening to barbecue for supper, and eat on our own private beach, gazing up to the village of Safed, sitting like a bright jewelled crown on top of the nearby mountain, and briefly in a village near Jaffa, where Marhy's aunt took great pleasure in dressing me in some of her traditional clothes and teaching me how to make pitta bread and cauliflower curry. An apartment had been bought for this aunt by her family, in a newly built block in a quiet residential area, but she preferred to stay in her tiny old house just outside the town, cooking on an open fire in a clay-floored hut in the garden, with a hole in the roof for the smoke to escape. She'd divorced her husband and lived life her own way, marching to the beat of her own drum and singing to her own tune. I have a photograph of the three of us squinting into the afternoon sun in her lovingly tended garden and can picture her brown, heavily lined face, her wide smile with its flash of gold and hear her infectious, joyful laughter. Such precious memories.

Although I was introduced (by my creepy taskmaster at the Nophit hostel, Joski Ben David, funnily enough) to someone who was interested in employing me in some capacity at Jerusalem University, I never did teach English in Israel (I can hardly count a few attempts I made at teaching some uncontrollable children in Eilat privately – to everyone's relief the project was brought to a premature conclusion). What I did do, however, was teach myself some rudimentary Arabic and Hebrew. It was in the latter language I made more headway, as I was using it in the workplace from day one... Good Morning. How are you? Everything alright? Fine, thanks. Hand me that knife! Watch out, it's hot! and so on. It's a theory of mine, not an original one I dare say, that if a language is learned in real, dynamic situations and is regularly recycled, it will embed itself so firmly in the memory that it will be retrievable more or less as long as one lives. I have certainly found that my basic Hebrew comes back to me quite effortlessly on the odd occasion I have needed it, whereas with German and Latin, both of which I learned formally and passed various exams in, yet rarely if ever held a conversation in, I struggle greatly to remember anything much at all. I do remember one phrase in Latin – *te amo, miles* – 'I love you, soldier', which I have not had occasion to use to date, but you never know – it could come in handy yet. As for German, one phrase, in particular, comes back to me from time to time from one of Goethe's poems: '*Streben, streben... immer aufstreben*', which might be translated as 'always strive towards your goals, strive to fulfil your ambitions' or into today's lingo possibly 'onward and upward!'

Blowing kisses to the desert sand and swiftly setting sun, I left Israel by ship in the summer of 1980, accompanied by the bold Laura Brickell, the friend I'd made working at *Le Bistro*. Laura was a little taller than me with short wavy, chestnut hair, a good complexion, pearly white teeth and piercing blue eyes, which had a slightly dreamy look about them when she wore her contact lenses. She had wonderful long shapely legs, which she often showed off by wearing seductively short shorts, and on catching sight of my own legs for the first time, she exclaimed, 'My God, Carrie, you've got fantastic pins – for goodness' sake, if you've got it, flaunt it!' I'm not sure I ever did really work Laura out. She loved good food, wine, dancing and sex and though some might have considered her a happy-go-lucky type of girl, she could be pensive, shrewd and serious with an unusually clear idea of what she wanted in life. She had a number of lovers in Israel, some of them much older men, but not really sugar daddies, though they might have been willing enough to behave so, should she have wanted them to. She formed one great attachment to a young Yemini man of slender means – I believe she really loved him, but she knew she'd have to leave him as he clearly was not husband-material, a phrase I heard for the first time from Laura. She adored little children and had a thing about their chubby calves, claiming it was all she could do not to grab them and take a bite. Having been brought up in a hotel in Bristol with her two equally stunning-looking sisters, she was very much at home in the catering world and was a highly accomplished silver service waitress. It was through me that she became interested in the idea of teaching English as a foreign language, and did in fact qualify and take up a teaching post in Sicily after we went our separate ways. We corresponded for a while and I learned that she was finding all the preparation required to do the job properly was getting her down and cramping her style. She was planning to resign at the end of the term and give up teaching altogether. 'Well, a girl's got to have fun!' she wrote, by way of explanation. My life became rather hectic around that time and I failed to respond promptly enough to one of her letters, so I was struck off her list of friends. Clearly, she was hurt, as I was told she felt her letters had become redundant. I was sorry we lost touch. I've tried and failed to trace her, but am fairly sure that she would have achieved her ambition to have a large family and quite possibly a well-run hotel somewhere by the sea with a climate warm enough to wear short shorts the year round. I really do hope so – I admired her spirit and occasionally dream that we run into each other in unlikely places.

After island hopping in Greece and hitch-hiking around France, Spain and Portugal, Laura and I returned to Northern Europe via Andorra, where we bought a cassette player and a cassette of Bob Marley's latest album *Uprising* (we'd just seen him live in Toulon), which we played almost continuously on the last lap of our journey up through France. We ended up in Aarhus, the second-largest city in Denmark, where we'd been told there would be work for us in the marquee bar during the autumn jazz festival and then at Jacob's Barbecue, an upmarket restaurant, owned by a very enterprising Israeli, Jacob, one of whose many brothers Laura had known in Israel. We couldn't believe our luck when we arrived at Jacob's – we were greeted like long-lost friends by two of Jacob's siblings, Shimshom and Yeheskill, and shown our accommodation, which turned out to be their own luxurious flat on the first floor of the stunning eighteenth-century building, which housed the various function rooms. Our working hours were quite long, but the work was so enjoyable that it often didn't feel like work at all. What a contrast to my teaching job in Crete, where each minute felt like an hour and each day like a week. Our efforts at learning Danish at Aarhus University were perhaps admirable, but we failed to make any significant progress – partly, in our defence, as our teacher appeared to have quite a serious drink problem, arriving late if at all for class, reeking of beer or spirits, and without any discernible lesson plan or procedure. What is more, most Danes we came across in the workplace or in public, particularly the women, seemed to be virtually fluent in English, so there was no real demand for private English classes. Consequently, in Aarhus, as in my previous port of call, my TEFL qualifications continued to lie fallow and another year or so went by without my gaining so much as a smidgen of vital language-teaching experience.

The next time I set foot in a classroom was in the Spring of 1983 at the Brighton and Hove School of English, a reputable language school run by Giggins and Shoebridge, two dedicated EFL gentlemen, who had published their very own book of drills, *Tense Drills* published by Longman, which I confess I never did get round to using. My interview for the job had been with the

Director of Studies, Duncan Shoebridge, a charming, urbane and dapper gent if ever there was one. On that first meeting I remember being impressed by his jet-black hair, slicked back with some sort of 'brilliantine', his well-cut suit, shiny black leather shoes and, to cap it all, in his crimson silk tie, a sparkling diamond tie-pin. Thankfully, I was not grilled on the intricacies of English grammar. I had been quite crestfallen to have been rejected at another Hove language school sometime before this by another DOS, the legendary Ian Pitkeathly, for failing to give the correct order in which the woefully complex English verb tenses should be taught. 'Well,' said Duncan after a fairly relaxed chat about my work in Crete with the diabolical children, 'if you can handle Greek teenagers, I think you can probably manage our Spanish groups – you can start on Monday.' The work was only for a few weeks over the busy summer period, mainly with Spanish youths from Madrid, but it was another important small step in my early EFL career, and though I don't think I did a very good job at all, I have always been grateful to Duncan for employing me and for writing me the loveliest letter of reference, which still sits in my folder of documents, along with the one from poor Loula Acetaki and half a dozen other bosses over the years. Duncan's signature, with its rococo loops and elegant swirls, was if anything even more flamboyant and eye-catching than his diamond tie-pin. What a dear man. End-of-service letters of reference aren't used anymore, I believe, and in some ways, I feel this is rather a pity. There was something uplifting about getting a good one, with an appreciation of one's efforts and possibly a string of glowing adjectives to bolster one's confidence in years to come, before daunting job interviews, for instance.

It was some time before I found myself standing in front of a language class again – a good two years or so. I can't say I had actually enjoyed my time with those surly Spanish teenagers on their summer course at Duncan's school. The fact was they didn't want to be cooped up in a language class being made to study irregular past participles and baffling phrasal verbs, when they could have been out in the sun on the beach, communing with the local talent and generally having fun. So, when, towards the end of the course, the opportunity of wielding a knife for a living presented itself, in a highly reputable vegetarian restaurant, Food for Friends, I jumped at the chance. It was whilst chopping vegetables at a feverish pace and stirring vats of peanut chilli sauce in the chilly sous-sol of this restaurant that I met and became instantly enamoured of a certain Rick Stiles, with whom I was to spend the next ten years. We decided to tour the world, teaching English along the way, and to this end Rick undertook and passed the same TEFL preparatory course that I had done a few years previously.

After an interesting though somewhat gruelling four months or so travelling on a shoestring in India, mainly in Rajasthan, we went on to explore Thailand, then travelled down through Malaysia and Singapore to Indonesia, where we tried and failed to find work teaching English, mainly as we had arrived at the wrong time of year. Our original plan had been to spend a whole year in India and South East Asia, then head on over to Japan, partly as we'd heard stories of people being extraordinarily well paid for teaching English there. By the time we got back to Thailand from Indonesia, however, from where we would have caught a flight to Tokyo, our funds were getting seriously depleted and so we found ourselves applying instead for teaching jobs in Bangkok.

Chapter 8

Thailand First Time Round

Arriving from the crazy, filthy, frenetic yet fascinating and indeed often beautiful cities of India, Bangkok seemed to me, that first time back in the mid-eighties, to be some kind of haven, filled with abundant, freshly washed, exotic fruit, gleaming gilded-roofed temples, lush tropical vegetation, clean toilets, delectable, cheap palatable food and gentle, smiling people – after our money too no doubt, yet, if so, it seemed with more grace and subtlety. I have since come to love India dearly too, with all its cultural diversity, vibrant colours, stunning temples and wildlife – its people no less – but travelling there as we did that first time on a very low budget, getting constantly sick from the enticing yet often toxic roadside food, queueing for hours on end at railway ticket offices only to be told unceremoniously that there would be no third-class tickets until the following day, emerging from train stations and being swamped by hordes of raggedy boys and men of all ages, vying for business and desperate to take you to a particular guest house so they could earn the commission that would pay for their evening meal – it was all such hard work and utterly exhausting. Thailand by contrast was far easier and less stressful. Even the *tuk tuks*, the Thai equivalent of the Indian motorised trishaws, though no doubt equally hazardous, were so much more inviting, painted as they were in rainbow colours and dotted with flashing, coloured lights. They were just like something out of a fun fair, as was the ride itself. Rick loved them and would leap in with gay abandon, refusing to entertain the idea that he might end up flattened on the road in the prime of his life.

Looking back, I am so thankful that we ended up in Thailand and not Japan. Neither of us were experienced teachers; we were both cutting our EFL teeth, so to speak. Rick had only just passed the RSA Certificate course and hadn't taught at all. There had been a shift in methodology in the language teaching world and the *communicative approach* was now all the rage. With their trusting, almost childlike demeanour and lack of inhibitions, I feel sure the Thais were far better 'guinea pigs' for us to try out our innovative classroom ideas on than the very much more reserved and cautious Japanese language learners would have been.

Our first employer was a prepossessing, graceful and elegant Thai lady of a certain age called Wipapan. She owned a school called the Universal Language Centre (ULC) just around the corner from our spanking new Lek Guest House, on Khao San Road, which in those days was relatively sedate compared to the bustling, effervescent and kaleidoscopic street it is today. Situated just opposite the massive and imposing Democracy Monument, the school was on the third floor of a huge old building, whose windows looked out onto one of the widest, grandest and busiest avenues in the city, *Rachadamnoen Klang*, built by King Rama V in 1899 to connect Dusit Palace to the Grand Palace. The latter, an architectural wonder of golden stupas, walls and pillars encrusted in shining multi-coloured mosaics, was the official residence of the Kings of Siam from 1782 until 1925. It was here along *Rachadamnoen Klang* that major processions took place on auspicious days in the Thai calendar, drawing thousands of spectators, so that the whole stretch of road from the Golden Mount Temple at one end to *Sanam Luang* Square at the other was a sea of teeming humanity.

The classrooms were positively cavernous and furnished with scruffy, old-fashioned furniture, school desks with names carved into the wood and squeaky old blackboards. Copying of worksheets had to be done using a duplicating machine that looked as though it had come out of the ark. We sometimes spent our own hard-earned money on photocopying at a nearby shop, as it was a lot less bother, even if you had to queue on the street in the noonday sun. Wipapan was an unusual employer, quite relaxed about our teaching arrangements, yet punctual with payment, meagre though it was. She had recently lost her Canadian husband, something of an academic we gathered, who had started the school several years earlier. She appeared to be missing him greatly; in any case, her heart didn't seem to be in the job. I don't think I was much of an asset to her school. I coped poorly with small classes of mostly uninterested young boys and failed to make a significant difference to a private student's pronunciation, an earnest dentist whose English girlfriend mocked him in English pubs as he was unable to pronounce 'A packet of Smiths crisps please'. The most embarrassing moment came when I was asked to give private French lessons to a very smart and rather serious mature Thai businesswoman. I hadn't felt I was being dishonest when I had written in my CV that I had 'a good working knowledge of French', having studied it formally for thirteen years at school and university, and then having lived in Paris for the best part of three years. It soon became evident, however, that the student's French – at least the type of business French she required – was significantly better than my own. We agreed quite amiably to call it a day at the end of the first hour.

I was rather more successful with my classes, most of them one-to-one sessions, at a large company a short bus ride away from Wipapan's school, across the Chao Phraya River, that manufactured ladies' underwear. My students there included the boss's daughter, Daa, a very pretty, petite and surprisingly modest young woman of around twenty-four, recently married to a similarly affluent young man, who also worked for the company. During the course of our lessons, I learned that Daa's parents had started off married life selling brassieres and other assorted underwear from their boat in the floating markets along the Bangkok canals or *klongs*. Daa herself amazed me one day by admitting she had never been on a boat on the river herself or even taken one of the ubiquitous river taxis. For that matter, she confessed, she rarely took public transport of any kind, as she was driven everywhere in one of the family's BMWs. What a phenomenal leap up the commercial and social ladder within one generation. I also taught Daa's lifelong friend, Mee, an equally likeable if less flamboyant young woman, from a working-class Chinese family, who was employed in the company's accounts department. At Daa's suggestion, the three of us would sometimes jump into a taxi after our classes and head off into the horrendous, cacophonous, slow-moving rush hour traffic for an early dinner together. Our favourite was a hotpot restaurant, the type of place popular throughout the Far East, where you sit at a table around a small cauldron of simmering broth, are given individual bowls, tongs and fishing nets, ordering various plates of uncooked chopped meat, leafy vegetables, noodles and raw egg, which you then cook yourselves, scooping each morsel out of the bubbling brew when you think it is cooked, dipping it into one of the many chilli-ridden sauces provided in small bowls. I rather preferred the Taiwanese version, known as *horgwor*, meaning fire pot, partly as the atmosphere in the huge steam-filled halls there in winter was so vibrant. These places would be packed with families at the weekend and the sound was deafening, which didn't really matter so long as you were hungry and were intent only on eating, not on making polite table talk.

On one occasion, Mee surprised me slightly at the end of our lesson by asking if I would like to join her and her boyfriend for dinner that weekend at a riverside seafood restaurant. I was of course to bring Rick too. I accepted graciously and bought a new peach-coloured silk blouse for the occasion. I learned from the taxi driver that this was one of the top seafood restaurants in the city and was frequented by well-known actors, politicians and other VIPs. The table Mee had reserved was perfectly situated overlooking the river, brightly lit dinner cruise ships gliding by along with long, dark, silent, faintly sinister cargo vessels piled so high with coal, cement, grain and other goods it appeared as though the whole lot was about to sink forever into the murky depths. Mee was looking particularly elegant for our soiree in what I suspect was a brand-new outfit and she appeared rather more self-assured and relaxed than she generally was at work. When asked what we would like to eat we replied that we would be very happy to have whatever they suggested. A short conference took place and when the waiter arrived to take the order it seemed as though enough food for many more than four slim people was being ordered. Before long an array of wonderful dishes started to arrive, including *prik tai torp*, deep-fried peppercorns, still on the branch; *pak pak boong*, braised morning glory with oyster sauce; *kung kasap*, enormous prawns in their shell; *yam woonsen*, glistening glass noodles with seafood marinated in lime juice, chilli and coriander; and the piece de resistance, *pla dumkap ching*, a magnificent large white fish, cooked with ginger, garlic and spring onions. All of this was washed down with copious amounts of Thai beer and local wine. It was a wonderful evening. There was a warm, easy atmosphere and I was very touched that my student should have invited us for what must have been an extremely expensive meal on her meagre salary, flatly refusing any contribution from us when the time came to pay. I have never forgotten this kindness and generosity. I feel sure Mee would have married her quiet, intelligent boyfriend, and I sometimes wonder if their children became friends with Daa's children, despite their very different backgrounds.

It was to the very same restaurant that we were taken a few months later by a pair of adorable and equally generous female business students of mine, Wilawan and Wacharee, both prone to fits of giggles for no apparent reason. They wanted to thank me for teaching them so patiently over a two- or three-month period; neither had an aptitude for languages but I did my best to find engaging materials with an element of humour where possible and we always seemed to have fun, even if I was not convinced that much progress was being made. I'm pretty sure my boss, David, realised I was deviating considerably from the rather dry binder of business materials I'd been given for this course; he even said, after reading the students' feedback, 'Well, I'm not sure how much their business English has improved, but they seem happy enough with everything.' This time the food was, if anything, even more lavish and plentiful. I remember one of the dishes being a rare treat of fresh crab – *poo sob* – I was encouraged to eat every morsel, including something they called the 'cream' from somewhere inside the head. It all tasted pretty good, but something was evidently amiss, for that night I was violently ill and, in the morning, I was in a very poor state indeed. Rick had reluctantly had to go to work, and soon after this I made my way gingerly to the bathroom, half leaning against the wall as I went. On my return to our room, I keeled over backwards in a fainting fit – I must have been totally dehydrated.

As chance would have it, one of our Chinese neighbours, the daughter-in-law of our landlady, in fact, saw me behaving theatrically from the courtyard below and came rushing upstairs to find out what had happened. Seeing I was barely conscious, she summoned her husband to help and, after trying to revive me with smelling salts (actually a Vicks stick), together they proceeded to dress me and bundle me into their clapped-out old car, driving me, thankfully, to the best hospital in the city, the American Hospital. Following an examination and x-ray, I had my head stitched up and was given a first-class private room with its own en suite bathroom and extra bed for my spouse, should he care to spend the night at my side. I was hooked up to a drip of salt and dextrose, which slowly flowed into my body until I'd absorbed several litres. I don't think I'd ever felt so pampered and well cared for – I was washed and powdered twice a day and had my temperature and blood pressure taken virtually every hour. There was a small window in my door and there appeared to be a nurse posted just outside to keep an eye on me day and night. As a child I'd always felt envious when I listened to radio programmes broadcast from the wards of children's hospitals – finally, my dream had come true. My doctor was none other than the current TV celebrity Dr Picharn, a little like the American heart-throb Doctor Kildare, only darker and rather less professional. It was actually quite hard to believe that Dr Picharn was a certified medical practitioner, as each time he came to my bedside, accompanied by a flurry of excited young nurses, he made virtually no reference to my diet or recovery plan whatsoever, confining his questions to unusually personal ones. He was especially anxious to hear my assessment of his level of oral English. The menu I'd been given resembled a large coffee table book, with an almost overwhelming choice of cuisines ranging from spicy Chinese Szechuan to Halal, Kosher and Western, including a full English breakfast, so I felt I needed some guidance about what food should be chosen and what was to be avoided. 'You may eat whatever you wish,' he replied nonchalantly. 'Now, tell me, how do you feel about the British monarchy?' There was no doubt he had charm and charisma and I enjoyed my brief bedside encounters with him. When the time came to pay the substantial bill, however, I couldn't help but protest when I saw that by far the most costly item was 'visits from Dr Picharn'.

The first visitor to arrive at my bedside that first day in hospital was not my dear Rick, but a short, tubby, rather odd American teacher from our school called Richard Hunter, a young man who had made no effort to hide the fact that over the past few months he had developed a raging crush on me. To Rick's mild annoyance, Richard had asked a few weeks earlier in the staff room if I'd be willing to combine our classes one afternoon to re-enact a traditional Western-style wedding for the educational benefit of the students. Having found pictures and explanations of our wedding traditions to have been quite adequate with my own classes up until then, I politely declined his request, even though Richard had spruced himself up considerably, since a complaint in an end-of-course survey that he wore the same rather scruffy clothes to work day in day out. Wounded and indignant, Richard had gone out and found – goodness knows where – some very formal clothes, including an extraordinary, outdated suit with matching waistcoat in an unsuitably warm, tweedy fabric, which he then started wearing each day for work, despite the daily average temperature hovering around the thirty mark. It was the very same old get-up he was wearing now for his hospital visit. He bore a huge bunch of red roses and greeted me like the adoring husband he dreamed of being. Thankfully, Rick didn't feel threatened by our clownish colleague and when he arrived a few minutes later showed simply surprise and mild amusement at the sight of this small, faintly ridiculous man perching eagerly on the side of my bed. When the time came for Richard to move on from Thailand a few months after the hospital visit, Rick even suggested we take him out for a farewell dinner. He turned up at the enchanting open-air Northern Thai restaurant we frequented in the same comical outfit, talked loudly over the little orchestra that was playing on a small platform beside us, and astounded us by cramming all the left-over bread rolls from our bread basket into his old duffle bag, whispering confidentially, 'You never know when you might need them!'

Rick soon found a more interesting and challenging job to the original one at Wipapan's rather half-hearted school, at the Home of English just across the road, a huge and successful operation run by a middle-aged couple, the Kanits, known to all employees as Mother and Father. Each year they treated the whole staff, along with their partners, to a weekend holiday with games and sports events organised, in which extreme team rivalry was encouraged. The year Rick worked there the annual jolly was to Kanchanaburi, a couple of hours' drive to the northwest of Bangkok, not far from the Burmese border, where lodgings had been rented in quaint bamboo and rattan houseboats, moored to the banks of a meandering River Kwai tributary. We boarded one of three large, luxury, air-conditioned coaches beside the Democracy Monument at 7 am and almost the moment we set off were served a breakfast of hot dogs, cakes and iced fizzy drinks. We were then given song sheets, in Thai, and coached in the cheering and clapping rituals for the Blue Team. Snazzy new T-shirts and directors' caps were also distributed to be worn at the sports do that evening. Our blue team actually won with Rick almost killing himself in the tug-of-war and our blue couple performing admirably in the eating and drinking competition. There was also a hysterical marathon sack race and a shoe-finding event plus much singing and chanting between events from the three teams. To my horror, I was asked to be one of the cheerleaders and was given white gloves and some giant, electric-blue taffeta bunches to shake at the team, spurring them on to ever greater efforts. The whole two days were organised superbly, with a great variety of activities and entertainment, including singing, dancing and an uproarious drag act on Saturday evening, walks in the tranquil forested hills and a boat trip up the lazy brown river. Any moment we felt the tiniest bit thirsty or peckish, iced drinks and snacks would materialise under the vast swaying bamboos, served by a team of gracious, smiling Thais, who were working for Khun Kanit, converting the area into what would ultimately be a luxury mountain holiday resort. Kanit himself was a thoroughly good-natured and jovial character who clearly loved his patriarchal role and to all accounts was the most remarkable employer. He'd started out as a poor English teacher from the south of the country and at one time rented one of the rooms at ULC to give his lessons. At the time we were in Bangkok, he owned one of the largest language schools in the city, with many of his students doing correspondence courses. Staff at his school had excellent conditions and all kinds of perks, such as these holiday weekends, free food at 'The Home', free classes in languages other than English and so on.

The young Thai ladies who taught at the school almost all had degrees in English and were relatively advanced speakers of the language. Like many adult Thais, however, they had a childlike quality; in some cases they were simply immature and bashful, especially in the presence of Rick, on whom many I suspect had crushes of varying degrees. Although I tried to engage with Rick's Thai colleagues, I found they were mostly quite awkward and reticent in my presence, so, in short, not of much interest to me conversationally. As it turned out, some had the most incredible tales to tell of atrocities committed under the military dictatorship during the peaceful student demonstrations a few years before we set foot in the country. Many, according to these young ladies' accounts, had been hanged from the trees surrounding *Sanam Luang*, the field where kite-flying competitions took place each year opposite the Grand Palace, not so far from Khao San Road, where we had stayed when we arrived from India. Others had fled to the forests outside the city, where they had scratched a living feeding on berries and other fruit along with occasional food packages smuggled in to them by concerned relatives, until the heat was off. These horrific stories were only told to Rick in the utmost confidence after his inner circle of teachers had known him for six months or more. There were many other stories, some concerning King Bhumibol, the world's longest-reigning head of state, who was on the throne at that time, stories that were only ever told in hushed voices behind closed doors. Thailand, for all its charm and beauty, its smiling, friendly people and ubiquitous temples with their hushed, tranquil, incense-perfumed inner sanctums, has a very dark side. There is an underlying current of violence in Thai society – life is cheap, we learned; a hit man can be hired for a small fee. Even the beloved royal family, of whom there were photographs on the walls of practically every place we ate or drank in, reputedly had blood on its hands.

In due course Rick and I both got jobs at ELSI (English Language Schools International), a highly reputable teaching establishment, linked to an American university, situated the other side of the city to our home in *Ban Kung Pom*. Rick continued working at the Home of English, whereas I had to resign from ULC, which Wipapan was most understanding and civil about – after all, she was only able to pay me ninety *baht* an hour, less than two pounds at the exchange rate back then, which was a fairly paltry sum even by Thai standards. The new school was right opposite the Children's Hospital, just up the road from the enormous roundabout that surrounds the Victory Monument, an obelisk erected in 1941 to commemorate the Thai victory in the Franco-Thai war. I learned to say this in Thai – 'anusawari chai' – in case I ever needed to take a taxi there. Conveniently, however, there was a bus stop at the end of our road at which we could catch a 39 bus that took us all the way over there. Buses in Bangkok only ever stop for a few seconds, so we had to learn to jump on and off pretty snappily. As Thailand is warm most of the year, if not baking hot, the regular buses, as opposed to the more expensive air-conditioned ones, had open windows so that the air circulated pleasantly and kept people cool. There were several humpback bridges along the route, crossing the canals that carve up the city. No one took any notice of speed limits in those days in Bangkok – during rush hours the traffic police were stationed at crossroads frantically waving traffic on to ever greater speeds with whistles and batons. I remember sometimes feeling quite exhilarated sitting with my head half out of the window as the bus hurtled along leafy avenues and over bridges – I would even forget at times that I was work bound. On one particularly hairy ride I remember commenting to Rick on the recklessness of the driver, suggesting he might be on some kind of amphetamine. 'He can't help it,' Rick replied '… it's just his nature!' Although our paths often crossed at ELSI, our schedules were quite different, so we mostly travelled to and from work separately. From the moment I arrived in Thailand, however, I had felt safe and in some strange way 'at home' – students told me on more than one occasion that I was not like other foreigners or 'pharangs', that I was more like a Thai in disposition, that I must have been Thai in a former life – which I took to be quite a compliment.

Fairly early on in our Bangkok sojourn, I had been working late and found myself queueing for my bus in the dark along with hundreds of other commuters. Two number 39 buses went by without stopping as they were full to bursting point. I had very little cash with me as I'd been warned by students to take the minimum amount required if travelling by bus; crazy though it may seem, I only had enough that evening literally for my bus fare home. At last, a bus came along that still had some standing room, so on I hopped and muscled my way in, away from the door in the hope of getting a seat at some point. Within seconds, a small pair of hands relieved me of my heavy work bag – this was a common occurrence in Bangkok and I had no fear, as, even if I got separated from my bag for some time, I knew that it would come back safely to me by the end of my journey. Sure enough, after ten minutes or so I managed to get a seat and my work bag was handed back to me. I gazed out of the window, thankful to be off my feet, enjoying the cool evening breeze and simply being there in the midst of sixty or so Thai fellow workers, also tired and homeward bound, not one of them giving sideways glances, though they were no doubt curious about this youngish blonde foreigner in their midst. If ever I happened to look over my shoulder for some reason when travelling by bus, I would momentarily catch dozens of eyes upon me, then look swiftly away. What a contrast to the brazen stares I would be subjected to in other countries, among less sophisticated crowds.

After I had been on the bus for half an hour or so, I started looking out for familiar landmarks – the most distinctive one being, of course, the Democracy Monument. Once this came into sight it meant I had to get off at once. A growing unease enveloped me as I realised nowhere looked in the least bit familiar; on the contrary, instead of large inner-city buildings and temples, it appeared we were bowling through some swampy residential suburb, and at the same time it occurred to me that I didn't have a single baht on me to pay a taxi to take me home. As my face and whole demeanour must have started to register mild panic, the young man sitting next to me, a soldier in uniform, who miraculously spoke quite good English, asked me where I wanted to go and when I told him, immediately stood up and told me we should get off at the next stop. He instructed me to follow him, and as I really had no choice, I did so, and we ended up negotiating a dark path between patches of tangled, tropical undergrowth, which led us to a stretch of brownish grey slow-moving river. I was told I needed to wait for the ferry in order to cross the river, then would be quite near a bus stop, where the number 59 bus would stop and take me back in the direction I needed, right to the Democracy Monument in fact. I confessed, shame-faced, to my escort that I didn't have any money at all, upon which the soldier immediately dipped into his pocket and handed me a few notes that he said would be enough to get me home. I thanked him profusely and surprisingly soon after we'd bidden each other farewell, a small ferry boat with a handful of people in it chugged up to the landing point and I boarded, along with a couple of elderly folk, who seemed to materialise out of nowhere. My only fear as we made our way across the muddy, plant-clogged waters under the starry sky that night was how anxious Rick would be and how helpless he would feel, not knowing what had happened to me. These were the days long before mobile phones. In due course the bus did arrive and after what seemed an eternity the familiar roads and landmarks appeared and I scurried from the bus stop up our road past the temple and late-night food stalls to our home. Rick had, of course, been worried, but not unduly so – I seem to remember he had more or less guessed what had happened and we collapsed onto the bed in our spartan blue room, falling almost instantly into a deep restorative sleep.

One weekend we were invited to a military banquet given by two of our private students who worked for the Thai Intelligence Agency. Their names were Ike and Pradit, though we quickly rechristened them Tweedle Dee and Tweedle Dum. They were an easy-going and rather killing pair who had decided that Rick and I were great friends of theirs. They were forever offering to perform unlikely favours, which we'd never have dreamed of asking of them. Ike had recently been promoted, so he was having a lavish celebratory do at his home near us, to which countless military big-wigs – colonels, generals, majors and so on – had been invited. We knew full well that we, the token *pharangs,* had been invited as a status symbol, to demonstrate how cosmopolitan and sophisticated they both were. Not that we really minded; such occasions were always interesting and educational, if a little tiring. Rick had gone along a couple of hours before me, as I was giving a private lesson, and by the time I arrived, the men (around thirty of them), who were seated around a large table on the veranda, were well into the whisky and soda and trying to extract promises from Rick to visit Soi Cowboy and Pat Pong Road with them (both red-light districts) in search of a 'long-haired dictionary' to improve his Thai.

After a grand hand-shaking tour of the table, giving me an inkling of how royalty must feel on social occasions, I was seated beside Noo, 'the big boss', at one end of the table, a diminutive man with a delicate complexion, liquid brown eyes – slightly bloodshot by now – and tiny manicured hands. It was just as well I had built up a good appetite, as I was brought dish after dish of exotic food, which, as Noo became increasingly inebriated, was virtually fed to me. He was a much-travelled man and was quite reasonable company, certainly very attentive, until the whisky began to really take its toll. Unfortunately, Pradit, who was also a bit worse for wear towards the seventh hour of drinking, became a bit of a pain, whispering in my ear that his rank and transfer to Europe depended solely on Noo's decision and not to forget to tell him what a good student he was. He was actually an extremely good student but it all seemed a bit obvious, especially as Noo had very probably overheard Pradit's request. I had in fact already said words to this effect earlier, so didn't bother to repeat them. By the time we left the gathering we had been assured that we were 'as family' to just about everyone present, and that *no* request would be too much to ask from them. Noo gave us his personal number 'for emergencies' and even murmured something about arranging our visas for us so we didn't have to bother making the trip to Penang, but of course we didn't take him up on this. (We actually looked forward to our visa trips to Penang, where we would stay in the captivating old Chinese quarter. The streets there teemed with life, woks sizzling in the open-air food stalls, gnarled old men slapping down mah-jongg tiles with a flourish, toddlers gurgling in playpens on the pavement and cycle rickshaws honking as they wove their way between the bustling crowds.) Our main worry now was how we were going to get home with Pradit in his drunken state. Luckily, the clutch of his gleaming black BMW mysteriously packed in, so we were lent someone else's private chauffeur and air-conditioned car, and were finally driven home safely. Rick had spent over seven hours at the table and had done very well to remain fairly sober. I had found five hours quite enough – all-male company, Thai or otherwise, can wear rather thin after a while, I find. There were very few women there that day and those present didn't speak any English and stayed indoors, except for Noo's wife, a severe-looking woman with a tic, who actually turned out to be very amiable.

Another weekend I was taken out to lunch by a fashionable young Chinese businessman, who owned a small chain of shoe shops. I'd bought a pair of shoes from him one day after work and had got chatting to him, learning that he'd spent two years studying English in Torquay and Exeter and might like some English lessons to keep in practice. He also exported clothes and latex and I'd been asked to meet him at the restaurant to look over some business letters he'd written in English. When I asked him what the main use for the latex was, he seemed a little embarrassed to tell me that it was used 'for something which is sometimes necessary when a man and woman make love'. He didn't appear to know the word for condom, and covered his embarrassment by scribbling madly in his notebook.

Our blue room had come to be our home thanks to a very young American woman who worked with me at ELSI called Marsha – or Bathroom Marsha as she became known, because of the inordinate amount of time she spent in the little bathroom that adjoined the teachers' staff room. She was married to a Thai karate teacher and had told us, while we were still living at the Lek Guest House, that a room had just become vacant in their building, which was owned by a Chinese family. We were more than ready to leave our noisy hotel accommodation in Khao San Road, Banglamphu (later to become a weekend hotspot for young ravers, both *pharang* and Thai alike), and found that by paying monthly for our modest accommodation in Ban Kun Pom, we were saving quite a bit of money. It was some time before we discovered that we had in fact moved into a red-light district, although admittedly on the very outskirts of one. Such districts are characterised by an abundance of short-term hotels with large neon numbers on their façade to distinguish them and rooms that can be rented by the hour. It never ceased to amaze us when we spotted corpulent, cigar-smoking Thai monks bound for such hotels in large black cars with tinted windows. My students would often ask where I lived and on me replying Ban Kun Pom would look vaguely uncomfortable and refrain from further comment. Finally, one of them told me during a break that our area was 'not a good one', explaining why and laughing. It was really not such a big deal, however, as Thais are surprisingly open-minded about ladies – or gents – of the night and their trade, the stigma, apparently, not being as great as it is in the West. Similarly, Thailand was ahead of its time with its attitudes towards gay, cross-dressing and non-binary individuals. Several of my students spoke with lighthearted affection and no embarrassment whatsoever of brothers or cousins who were gay or cross-dressers or both – *catoys* as they were then known in Thai. There was even a popular radio channel with tips on make-up etc. for ladyboys and drag queens.

The room we rented in the red-light district was sparsely furnished and painted pale blue, both walls and ceiling. We would always have fresh flowers in the room to brighten it up, usually roses or chrysanthemums, but occasionally orchids or even lilies – at 15p a bunch they were hardly a luxury. It was only after living there for some time that I realised each piece of new clothing I had bought – mainly for work, as I knew Thai students would notice if I wore the same old outfits – was of a similar hue. I had been subconsciously harmonising with my surroundings, modest though they were. Our building was opposite a newly painted Buddhist temple and next to this was a small school that broadcast loud, rousing songs in the morning, supposedly to pep children up for the academic day ahead. Fortunately, we were already up and practically out of the door by the time the music started, which was just as well as had we been night workers of any sort there would have been little chance of sleeping through it, such was the volume. Ours was a newly built block owned by a seemingly dysfunctional or at least rather miserable and reserved Chinese family, who lived in a two-storey house just next to us and of whom we caught glimpses from our balcony from time to time. The only family member we exchanged greetings with on a daily basis was the plump, overworked daughter-in-law, Po, and it was she who quite possibly saved my life when I had food poisoning, by noticing me fainting on our fourth-floor balcony as she attended to an enormous pile of hand washing that she wearily distributed between several large coloured plastic bowls in the front yard.

It was a relief when the rainy season started up around May, as the rain cooled the air down wonderfully and even the torrential downpours, resulting sometimes in instant flooding, were not really a problem if one had an umbrella and plastic shoes (I found an excellent pair of white ones with a strap and a small heel at Bata budget shoe shop that I felt were quite respectable and certainly good enough for work). Besides, it didn't generally rain for long – perhaps an hour or so, then the clouds would clear, the sun would come out and before you knew it the skies were blue and cloudless again and everything sparkled after its thorough dousing. I set out for the bus stop one morning not in the plastic Bata shoes, however, but in some smartish, black, leather ones with four-inch stiletto heels to offset an outfit I was wearing for the first time; it consisted of a long black full skirt I'd had made for me by a tailor in Banglamphu and a snazzy cotton knit top with wide black and pale blue horizontal stripes (the blue matching our room perfectly). With it being the rainy season, there were large puddles all over the place, which slowed me down somewhat, so by the time I got to the end of our road I noticed to my horror that my bus was already approaching along the main road and realised I would have to run if I wanted to catch it. I simply hared along, as though my life depended on it, my eyes on the bus rather than on the ground below. I remember thinking that by the time the large collection of people who were waiting at the bus stop had all boarded I should have just about reached the boarding point. Wishful thinking! What in fact happened was, rounding the corner from our narrow, sodden street onto the main verdant thoroughfare, I got the heel of my left stiletto stuck in the metal grid of a street drain and went simply flying into a huge muddy puddle at the side of the road in full view of the crowd at the bus stop. One thing I had to be thankful for was that my new tailor-made skirt was made of the best gentleman's suit fabric. Though not obviously so, the fabric was quite thick and robust and possibly saved me from the cuts and grazing I might have suffered had I been wearing something in an inferior, flimsy fabric. My work bag, containing carefully corrected student essays, had been flung during my nosedive into the road, causing a fair bit of swerving and cursing by rush hour drivers. Picking myself up from the puddle and retrieving my bag, I swiftly assessed the situation. At that moment an old taxi cruised into view and, though I would never normally have considered taking a taxi to work, public transport being perfectly adequate for me as a simple working woman, I considered this to be a perfect occasion to splash out and before I knew it, we were on our way, overtaking the bus I should have been in, along with its careworn cargo of commuters, who had just been treated to a dramatic free show before their working day had even begun. As it turned out, the taxi I had chosen was probably one of the ropiest in the whole city. It rattled and whined and the driver, viewed in the rear-view mirror, appeared shifty with bloodshot eyes and dishevelled hair. Perhaps he had just been released from prison – I'd been told by students that here and elsewhere in Asia the one job ex-convicts managed to get without too much trouble after their period of incarceration was taxi driving. On this occasion, I was driven without mishap to my destination. A year or so later in Taipei, travelling in a similar type of beaten-up vehicle, I was less fortunate – but more of that later on.

The director of studies at ELSI was a slightly eccentric yet very good-natured Australian of Irish descent with a timelessness about him called David Rodgers. When I came to work for him, he'd been in Thailand for many years, seven of which had been spent outside normal society, training to become a Buddhist monk. His reason for leaving the monastic life was never revealed

– perhaps he missed female company – and he maintained a relaxed distance from his staff, though was never aloof. Still a practising Buddhist, he understandably showed a preference for ex-monks in his selection of teachers, and there were in fact two working at the school when we arrived. The years he'd spent in the monastery, where part of the training, we learned, included watching bodies decompose, had evidently stood him in good stead for the often stressful job of managing a busy city language school. Whatever the calamity – and there were a few of them during our time there – he remained unruffled and dignified and never lost his sense of humour. Once he had decided to employ a teacher, he gave them free rein and let them get on with the job. As a relatively inexperienced teacher I welcomed this freedom and trust that had been placed in me and worked hard to get to grips with the materials provided and try out new and amusing activities with the young students, many of whom were from hard-working Thai Chinese families and hoped to continue their education in the United States.

Others, however, abused the trust David had placed in them and behaved outrageously, considering they were being quite well paid to teach English to mainly deserving young people. To begin with, there was Johanna, a tall, willowy, auburn-haired woman – American, as most of our colleagues were – who, it transpired, had spent every afternoon for weeks on end handing out Scrabble sets to small groups of students, letting them entertain themselves while she occupied herself – day-dreaming, reading, writing letters, who knows. It was some time before one of the students finally complained to David as she felt that possibly she wasn't getting her money's worth. Then there was Rory, another American, a very private, hyperactive individual who looked rather more like a film star than an EFL teacher; on one occasion he did actually claim to be an ex-actor. Wherever he went he carried a sleek James Bond-type case, the contents of which were a constant source of speculation and amusement to my colleagues; despite his bulk, he appeared to glide around the school rather than walk and his expression led one to believe he knew something quite mind-blowing that no one else was privy to. One afternoon a student ventured into the staff room and went up to David's desk. Rory, it seemed, had not turned up for his class, which had been due to start almost half an hour previously. An enquiry in the office below revealed that Rory had been seen entering the building at the expected time, although he had up until that day been late no fewer than six times. A search was made and Rory was finally located sitting peacefully on the ground under a tree in the garden, a glazed expression on his handsome face, in a state of drug-induced euphoria. As his James Bond case lay beside him with the lock undone, David took the liberty of looking inside – it was full of what appeared to be a comprehensive selection of designer drugs, complete with syringe, hip flask and chillum. Needless to say, both Johanna and Rory were relieved of their duties at the school, but they were personable colourful characters and were missed after their departure.

There were soon others, however, to take their place. There was baby-faced, freckled Kevin from Manchester, with his lurid T-shirts and his idiosyncratic use of pronouns. He'd just been employed as an extra in Roland Joffé's *The Killing Fields*, a film I never dared to watch, dealing as it did with horrific events that took place during the civil war in Cambodia in the early seventies. It would all have been a bit too close to home. Another vibrant figure to join us was Edie Scoropad, a brassy, blonde Canadian, whose good-looking, clean-cut though slightly introverted husband, John, was doing an advanced course in gemology. It was really Edie's bravado and charisma that got her the job, as she had no teaching qualifications whatsoever. She had been a successful cheerleader in her time and one of her occupations back in Canada had been hosting ladies-only house parties, at which she sold sex toys, rather like Tupperware parties in the UK in the sixties. We became quite friendly with Edie and John, and the night before we left the country, they insisted on taking us on a tour of the sex clubs of the *Pat Pong* area, which they frequented regularly during their stay in Bangkok, as they found it spiced up their love life no end. It was an interesting experience from a sociological point of view, and I don't regret going at all, but I think once was probably enough. Distressingly young Thai country girls performed a variety of tricks involving darts, candles, bananas and live snakes. We weren't at all sure we wanted to witness the live sex show, but were actually pleasantly surprised to find it featured a tall, arresting Thai couple, who thankfully appeared to like each other immensely and performed a surprisingly tasteful balletic sex 'dance' to languorous music.

Other members of our colourful, cosmopolitan staff included Len, Martin, Alex and Donna. Len was from somewhere 'up north', Leeds perhaps, a highly intelligent Oxbridge-educated man, who'd developed a heroin habit in his early days in Thailand; he had ended up getting gangrene and losing part of one leg. He was evidently a gifted teacher as his students adored him and never complained when he hobbled into class on his crutches late and lit up a cigarette, usually smoking out of the window, and ad-libbing his lessons shamelessly. Martin was also a fellow Brit, a tall striking-looking man with come-to-bed eyes and an extremely high libido, which he spent most of his time outside the classroom trying hard to satisfy, or so it seemed. He lived within easy reach of some of the most notorious Bangkok pick-up bars, just off Sukhumvit Road, in a modest block of flats called, rather appropriately, Rabbit Court. He kindly put Rick and me up for a few days just before we left the country and my enduring image of him is him sitting on a bench in the sun after breakfast outside his flat, wearing nothing but the skimpiest pair of shorts imaginable, which he may as well not have worn at all, as his famous tackle had, totally unbeknownst to him, escaped the restricting garment in search of a few golden rays.

As for Donna, a greater contrast to Edie could not have been found – apart from their shared Canadian nationality they had nothing really in common at all. Donna was married to an upper-middle-class Thai and led a sheltered life it seemed, being escorted to and from work in a chauffeured family car to spare her the indignity of having to take public transport. Her thick, brunette hair was stylishly coiffed and she was always immaculately dressed in tailored silk suits with matching accessories and expensive jewellery. Despite living so far from her native land and working in an international working environment, Donna was not what you might call a woman of the world. She seemed rather forlorn and perhaps a little lonely, so one Friday evening we asked if she'd like to join us for dinner at the Northern Thai restaurant near our school that we liked. She wasn't sure if she'd be able to – perhaps she had to get permission – so I took her phone number and told her I'd 'give her a ring' later on. She looked at me with a puzzled expression, never having heard the British idiom. It was also Donna who initially failed to comprehend when I asked one day in the staff room if she could lend me her 'rubber' – it was a learning experience for both of us.

At one point during my employment at ELSI I was given a dreaded split shift, which meant a lot of to-ing and fro-ing on the local buses. I would sometimes stop on the way back to our room at a roadside stall for sticky rice wrapped in banana leaves. The rice generally had a spicy pork filling, but there was also a sweet version with sugary red beans, a bit reminiscent of a jam doughnut. It made an easy and tasty lunch and I would then invariably lie down for a short siesta before setting out for the evening shift. I always found it incredibly hard to get up and get going again when my alarm went off. It was sometime later that someone told me sticky rice had well-known soporific properties and that Thai mothers would give it to boisterous, overactive youngsters to calm them down and get them off to sleep. One afternoon I was in quite a deep, sticky-rice-induced sleep when the alarm went off so, instead of rising promptly to dress for work, I allowed myself to doze a little longer. The next thing I knew, I awoke to find it was dark outside and that I'd overslept quite badly. I simply leapt up, grabbed the first thing I found hanging in the wardrobe, a black cotton dress I had bought in Bali with embroidery around the neck and hem, shot out into the night and scurried up the road to the bus stop. My bus crawled along in the rush hour traffic and I kept looking, mortified, at my watch as I knew the business class would already be there sitting waiting for me. After bursting into the classroom a good half hour late for a two-hour class, I strode purposefully to the front to make my apology. To my astonishment, I was welcomed with a hearty cheer from the entire class and I turned to face a room of beaming, youthful faces. Living in the city themselves, they were all too aware of how dreadful the traffic was and how it could sometimes delay the most punctual of people, and as I had never arrived late before, I was immediately forgiven. What had provoked their joyful outburst on my entry was a detail of my new dress that I had completely forgotten about – it had quite a dramatic slash up one side, or possibly up both sides, giving the class more than a glimpse of my pale, bare legs for the first and last time.

One member of this smallish business class was an attractive, sweet-natured, conscientious young woman called Choum, tall for a Thai, with large roundish eyes and a radiant, infectious smile. She was an only child, the daughter of a judge and a lawyer, and was attending an English class as she wanted to fly for Thai Airways. She came to class one day over the moon as she'd been offered a job working on domestic Thai Airways flights, and was to start work almost immediately. A few weeks later, just as I was about to start my afternoon teaching, I glanced down at the *Bangkok Post*, which was lying on Rick's desk in the staff room, and there on the front page was a black and white photograph of Choum, along with two other young Thai women, fellow cabin crew, or air hostesses as they were then still called. She and her colleagues had died in a plane crash on her very first flight from Bangkok to Phuket the previous day. The plane had apparently flown into a mountain in the mist shortly before arrival at its destination. I was so shocked, I barely knew what I was doing – I looked across the staff room and my eyes met those of David, who was sitting at his desk, unaware of the news at that point. He summed up the situation instantly, told me not to worry about my class, that he would teach in my place, and, after grabbing some board pens and a couple of books, headed off upstairs. I can still see Choum's face now in my mind's eye, the serious black and white picture in the paper contrasting starkly with the vivacious, animated expression she always wore in my classes. It was so terribly sad.

Regrettably, we never really did get to know David Rogers socially, one of the reasons being that we lived at opposite ends of the city. Lacking an underground system, on account of the marshy ground it is built on, Bangkok was extremely hard to get around in those days, particularly in the rush hour. In more recent times, the overhead railway system has improved things somewhat. I did once arrange to meet David for dinner at a large and famous hotel, the Ambassador, on Sukhumvit Road. We were no longer living in Bangkok but I was there on holiday and my mother had joined me for a spot of winter sun herself. My memory is a little hazy here, but I think I must have rung the school to say hello to David and it was he who suggested that we meet up at this particular place. It was some distance from our hotel and we had spent what felt like an age in a scruffy old taxi wending our way through heavy traffic to get there at the appointed time. After stopping briefly to inspect the peacocks and other exotic birds in the cages lining the approach road to the hotel, we ascended the wide flight of steps into the lobby expectantly. Half an hour passed, but there was no sign of David and the immaculately turned-out receptionist assured us that no message had been left. A thought suddenly occurred to me that perhaps we had agreed to meet at the actual restaurant rather than in the main lobby. Aware that the hotel had not one but several restaurants, I asked at reception for a list, which was duly produced. I then had to decide which of these several restaurants David would have been most likely to have suggested. In the end, I plumped for the Thai buffet as we felt Italian, Japanese or Korean barbecue would have been a little odd, given that this was my mother's introduction to Thailand and the tropics. The moment we entered the restaurant, I spotted David, seated in a candlelit booth, deep in conversation with a sultry, sophisticated-looking Thai woman, who was gazing intently into her chaperone's eyes. They seemed so wrapped up in themselves that, at first, I hesitated to intrude upon their intimacy, but having flapped about trying to find the man for what felt like hours – valuable hours as my dear mother's visit was a short one – I marched across the restaurant floor with Mum a few steps behind me and made my way up to their table. I naturally expressed my pleasure at seeing him and asked how long they had been here. It became clear at once that he was surprised to see me in this place and had evidently forgotten about our arrangement altogether. Having always treated David with a great deal of respect, he being after all my boss in the days when I considered myself a novice EFL teacher and quite lucky to have a paid job at all, I wished them a pleasant evening and started searching for a good table for my mother and myself – at some distance from the amorous couple.

Rick and I created a good life for ourselves in Bangkok; there was a gentle rhythm to our days that suited us, but time slipped by just a little faster than we'd have liked, as it always tends to when you are enjoying being alive. We both learned to accept the traffic, the pollution, the heat and the floods, the low pay for our work and even the mosquitos who drew our blood at night. We lived happily on street food, dining each night at a tiny, open-air food market at the end of our road, ordering simple dishes of rice or noodles, with chicken or pork, and a glass of freshly squeezed orange juice with a little salt (*gua nit noi*). The only time I ever got ill was dining at the expensive upmarket riverside restaurant. We were happy there and came to regard it as home; I still think of Thailand as my second home.

Chapter 9

Further East to Taiwan

Much as Rick and I loved Thailand, after the best part of a year, we were becoming increasingly aware that, despite the low cost of living and our very frugal lifestyle, we were saving next to nothing, peanuts in fact. Although we rarely discussed the future, we knew that many others of our age considered these years to be their peak earning years, a time to be putting something aside for the future. It was beginning to feel as though we would never save enough to get set up in Japan, our original destination, so when David informed us casually one day that there was a sister school in Taipei in need of teachers and that we would be paid quite a lot more than we were making in Bangkok, we naturally gave it some serious consideration. At that point, I really knew nothing about Taipei – or even about Taiwan for that matter, politically and otherwise. I expect Rick was slightly better informed, being more tuned in to world affairs than I was at that time. We decided to finish the term at ELSI and head for Taipei, but as the term progressed, we considered all the things in our Bangkok lives that we would miss – the climate, the people, both our teaching colleagues and the various Thais we came into daily contact with, food vendors in the little market where we ate each evening, cheery office staff in the school, other locals we'd become friends with in guest houses and restaurants in our original stomping ground, Banglampu. We put off our departure for another term and decided to enjoy the here and now, whether we were making money or not. Taiwan could wait.

When we did eventually come to pack, we realised we had accumulated quite a lot of fluffy, frivolous, rather childish gifts, mainly from students – pencils with animals bobbing on top, pink tasselled tissue-holders, Disney picture frames, 3D bookmarks, key rings containing beetles suspended in plastic and so on. We decided to wrap them and redistribute them, calling them leaving presents. Most people seemed quite touched and beamed as these gifts were handed over and opened. There was just one retiring young lady, however, a filing clerk at our school office, who looked a little crestfallen when she opened her small package; I think it may have been a picture frame. She smiled wanly, murmuring her thanks, and put it gently to one side. It was only that evening, when I went over the events of the day in my mind, that it dawned on me that quite possibly it was this very colleague who had given me the awful thing in the first place. I still feel bad about it today when I think of her meek, bemused, downcast expression.

Our first resting place in Taipei was a kind of travellers' hostel with poorly lit, functional, single-sex dormitories, which meant, to our dismay, that, for the first time since setting out from the UK, Rick and I had to sleep apart. At the time it felt quite unnatural and unreasonable. In the small, grubby kitchen there was a large communal fridge with an ill-fitting door, which meant cockroaches could get in at night and feast on our food, some of it expensive Western delicacies we'd splashed out on to make up for not being able to share a bed. The first night I slept at the hostel I went to the fridge in the early hours to get some cold water only to be greeted by an alarming swarm of the winged black beasts flying straight out at me. From then on, I made sure I had a bottle of water beside my bed to last me through the night. The other facility in the hostel was a small room containing an antiquated washing machine, which tended to flood, not only the room it was in, but half the large inner communal area too, which took forever to mop up. It was in this latter room that the all-night mah-jongg sessions took place – noisy affairs as the players, mainly aging cronies of the owner, would slap the ivory tiles down on the table with a flourish and, as the men became steadily drunker and redder in the face, they would completely forget that there were people paying to sleep in the surrounding rooms, if they ever gave any thought to this at all.

Compared to Bangkok, we found Taipei ugly, evil-smelling and depressing – the streets lacked greenery, the pavements were cracked and uneven, treacherous to negotiate, cluttered as they were with countless old bicycles and motorbikes. Buildings seemed to have been thrown up willy-nilly using the cheapest materials; everywhere you looked you saw bare, unfinished concrete walls, rusting pipes, windows with bars reminiscent of Sing Sing in Eilat. Anything of any age or architectural interest had been or was in the process of being demolished. Our timing for the ELSI school term was once again all wrong and we were told it would be several weeks before there might be some work for us. Keen to take up our coloured chalks and get back in the groove sooner rather than later, we decided to hunt for a job elsewhere. After days tramping the sad, soulless streets and attending job interviews, only to decide we didn't want the jobs being offered anyway, the last thing we wanted to do was return to our prisonlike accommodation to sit in our separate dormitories, bewailing our forced celibacy and counting the cockroaches.

We did, however, meet some interesting people at the hostel, some of whom became good friends. The most colourful character in residence when we arrived was a tall, blue-eyed charmer, a disarmingly good-looking young American from one of the southern states called Doug, who I believe at this time was making money modelling. He was extremely friendly and gregarious, which meant a lot to us, as our first days in Taipei were not the happiest – we were more than a little homesick for Bangkok and had failed to secure the job we'd hoped for. At the end of our first week in the crumbling capital, to our delight, Doug suggested we all go out on the town and promised to take us to the very best hot spots. At one such place, we were introduced to an equally convivial, highly effeminate young Taiwanese, Eric, who managed the bar with great panache. We drank copious cocktails, exchanging life stories, dreams and aspirations and when we left Eric kissed us fondly and made us promise to return the following weekend. By the following weekend, he was dead – of AIDS. It was Doug who broke the news – he seemed pretty cut up about it, and it was only then that it dawned on us that Doug himself may well have been gay or perhaps bisexual and that Eric had very possibly been one of his lovers. Lacking the internet in those days, there was no quick and easy way to do some research about the transmission of AIDS and we were painfully aware of the fact that Eric had kissed us both on the cheeks, French style, before we left his club. Might we have caught it? Were our days now numbered? We didn't have much time to brood about it, however, as, following a tip from someone we'd met on our night out on the razzle, we went for an interview at a new school that was being set up in the city centre called the Emerson English School. They were looking for experienced EFL professionals to work initially as curriculum designers and then as supervisors. It all sounded very promising.

We were interviewed jointly by two Americans, both of whom were called Mike. It was a bit like the old good cop, bad cop scenario. The taller better looking of the two Mikes sat sideways in his chair in a pose of utmost relaxation, bizarre for an interview, quizzing us gently about our qualifications and experience, while Bad Mike looked on tensely and seemingly far from benignly, asking for extra information here and there, clearly against us from the start. Fortunately, it was Good Mike who then had more clout, holding, despite his rather dubious academic background, the superior position of Director of Studies (DOS), while Bad Mike, who was fresh from an interesting-sounding MA TEFL course in Hawaii, was only Assistant Director of Studies (ADOS). Had the roles been reversed I strongly suspect we would not have been asked to 'start work tomorrow'. We later learned, that one of Bad Mike's tutors in Hawaii had worked closely with Lozanov, the Bulgarian psychologist who developed a language teaching method Rick and I were fascinated by called Suggestopedia. (The name combines the terms 'suggestion' and 'pedagogy', the main idea being that accelerated learning can take place when accompanied by de-suggestion of psychological barriers and positive suggestion.) Sadly, we were not to benefit from these connections as Bad Mike made no effort to develop a collegial relationship with us at Emerson; indeed his arrogance prevented him from mingling with the teaching staff much at all.

Although Rick and I had been taken on at Emerson as curriculum designers, neither of us had had any relevant previous experience whatsoever. We were both assigned to intermediate levels and set to work examining the mainly American materials that had already been ordered, trying to look competent and conscientious, whilst really muddling through and making it up as we went along. A fresh-faced young American with closely set eyes, David Swensen, straight out of college we guessed, a colleague of Good Mike in a former work setup, was put in charge of elementary levels, while the advanced levels were assigned to another American, an assertive and enviably energetic woman with stylishly cropped fair hair and a deep knowledge of astrology called Pat Ghelle. David arrived in our open-plan office/staff room each morning with a large paper bag from McDonald's, containing two full-sized meals, which he called breakfast. Much as I dislike the whole idea of McDonald's, I can hardly criticise, as I too developed something of a passion for McDonald's fillet of fish whilst in Taipei. I believe it could even have been an addiction, as there were evenings during the foul, cold wet winter we spent there, when I would rise from our bed after retiring, dress and surge out into the night, walking three blocks for an overpriced fillet of fish. I always put it down to something they added to the tartare sauce. David, like many of the other American teachers working in Taipei at that time, had had no formal training in EFL, and had come to Taiwan to learn Mandarin, as it was said that the Taiwanese spoke with an excellent standard accent and Taipei had good affordable language schools for foreigners, the best known of which was called Shir Dah. What all these young Americans lacked in training they made up for in self-confidence, articulacy and sometimes charisma. David's looks and clean-cut appearance stood him in good stead, and when student numbers started to soar, he eagerly took on a double teaching load, which meant extremely long hours, but he met the challenge admirably, fuelled by McDonald's take-aways, and was always good-humoured and fun to work with.

The courses at the new school were well advertised and the school's prestige was boosted by two Chinese professors of English, rivals as it later turned out, whose names were linked to the enterprise. Although their role was ostensibly to offer their academic expertise, we always felt the tedious, self-important pair were very much more of a hindrance than a help. The modern building that housed the school was rented from the Catholic church and was well located, just off a major thoroughfare, where there were frequent buses to other parts of the city and a multitude of restaurants, both the hole-in-the-wall type and everything else from street market food through to plush and fancy dining joints. A day or so after landing the job, we were fortunate enough to hear of a room for rent right opposite the school above a dumpling shop, overlooking a small park, where old folk performed tai chi first thing each morning. The flat itself was rather austere and unappealing, but our room was quite spacious and had its own bathroom, which to us at that time was the height of luxury. The upper walls on two sides of the room, however, were made of sheets of ill-fitting glass, which meant the room became horribly cold and draughty in winter. We sublet from an earnest young Taiwanese couple. Mayman was an epidemiologist, a petite and precise sort of a woman, pale and rather emaciated, as was her husband, whose name like himself was unmemorable. It was evident from the start that it was Mayman who wore the trousers. Strangely, it seemed to us, with her background in medicine, her knowledge of maladies and microorganisms, she showed scant concern for hygiene in her own home and did little to keep the communal kitchen clean, besides taping up nasty brown paper on the walls around the cooker to catch spitting fat from the wok and splashes from food preparation mishaps. We learned sometime later that Mayman had a younger sister, who was born in the Chinese year of the tiger. As the mother was a tiger too and it was well known in Taiwan that it was not advisable for two tigers to cohabit, the unfortunate baby was farmed out to a poor country relative and received virtually no education at all; I'm not even sure if she was literate. She once came to visit and we were quite shocked to find she did indeed look and behave like a lowly, country bumpkin, cowed into submission by her older, educated and relatively well-to-do sister.

We had no sooner cobbled together what we thought looked like a decent enough syllabus for the various levels we offered at our school, than our first students started arriving; they were hastily given placement tests, grouped on paper into classes and allocated to teachers. Most of the teaching materials that had been ordered before and since our arrival were based on what was at that time a relatively new approach to language teaching and learning – the communicative approach. This was based on the idea that learning a language successfully comes through having to communicate real meaning. The focus, therefore, is on the use of language in everyday situations, on the functional aspects of language, rather than on the structures used, as in previous methods, such as the grammar-translation method we had been subjected to at school in French lessons, for instance. Amongst the many books piled up on the table in our teachers' resource room was one that had come out just before our arrival in Taipei, *The Natural Approach* by Stephen Krashen, a linguist and professor emeritus at the University of Southern California, and Tracy Terrell, also an American education theorist. The natural approach was a comprehension-based language learning methodology that emphasised the idea of exposure to the target language and the lowering of affective or emotional barriers to learning. Rick and I took it in turns to read this book and liked the ideas it contained so much that we got our DOS Mike to order multiple copies so that all the teachers we employed could have their own slim volume, which they were required to read and digest before they started teaching. Such was our zeal for the natural approach at this time that I do believe, given the chance, we'd have made our poor 'newbies' sit comprehension tests on the contents of the book. I think perhaps one of the reasons this approach appealed to us so much was that, with the emphasis off grammar and the main focus on authentic communication and the lowering of inhibitions, there was so much scope for fun in the classroom in the form of language games, competitions, role plays, the performing of humorous sketches and discussions revolving around memories, hopes, dreams and so on. The natural approach and the communicative approach, we decided, dovetailed beautifully.

I remember starting my first class at Emerson with an attempt to explain the theories behind this innovative type of teaching. At the end of what I had hoped was a clear and concise explanation, a very confident young woman called Lucy, with a mop of curly black hair (almost certainly permed as this was the early eighties) and a smooth, milky complexion reminiscent of ivory, piped up, 'Excuse me, Ms Carrie, but what *exactly* is your meaning?' I started all over again, trying desperately to make the ideas more accessible to students who had been educated almost solely so far via rote learning, and this time I was given the benefit of the doubt. Despite my time teaching in Bangkok, I was still fairly green when it came to classroom management, and Rick was greener still, but we had the energy of youth, were fervent about our work and were impatient to try out all these exciting new ideas on what turned out to be the most willing, receptive and altogether lovely set of young students you could possibly hope to teach.

Improvisation and role play were very much part of this new methodology and we were forever dreaming up imaginative new scenarios to engage our young learners. One role play that worked particularly well and so sticks in my mind was the one where the students were put into pairs and told to imagine they were animals – lions, giraffes, buffalo, snakes, etc. The pairs were of the same species and were related. One member of each pair had been captured and had spent the last ten years in captivity at London Zoo, whilst the relative had continued to live precariously in the wild. The pair had to imagine that they were meeting in a dream and were exchanging tales about what had gone on in each other's lives. To set the scene I would lower the lights and play soft, dreamlike, hypnagogic music. This was one of many such activities where I would ask the students to relax, forget the outside world and put their trust in me, however odd my ideas and instructions might seem. I was well rewarded for my efforts – my first class of Taiwanese students became such devotees that at the end of the course they trooped down to reception *en masse* and more or less insisted on continuing with me as their teacher before parting with any more tuition fees. As a result, I taught several individuals from this first class for six months or more, witnessed significant progress in their English and became quite close to them during this time.

One of the stranger students in that early batch at Emerson was a little older than the others and went by the name of Summer. He seemed rather shy and inhibited at first and tended to mumble when spoken to in class, so badly so in fact that it was impossible to understand him much of the time. One day I kept him back after class to have a quiet word. I seem to remember telling him that we 'used our mouths' more when speaking English and proceeded to speak to him moving my lips and mouth in a rather exaggerated way so as to articulate the sounds ultra-clearly. He certainly appeared to take all this on board and to my relief showed no sign of being offended. From that day on, almost miraculously, Summer spoke significantly more clearly and, encouraged by the better reception and communication he was enjoying in class, he underwent a gradual character change, appearing altogether more relaxed and even giving us occasional radiant smiles. Such was the increase in his confidence that one day Summer opened up to the class in rather an exceptional way. We had been discussing supernatural experiences, a favourite topic with the Taiwanese, nearly all of whom respected the local customs during Ghost Month (e.g. not swimming in deep water or showering around midnight) and had some good ghost stories to tell, many from first-hand experience. Summer had served his time in the army and may well have had some traumatic experiences during those two years that had left their mark. On this occasion, he proceeded to tell the class quite graphically and believably how he had seen an armed soldier walking right through one of the walls into his house and out again the other side. Everyone listened spellbound. The fact that I remember this story so vividly testifies to the growing communicative competence of my elementary student, who had at one time been practically incomprehensible on account of his pronunciation problems. At the end of his three courses with me, Summer came and shook my hand and gave me a letter, which I believe I still have in one of my boxes of memorabilia. In it he told me how studying English in my class had literally changed his life. He had found that as his confidence about speaking English grew, his confidence in other areas of his life had grown too, and that consequently he was a very much happier man. It was wonderful to receive such a letter and as a result my own confidence as a teacher, I'm sure, went up a notch or two too.

One of my chief objectives in those early days in Taiwan, and ever since for that matter, has been to create the sort of atmosphere in the classroom where students feel sufficiently relaxed to experiment with the language, without fear of making mistakes, and to talk about anything they wish, even quite personal things, without fear of ridicule or judgement. I daresay at times if an outsider were to enter my class (or to hover above it unobserved in a virtual classroom, as I once had described to me by a colleague who had done his MA in media-assisted TEFL) they might think they had accidentally stumbled upon some sort of encounter group. There were two Jennys in my first group of students – young Jenny and older Jenny. It was from young Jenny that I learned she had opted for a caesarean section at the birth of her son, so as to make sure he entered the world at an auspicious moment in the Chinese calendar. Apparently, this was quite a common practice, such was the strength of the superstition amongst Taiwanese of childbearing age at that time. While most ancient Chinese superstition was stamped out on the Mainland during the Mao years, it remained alive and kicking in Taiwan when we lived there. Lifts in buildings didn't have fourth-floor buttons, nor would you find a house number four as the words for four and death in Mandarin differ only in tone. This Taiwanese tetraphobia was far stronger than Western misgivings about the number thirteen, for instance, and even had a bearing on property values. Renting a fourth-floor flat was often significantly cheaper than renting one on any other floor.

On another occasion, the older Jenny, a retired primary school teacher, a rather glamourous and cultivated woman, with a sparkle in her eye, a zest for living and a clear love of people from all walks of life, told the saddest tale from her early teaching days. It concerned a pupil of hers, a very bright and gifted child, who almost always got top marks for her work. One day she was awarded a nine instead of her usual ten for a piece of homework. Her reaction was so extreme that Jenny followed her discreetly out of class at the end of school that day and found her sobbing behind a school shed. It transpired that this girl's parents were obsessed with her school marks and would beat her if she didn't get full marks for each piece of homework. Tears welled up in Jenny's eyes as she recounted the story and by the time she'd finished I doubt there was a dry eye in the room – I was so busy trying to suppress my own tears I didn't really look to see who'd been similarly affected. The bond that formed between us all in that group was exceptional and one of my most rewarding teaching experiences.

One of the lovely things about teaching in the Far East at

this time was that Rick and I were still relatively young (we were both in our early thirties), so the age difference between us and our students was sufficiently small to make socialising together outside school hours quite natural and even desirable. Barely a weekend went by when we didn't have an invitation of some sort – a meal with a student's family, an outing to some local beauty spot, dinner in a restaurant or perhaps a birthday party. We almost always accepted these invitations; it would have seemed rude not to have done, and although at times I found it tiring having to engage in social chit-chat with students, lower-level ones in particular, especially if I'd been teaching all day, we had many a jolly jaunt and many a pleasant evening wielding chopsticks during our two years in Taiwan. Dining with students we experienced dishes we never would have done otherwise (deep-fried baby birds served in their nest, for example, though that is one delicacy I'd really prefer to forget). What is more, it was intriguing to catch rare glimpses of their home lives, some of which appeared not so unlike ours in the West, whilst others appeared quite exotic and Oriental in style. On one occasion we had a Saturday lunchtime invitation from a rather quiet young man in Rick's class. We had been given a time – right on noon, if I recall – but thought it might be polite to arrive slightly after this time; noon did, after all, seem a little early to be having lunch at the weekend. I believe we rang the bell around 12.20 pm. The door opened almost instantly; it was as though our young host had been standing just there on the other side of the door, waiting impatiently for us to arrive. There was a fixed smile on his face, betraying a malaise that had us wondering what might be wrong. It was a humble abode, sparsely furnished and rather poorly lit with grills over the windows, often seen in Taipei and other Asian cities, giving the place a vaguely prisonlike feel. We entered straight into what appeared to be the main living/dining area and there in the centre of the room was a dining table simply laden with dishes of every description. Assembled around the table on uncomfortable hardwood chairs were the whole family, including an ancient-looking couple, whom we took to be the grand if not great grandparents. We got the distinct impression that the food had been ready and that everyone had been sitting there expectantly from the stroke of twelve noon, if not before. It was a lesson we learned the hard way, that whatever time a Taiwanese invitation is for, *that* is the time you arrive.

Eating with chopsticks was something we had to get to grips with from the word go, otherwise we'd have gone hungry. Lunch during the working week would invariably be eaten out with a group of our American colleagues. 'Let's do lunch!' was a common exclamation, usually made by David Swensen, whose McDonald's breakfasts would leave him ravenously hungry well before noon. For most of our stay in Taiwan, we were the only Brits on the staff, which grew remarkably in that first year from six to over sixty. By most of our American fellow teachers, we were openly treated as lovable eccentrics; it was only 'Bad Mike' who never warmed to us, for reasons known to himself only, so it was just as well that he was the one to get the boot before the first year was out and not us. There were a great number of excellent eating places within walking distance of our school and the variety of cuisines to be found was quite possibly unrivalled. Apart from the many types of Chinese food (ranging from tasty Taiwanese pork buns, street noodles and spicy Szechuan fare to outstanding Cantonese *dim sum*, Shanghainese soups and everything in between), there was superb, affordable Japanese, Indonesian, Burmese and Buddhist vegetarian fare, the last found in restaurants with giant backwards-facing swastikas hanging outside. More often than not we opted for *dim sum*, or *yum cha* as it's sometimes called, as it gave us the flexibility of ordering as we went along, choosing whatever looked tempting from the little trolleys that were constantly wheeled past the tables in the huge dining area. Another reason the *dim sum* restaurant was so popular amongst the male staff was that guests were greeted at the top of a wide, dramatically curving, red-carpeted staircase by the most ravishing Chinese beauties on the island, wearing high-heeled shoes and traditional figure-hugging silk dresses with slits right up one side revealing tantalisingly shapely long legs. Many of the *dim sum* dishes were pork or prawn based, but there were also health-giving plates of vegetables with ingredients such as asparagus, morning glory, pak choi and other green leafy vegetables in oyster sauce or other delicious, no doubt MSG-enhanced sauces, along with my favourite of all, squares of golden Hakka fried turnip cake, made from shredded daikon radish and rice flour laced with tiny morsels of sausage and shrimp.

The rice in Taiwan was unlike rice I had ever eaten elsewhere before or have done since – it was, I was told, of the very best quality, moist, large-grained and with such an exquisite taste that one could easily eat bowl after bowl of it just as it was, as the hungrier males often did. It outshone even Thai fragrant rice, which is not something to be sniffed at. The more expensive dishes, such as the ones involving fish or king prawns were naturally the ones to disappear most quickly from the Lazy Susan, which would revolve steadily as one ate, hence the need for swift mastery of one's chopsticks. To begin with, I would carefully spear the morsel I was set on with one of my chopsticks and proceed to eat it as one might chicken kebab on a skewer. This I later learned was considered by the Chinese to be the height of bad manners, along with sticking one's chopsticks vertically in one's bowl of rice as this is associated with death. It didn't seem to bother our American colleagues, however, and it was in fact a candid, well-meaning student of mine – the same Lucy who had requested a clearer explanation of my teaching methods – who later pointed it out. These dim sum lunches were invariably accompanied by jasmine tea, although a little beer was consumed on occasion, especially if it was the end of the week. If Japanese cuisine had been the choice of the day, however, it always seemed a bit of a crime to eat sushi or sashimi without the complement of *sake*. The thing about *sake* I've always found, perhaps on account of the fact that it is normally consumed warm, is that it tends to make one tipsy quite quickly but then wears off again equally quickly and almost never gives one a hangover, even when large quantities are consumed. I don't recall ever having taught a class after a sake-fuelled lunch, but there were certainly times when I returned to the school to prepare lessons and so forth in an alcoholic haze, and I know plenty of teachers who rolled straight into the classroom from indulgent Japanese meals three sheets to the wind.

Two local delicacies that always cropped up during class discussions on food were 'thousand-year-old eggs' and '*chòu dòufu*' or stinky fermented tofu. The former were hard-boiled eggs cured, so I was informed, in horse urine, though I believe a cheaper version could be bought in the 7-Eleven stores, cured instead in tea until they became a similarly off-putting shade of brown. The latter was deep-fried fermented tofu, a huge favourite with Chinese the world over, so I understood. We had a *chòu dòufu* stand on the pavement quite near our flat that gave off an overpowering and atrocious smell. Depending on which shoes I was wearing, I would either take a deep breath and run past the stall or make quite a long detour around it, which involved crossing the wide main road and approaching our flat from the opposite direction. I was often told that the taste was nothing like the smell and that I really should try it. I'm quite sure Anthony Bourdain would have done. Neither Rick nor I, however, ever had the courage to do so, so I am unable to verify its palatability.

The internal politics at the Emerson Language School were

quite complex and heated interchanges could often be heard wafting across the open-plan office, almost from the very outset. One of our supervisors, Pat Ghelle, withdrew early on from her position, quite possibly anticipating conflict and trouble, if not out-and-out revolution, early in the first year. The Chinese professors became more and more difficult and demanding, until the order came that we supervisors, who also taught and were the best-qualified teachers, should write out detailed blow-by-blow lesson plans for the benefit of the rest of the teaching staff, some of whom had little or even no teaching experience at all. We saw it all as something of a joke – 'teaching by numbers' we used to call it. Not having very much choice in the matter, however, we set to work and proceeded to transcribe each of our lessons each day in minute detail, all handwritten as there were no word processors in those days. In the meantime, the two Mikes were fired, quite dramatically, and marched off the premises, whereupon Rick was asked if he'd be prepared to take over immediately as DOS. A little odd considering that I was the one with rather more experience in the TEFL world, but the fact is I wouldn't have dreamt of taking on the role had I been asked, one of the main reasons being that I'd come to realise I couldn't stand academic meetings with the pompous professors and would do almost anything to avoid them. Working as DOS, I knew, would mean daily meetings with the professors and no amount of money would have swayed me at that time. Rick slept on it and decided that for him too it was not worth the headaches he knew the position would provoke. As it was, he already suffered from crippling migraines every once in a while, and so he politely declined. The only member of staff who was willing to take on the role was an ill-qualified and rather irritating young American woman called Jana, who seemed to spend most of her time coaching her students to perform inconsequential Walt Disney-type sketches and the like. Fortunately, Jana didn't give us any trouble while she was DOS and let us get on with things. We had to admit we were quite relieved that another American woman, Karen, hadn't put herself forward for the post. Tall, bespectacled and humourless, with the distinct air of a prison warder, Karen had joined the school a few months after it opened and evidently had high ambitions. We felt there was something rather sinister about someone who claimed to have studied Russian and Chinese at university, as they felt it would be useful to 'know the languages of one's enemies'.

During that first year, student numbers grew exponentially, possibly due to the fact, I liked to feel, that my photograph was being used to advertise the school. To our great amusement, I could be seen grinning away, very much larger than life, plastered across the side of many of the city buses. The script below this advertisement was translated by one of my students and went something like this: Why is Carrie always smiling? She smiles because she loves her work and she loves her students – and indeed they love her too… and so on. Slightly nauseating, but also rather flattering, and seeing my image on the buses sail by caused Rick and me no end of mirth. With the school numbers now sometimes doubling by the week, more and more teachers had to be taken on. Recruitment often took place in a hurry and sometimes without the vetting that would have been preferable.

I think it must have been Jana who interviewed and employed Patrick O'Reilly. One Monday morning, there he was in our midst, a tall, self-assured, lanky young man, with Michael Caine glasses and a distinctive hooting sort of laugh, which he'd produce frequently, leaning back slightly as he did so. His attire was rather unconventional and was reminiscent of his Cockney peers, the bovver boys; he wore braces and trousers with turn-ups that showed a good few inches of lurid sock, along with black Doc Martens. Although he had no teaching experience to speak of, he was said to have a degree in English, and what he lacked in teaching qualifications he made up for with, if not exactly charisma, bravado. Being of Irish extraction, he certainly had the gift of the gab and to his credit, he picked things up fast. He threw himself into the job and took it upon himself to liven up the staff room with a seemingly endless repertoire of jokes and a fair bit of teasing of colleagues – he had a knack of homing in on people's weak spots. One morning he brought in to school a cassette tape of Frankie Goes to Hollywood and proceeded to play 'Relax' at high volume five minutes before we were all due to go and teach our first class. His rationale was that it was energising and would put us all in the right frame of mind to kick off our day's teaching. This continued for several days until one of the professors paid us an unexpected, early morning visit and put a prompt stop to the music, which I'm sure could be heard halfway down the street.

During those early days Rick and I had built up quite a reputation for our teaching and when Patrick got wind of this, he decided to see for himself what made us so special, what was going on, in my classroom in particular. Instead of waiting to be invited to observe one of my classes (for which I would have 'got out the best china' as it were and prepared a few extra, carefully devised activities and materials) he decided to appear unannounced – through the classroom window. My classroom was on the third floor and in order to get in Patrick had climbed out through the window on the floor below then scaled the drainpipe. Naturally, the students were thrilled by this unexpected entertainment and the intruder had everyone's rapt attention from the moment his feet touched the floor. He totally hijacked my lesson and ad-libbed his way through the rest of the forty-five-minute session, rather more in stand-up comedian mode than English language teacher. I tried to be good-natured about it all – to be otherwise would, after all, have no doubt been counterproductive – but there was a slightly unpleasant undercurrent in the staffroom for a while and it became clear, to Rick and me at least, that our resident joker harboured some sort of resentment and was perhaps unhealthily competitive. He settled down a bit once he found himself a Chinese girlfriend, Jennifer. She was a plain, homely sort of girl, but then Patrick was not exactly a James Bond lookalike himself (yes, I know that smacks a little of revenge), but they did throw some good parties, one of which was so good the police arrived somewhere around midnight as we were all pogoing with gay abandon to The Cure, lined us up against the wall, prodded us menacingly and ordered us all to go home and not to disturb the neighbours with our decadent revelry again.

It could well have been in Taipei that I came closest to meeting my maker in one of the most unpleasant of ways possible. In my second year in the city, I acquired some private students, an easy-going and sociable young couple called Vivien and John, who had a pretty, precocious toddler with attitude called Yaya. Sweet though she first appeared, this child became an out-and-out pest as she became venomously jealous when her parents directed their attention towards me instead of her. She would try all sorts of ways to get their attention back, banging loudly with spoons on metal toys, tearing pages out of books she'd just been given and, most effectively, if Vivien had forgotten to put a nappy on her, making large puddles in the middle of the parquet lounge floor. Vivien was a couple of inches taller than John, yet in the wedding photos they brought out to show me one evening I noticed that John was a good bit taller than Vivien. When I politely pointed this out, I was told delightedly to study the bottom of the photograph. The bridal couple's feet were festooned in artificial creeper and flowers, which they told me, between fits of laughter, concealed two or three fat telephone directories, which formed an effective pedestal for the grinning groom. We always managed to have fun during the classes, even though we must all have been quite tired, having put in a full day's work beforehand, so I was quite sad when the course came to an end and the time came to say our goodbyes.

Their home was the other side of the city from us, so for their two-hour lesson I would take a long bus ride to their little flat and a taxi on the homeward journey around 10.15 pm. On this last evening, Vivien and John insisted on coming down to the pavement to see me off. Normally I was very careful about the taxis I took as I had been warned by my Taiwanese students, as I had been by my Thai students, that many of the older, more dilapidated-looking taxis were driven by ex-convicts, taxi driving being one of the few jobs open to them after they had served their sentence. On no account I was told should I take such taxis, especially after dark, as these evil men had been known to abduct unwary women, rob and murder them, possibly raping them beforehand, or perhaps just poking their eyes out so that they wouldn't be able to identify the perpetrator. On this particular occasion, as I was busy saying goodbye to Vivien, John had hailed a distinctly old and nasty-looking taxi, which was waiting by the kerb for me to get in after our final farewells. For once, I decided to take a chance and make do so as not to make a fuss. We trundled along for a few kilometres until we came to the point where normally we turned right onto a bridge over the river. To my dismay, the driver went right past this turning and started to speed up a little. I immediately spoke out in my laughably minimal Mandarin saying this was not right, indicating in no uncertain terms that I was perturbed and wanted him to turn round. The driver ignored me, muttering something obscene-sounding under his breath, and continued to drive, steadily accelerating. I was beginning to realise I had made a grave mistake and that I was going to have to take desperate measures if I was to get out of this alive. After what seemed like an age, we came to a set of orange traffic lights but as we approached the driver put his foot down and drove straight through a red light. Now I knew for sure that I was in serious trouble. Another set of traffic lights loomed up, but this time there was a car in front of us, so the taxi was obliged to stop. Before we even came to a halt I leaped out of the car and raced away along the pavement until I came to an old man wheeling a cart of vegetables. To my horror, when I looked back, I saw that the taxi driver had parked his old banger and was hotly pursuing me. I attempted to explain to the baffled vendor that the taxi driver was a bad man (*boo hao shenshung*) but I was simply stared at as though I was quite mad and it became obvious that I was not going to get any protection from him. Unbelievably, the taxi driver started waving a handful of banknotes around in the air, indicating that he wanted me to pay for the distance he'd driven me. I got a distinct feeling that the old veggie vendor would have willingly helped the taxi driver rob me if I didn't cough up, so very begrudgingly I did so. It was some time before another taxi came along. Telling myself that lightning doesn't strike twice, I jumped in eagerly, and before I knew it, I was safely home, somewhat careworn but at least in one piece.

Winter was approaching and we were about to experience the coldest, wettest winter the people of Taiwan had endured for many a year. There was talk of freak Siberian winds and the buses all reeked of damp musty clothes. As the temperature dropped steadily, we realised we would have to buy extra bedding and even considered getting some sort of heater to use first thing in the morning, as we ate our breakfast, and in the evenings, as we undressed for bed. We were a little disconcerted to learn from our colleagues that the Taiwanese considered heating in people's homes to be decadent and so it was not the norm. Our young landlady, Mayman, certainly made no mention of the unusual cold, but I must say I didn't see her sitting on the sofa that winter. It was a typical, hefty, Chinese construction of dark varnished wood with green marble slabs where normally one would find cushions; the marble, as you can imagine, was positively icy to the touch. One of our colleagues, Li Ping, a delightfully eccentric young woman from Singapore, a dead-ringer for Popeye's favourite, Olive Oyl, who had acquired her excellent English through watching English films on TV, offered to lend us a two-bar electric heater. We accepted instantly and very gratefully, as by this time I had taken to eating breakfast wearing gloves and a scarf. We didn't see a great deal of our flatmates on the whole, but as luck would have it, the very afternoon we arrived home with our shiny, new, red electric heater there was Mayman, standing before us as we entered the living room, a look of pure horror on her face. 'You're not going to *use* that are you?' she asked in dismay, and when we said yes, that we were freezing in our room, and that we most certainly did intend to use it, she had little choice but to consent, imploring us, however, only to use *one* bar. Her concern was, of course, not that we risked becoming decadent but that her electricity bill would be sky-high.

I have never been a good sleeper and am particularly sensitive to noise of any sort when I'm trying to switch off and prepare for surrender into the arms of Morpheus. Soon after we moved into our humble abode, to our great consternation, a neighbour, whose room was just at our level in the next-door building not more than three metres away, took up the violin and would practice each night just when I was turning in for the day. I tried earplugs but to no avail – I was going to have to let the fiend know that he was affecting others' well-being with his appalling nocturnal fiddling. With the help of colleagues, I learned how to say 'Please don't play, I'm trying to sleep!' – in Mandarin approximately '*Bu yaw swejeaw, wor yaw tang le*' – and practised several times with Mayman until I thought I'd got it right. Sure enough, that night the dreadful racket started up at the same time as usual. I opened our window and shouted out into the night, audible I'm sure to the customers in the dumpling shop down below and to dozens of passers-by, the words I'd prepared. To my delight, the playing stopped, but I could hear Mayman and her husband howling with laughter just outside our door. Apparently, I'd got the sounds right but had used the wrong tones. What I had in fact said was 'I don't want soup, I want dumplings!' The neighbour must have thought he was living next to a psychiatric case and, perhaps fearing more hysterical outbursts, refrained from practising at that hour again.

During our time in Taipei, we had to make a couple of visa trips back to Hong Kong, which was a nuisance as it bit into our hard-earned savings and meant we had to take a day or so off work. We had a similar situation working in Bangkok, but we enjoyed our train trips south through the luxuriant tropical landscape to Penang, in the days before the eight-mile Penang Bridge was built connecting the island to the mainland. We were fond of Georgetown, the main city, where we stayed at an old Chinese hotel, whose bedrooms were separated by walls that stopped six inches before they reached the ground, which enabled tiny mice to run around after dark between the rooms. Hong Kong was a different story. We found the Hong Kong inhabitants, at least those we encountered in shops and on public transport, compared to the Taiwanese, to be abrasive, if not downright rude. The first time we stayed in Hong Kong, we stayed in a very low-budget hostel in a building well-known to backpackers, called Chung King Mansions. It was a good place to get work smuggling drugs, so we heard, and you would meet dealers of every description there. Our hostel was way up on the 19th floor; the lift was tiny and often packed with enormous Nigerian ladies laden with bulging bags of wares, talking loudly as though they owned the building. On our second visa run, we decided to splash out on somewhere a little bit more comfortable, having followed a recommendation from one of our American colleagues. We negotiated a price with the surly receptionist and were led to a room that admittedly was almost three times the size of the rooms in the Chung King Mansion hostel. There was actually room to put one's bags on the floor and it had its own tiny en suite bathroom. A large circular mirror was pointed out above the bed, which in my memory was also circular, and as he withdrew the receptionist muttered something unintelligible but vaguely threatening under his breath. When the time came to pay, to our astonishment the bill was far higher than we had negotiated. Yes, sleazy Uriah Heep snarled at us, the room we had stayed in was the special 'lovers' room' with the circular ceiling mirror and so of course we had to pay extra. I am rarely roused to public rage, but on the odd occasion when I am, woe betide my adversaries. I don't take kindly to being cheated and protested vehemently. Taking the amount that we'd originally agreed to pay out of my purse, I slapped it down on the counter and marched out, shouting a few expletives over my shoulder as I went.

I have never been known for my punctuality, and have in fact missed a few planes in my life, but on this occasion, we had actually arrived at the airport extremely early, mindful perhaps of the fact that we were both supposed to be teaching back in Taipei that afternoon. Approaching the check-in desk, we must have been asking ourselves if we'd got the right one, as there were no staff in sight and no other passengers around. All of a sudden, we found ourselves surrounded by smartly dressed, official-looking men with grave expressions on their faces. To our great surprise and horror, one of them then formally addressed us: 'Mr Stiles, Ms Evans, we have reason to believe you are smuggling narcotics. Could you come this way, please?' The next thing we knew we were being marched across the airport hall, apparently under arrest. It was not long before this that we had watched the harrowing film *Midnight Express*, about a young traveller who has drugs planted in his luggage, resulting in years of incarceration in a horrific prison somewhere in deepest Turkey. Having spent some time apart from Rick in Hong Kong and knowing that some of our American colleagues were partial to a bit of cannabis at weekends and could well have asked Rick to buy them some whilst in Hong Kong, I whispered to Rick as we crossed the wide departure hall, asking if he had bought anything while we'd been apart in the city, doing our own thing. He replied that he certainly hadn't but then, of course, he would have said this whether he had or not. As we were separated and ushered into different rooms at the back of the airport, I remember distinctly feeling that I might not see my dear Rick again for years to come, if indeed ever.

I then found myself closeted in a small, empty room with a severe and deathly pale and pasty young policewoman, who immediately told me to undress. As I removed each item of clothing, it would be snatched rudely from me and my captor would violently rip hems and seams apart with what looked like excessive zeal, appearing quite crestfallen when showers of cocaine failed to rain from my crumpled clothing. During the clothes search, I had been told to start doing squats and while I performed this increasingly uncomfortable exercise in the corner of the room, she started rifling through my luggage, pouncing on three or four large boxes of Tampax tampons as though she'd discovered hidden treasure. The reason I had bought such a large supply was that – like coffee – they were considerably cheaper in Hong Kong than in Taipei. She then went methodically through each box, opening each and every tampon and poking her finger inside the cardboard outer layer, ever keen to discover illicit substances. After watching my precious tampons being destroyed in this way for several minutes, I took a brief break from my now quite painful squats to politely suggest that perhaps at this point she could see for herself that these were normal, genuine Tampax tampons. This not unreasonable request provoked a furious outburst: 'I'm just doing my *duty*!' she hissed at me. 'Now shut up and *bend*!' By the time she had gone through all my tampons, torn up several more bits of clothing and dropped them disrespectfully to the floor, I had come to loathe her with every fibre of my being. I was told contemptuously to get dressed, take my luggage and get out.

To my amazement, as I emerged from that awful room, shaken and trembling with rage and rightful indignation, I beheld Rick looking extraordinarily relaxed, chatting and joking with the very policemen who had arrested us what felt like several hours previously. The police officer in charge of this operation was unexpectedly young, now I came to inspect him, and rather good-looking. Catching my gaze, he came over to me and offered what appeared to be a sincere apology for troubling us in this way. He explained that a lot of drug smuggling went on at this airport and that it was his responsibility to track down and detain the culprits. We were escorted to the plane, which miraculously was still waiting on the tarmac, our baggage loaded, and off we went back to Taipei. It was on the flight back that Rick told me what had happened in his room next door while I was undergoing my ordeal. On questioning Rick and inspecting his luggage, the police had realised quite quickly that an error had been made and that we were indeed the innocent young teachers on a visa trip that we had claimed to be. As the contents of Rick's luggage were gone through, they came across three large tins of ground coffee with the words PURE COLOMBIAN written in bold letters on the front. At this point Rick, who was doing his own naked bending exercises, stopped and smiled; as the chief of the operation looked up at him, Rick asked, 'Do you think I could take a photograph of you standing there with the tins of coffee, please?' The request was, perhaps not surprisingly, declined, but I gather there had been a good laugh about it, which explained the relaxed atmosphere and camaraderie I witnessed when I emerged from my own personal hell next door. Just over three hours later we found ourselves back at the school, heading towards our classrooms for the afternoon's teaching. The whole episode at Hong Kong airport lingered in my subconscious for days like a bad dream and every so often I would think someone was about to tap me on the shoulder and ask me to 'Come this way please…' I suppose I'll never know the reason we were picked on that day by the customs police, but I have a strong feeling it had something to do with the irascible receptionist at our budget hotel, miffed at missing out on a 'tip' for the round lovers' mirror above the bed – or perhaps he was just spiteful by nature.

Taipei lies in a huge basin surrounded by dramatic high mountains, which sadly can rarely be seen on account of the appalling pollution that plagues the city. On bad days, when we lived there, one could barely see as far as the end of a block and many of the cyclists and motorcyclists wore masks – something we had never really seen before, even in equally polluted Bangkok. Once in a while, there would be high winds during the night and as we stepped outside in the morning we were amazed and delighted to see clear blue skies and the outline of astonishing jagged mountains all around the horizon. The wealthier expats lived in opulent houses with swimming pools and tennis courts up in the foothills of these mountains, and as the hired hands did the food shopping, the only time many of these residents descended into the ground-level smog was to eat at one of the city's five-star hotel restaurants. Once in a while, at weekends, we got to live it up at some of these desirable residences, invited by good friends we had made at the hostel on arrival, Rita and Patrick. This canny pair were very clever at getting employment as house sitters for these wealthy folk, sometimes for fairly extended periods. The job also often involved looking after animals, usually guard dogs, who were accustomed to living outside but, in Rita and Patrick's care, tended to become spoiled and converted to pets. Many a happy weekend was spent up there in the pure air, reclining on sun loungers or expensive leather sofas, drinking beer or local plum wine, feasting, watching videos and putting the world to rights until the early hours. Patrick and Rita were total opposites in so many ways, yet they complemented each other perfectly. Patrick was a physiotherapist from Holland and Rita a Swiss florist; both spoke excellent English and were well travelled. We loved their company and the warm ambiance they created in those fancy mountain villas. We were very upset to learn one day, out of the blue, that they had decided to go their separate ways. They both came to our leaving party, however, drank copious amounts of my plum wine and vodka-fortified punch, and got back together, and it seems it was that very night that the first of their two boys was conceived. When I visited them a few years later in Berne I got to meet their two adorable sons, both of whom spoke several languages. Having had a Filipina nanny in the Philippines, where they lived after Taiwan, the boys picked up Tagalog as well as English, Dutch and Swiss German. It amazed me how easily they switched language depending on who they were talking to. Sadly, we lost touch, but I'm ever hopeful of running into them someday, if not on the street, in the ether.

Another friend of ours was a large, comely woman from California called Charlene, who applied for a job teaching at Emerson early on in our first year. Remarkably, she was still working at eighty years of age, and was game to try out some of the innovative approaches to language teaching, such as Asher's TPR (total physical response) classroom activities, which we encouraged our new teachers to incorporate into their lessons. Very sadly Charlene's demo lesson didn't go well and she was not taken on, as Bad Mike didn't feel she'd be able to adapt her more traditional style of teaching to our more up-to-date methods. We remained in touch, however, and one weekend were invited to a small house party up on the mountainside in Tien Mu, not a million miles from Rita and Patrick's house-sitting patch. We were very impressed by Charlene's attractive stone cottage, tastefully furnished as it was with her own things, which had been shipped out from the USA. We were given a house tour and shown her favourite room, the study, where she gave private lessons and communicated with friends using her brand-new shiny personal computer, the first of its kind we'd seen in someone's home. She proudly showed us how her word-processed letters and their replies could be stored in neat separate folders along with worksheets she designed for her Chinese students. Charlene was one of the original feminists; she'd dispensed with her husband when her four children were young and had brought them up herself, waiting until they were all standing on their own feet before packing up and leaving the States to pursue her greatest love, Chinese culture and language. She spoke fondly of her Chinese professors, one of whom was a guest that evening, but we got the idea that, although she may have been lonely, she would not give up her independence easily if at all.

She had gone to enormous lengths to prepare what I can only call a banquet for us and a handful of other guests. Course after course appeared out of her tiny kitchen – everything quite delicious and cooked from scratch in quantities that left one boggling. Each and every offer of help was spurned, so we obediently sat back and enjoyed it all while Charlene slaved away until she must have been utterly exhausted. The wine was free-flowing, Chopin played softly in the background, people conversed with ease, and before we knew it, it was long gone midnight. Thankfully, we had been invited to stay the night and had come prepared with pyjamas and toothbrushes; the small guest room was freezing but the bed had beautifully laundered French linen sheets and we had no trouble falling asleep. I will never forget the sight that beheld us on entering the living room cum dining room the following morning – it resembled a bomb site. Every surface was covered with plates, bowls, platters and cutlery. There were so many glasses it seemed as though there had been ten times as many guests as there actually had been. As there was no sign of our hostess we got stuck in clearing up and fortunately had made great inroads into the task by the time Charlene made a graceful appearance. She was such a kind and generous individual I have often thought of her since and have always regretted that she was not offered work at our school. Had Rick or I had any say in the matter, she'd have been snapped up eagerly, something, fortunately, we had the opportunity to tell her.

While Charlene was perhaps one of the unlucky ones with regard to employment at Emerson, Texan Dave Tetter was most certainly one of the luckiest. He stepped into the school with no teaching experience whatsoever and not a great deal of education per se, but, despite his lack of height and his oddly triangular body shape, being a serious, competitive bodybuilder, he radiated calm confidence and simply glowed with good health. With his impressively honed and bulging muscles, shown off to the full in crisp, white, short-sleeved shirts, his golden hair and year-round tan, though not the typical EFL teacher, he was more than presentable. Whatever went on in the classroom, Dave's end-of-course student evaluations were always good, if not superlative, and we had no reason to be dissatisfied. One day, to our surprise, he invited Rick and me, plus a few other teachers, to come to a bodybuilding competition he was taking part in that weekend. As we entered the hall, we were met with an overpowering smell of coconut oil and strains of AC/DC or possibly Guns N' Roses on the sound system. We took our seats really having little idea what to expect. There were several categories for both male and female competitors, who emerged from the wings, in turn, glistening with oil and posed in various positions to their chosen music to show off their curiously over-developed muscles. Exacerbated by the atmosphere of hushed reverence and the looks of keen anticipation on the faces around us, we all found it utterly hilarious and it was a tremendous effort to remain sitting upright and stifle our guffaws, which we knew if heard would be deeply insulting to the competitors. When Dave himself came on stage, some of us had to actually double up and bend down out of sight below the seats in front of us so as not to be seen convulsed with laughter. Seeing our earnest colleague before us, normally fully clad and carrying a pile of books, performing in the skimpiest of posing pouches, flexing his muscles in time to the music, it was just excruciating, and by the time the event drew to a close and we could safely escape out of the hall into the Taipei night, our ribs were positively aching with suppressed laughter. If laughing exercises one's insides in the way it is said to, then we all gave our innards a thorough work-out that afternoon. Not only that but in the short space of an hour or so, we released every shred of anger, tension and anxiety that had built up during the working week.

Outside work, one of the best things about Taipei for Rick and me, both being film buffs, was the underground video clubs. There was something vaguely disreputable about these places, even though the majority of us went to see art films if not plain Hollywood, rather than blue movies that I gather were available too. The deal was, on arrival you were presented with a menu for drinks and simple snacks along with one or more huge folders of movies to choose from. While the law forbade the rental of videos at that time in Taiwan, it did naturally permit the sale of food and drink, which was consumed in funky, private wigwams, each containing a comfortable sofa, coffee table and large TV screen – the entertainment was provided 'free'. We paid many a visit to these curious establishments, which I was particularly enamoured with, as they permitted me to see dozens of films I had missed out on over the years either through lack of funds or simply through being out of the UK when they came out. The most outstanding film I saw there was Ridley Scott's neo-noir sci-fi cult classic, *Blade Runner*. As we emerged that night around midnight with images of the futuristic, bustling neon-lit streets of Los Angeles still in our minds, it was as though we had stepped out into the movie itself, such was the grungy, stygian scene that greeted us, with its gaudy, flashing signs, its cold, clammy night air and its vaguely threatening ambiance.

When we first arrived in Taipei we had been struck by the ugliness and even what we felt to be the soullessness of the city. It was also unbearably hot and sticky. We'd been homesick for Bangkok, where we could escape the humid tropical heat by jumping on a river ferry and zipping down south to check for mail at the GPO. We found the general Taiwanese public, compared to the smiley Thais, rather surly, almost hostile and more inclined to stare. Everything from food to clothes and toiletries was more expensive and we seriously wondered if we might have made an awful mistake coming here. As time went by, however, we became more involved with our work and formed close relationships with our students, who, along with our American colleagues, showed us places to eat, brought us mooncakes at the Chinese New Year and wrote touching appreciative cards at the end of their courses. In the end, it was our Taiwanese students who made our work so rewarding and the friendships we formed that made our two-year stay such a memorable one.

One of the reasons we decided to move on from the Far East was that my hormones were starting to tell me in no uncertain terms that it was now or never if we wanted to have a baby. There really wasn't much difference between Bangkok and Taipei when it came to pollution; neither were places where one would want to bring a newborn babe into the world – its little pink lungs would have been blackened in no time. Rick was keen to visit his family in New Zealand. His parents had emigrated there from the Midlands when he and his brother were quite young. The decision had been made, apparently, while the whole family was stuck in a hot car in a traffic jam one bank holiday. So, the plan was to head back to the UK to see my family first, stopping off for a couple of weeks in Thailand for a much-needed break on the way, then travel on to Auckland, London then being one of the best places to buy cheap air tickets. The only thing was, all our savings – several fat wads of none-too-clean banknotes bound with elastic bands at the bottom of a Corn Flakes packet at the back of our wardrobe – would need to be somehow smuggled out of the country, as the laws at that time were quite stringent and only allowed you to take out a small amount of cash.

Fortunately, one of Rick's students, Piana, a delightful, vivacious woman with whom Rick sometimes played Chinese checkers at her modest home behind the family shop, said she could help. She promised to introduce us to someone who could assist us by giving us a cheque from an American bank, which could be cashed once we got back to the UK. She assured us that this was quite common practice and that she could vouch for the honesty of this money dealer. It was from Piana that we learned that 'every wise rabbit has a second bolt hole' – most sensible Taiwanese were steadily siphoning off money to overseas accounts in readiness for possible evacuation, should the mainland Chinese invade. At an agreed time, we met Piana outside her home and took a taxi across town to an area where most of the shops seemed to be jewellers. The one we entered was not distinct in any way from the others that lined the street. A brief word to the assistant behind the counter and we were led to the back of the shop, through a thick dark curtain and into a smaller room. There, behind a huge, mahogany desk sat an enormous, dignified, bespectacled woman with a steely look and an ancient abacus. A deal was done, and our savings of two years were handed over, not without a touch of anxiety, despite Piana's assurances, and in return, we were given two unusually small cheques, each made out for $9,000 from a bank in California. (The money was finally 'collected' by my bank in North Wales, Williams & Glyn, even though the manager called me into his office at one point and warned me that he thought it extremely unlikely that I would ever see the money again.)

Just a few days before we were due to leave the country, we received a letter from the tax office calling us in for an interview. Having already parted with most of our Taiwanese money, we went along at the appointed time with not a little trepidation, fearing we might be presented with a nasty bill. To our amazement, not only were we *not* asked to pay a thing, but we were told we were owed a tax rebate. In front of our very eyes one of the young female tellers counted out rather a lot of high denomination notes, which she solemnly handed over. There was enough there, in fact, to pay not only for our two-week holiday in Thailand but also part of our airfare back to the UK. We simply skipped off down the road, hardly able to believe our luck, anxious to get away before a mistake was discovered.

Packing was a nightmare – we had left it far too late to begin the process of sifting through clothes and possessions acquired over the past two years, deciding what to take, what to give away and what to send home by post. Our flight out of Taipei was quite early in the morning and we'd been up drinking with friends the night before. We were not in the best state, therefore, when our taxi arrived outside our building and hooted. We were very touched to see Piana and her whole family had turned out to see us off and one of the young American teachers, Mark Teague, who'd been so devoted to us, his British supervisors, he'd make any excuse to come over at weekends, just to hang out and be near us. He had an infectious laugh and the palest baby blue eyes. He'd been quite hurt when one of his students, a pretty young Chinese teenager, told him she couldn't bear to look him directly in the eye as it made her feel sick. Mark too had forfeited a lie-in on a Saturday morning to come and say farewell and wish us *bon voyage*, so we felt we had quite a send-off. Our only regret, as our plane rose up above the smog into the powder blue skies heading south towards Thailand, was that we had seen so little of the island while we were there, as Taiwan is supposed to have some stunning scenery. We felt at the time, however, that we were there to work and save as much as we could, and so rarely left Taipei city. Given the choice of a spell of post-employment R & R in either Taiwan or our beloved Thailand, there was really no contest.

Chapter 10

From London to Auckland via LA

Before ever setting foot in New Zealand, or Godzone as it's often called by its inhabitants, I had been told that living there was a little like living in a place where it's always Sunday afternoon, where there's a very limited choice of shoes and frocks in the shops, where most people are either shopkeepers, teachers or sheep farmers, but where you'll be quite happy living if you appreciate cheap drinkable wine and you're a lover of the outdoor life. It hardly made me want to jump on the next plane Down Under, but, as the decision had been made to visit Rick's parents and as I was always game to explore another corner of the globe, we went out and bought one-way tickets to Auckland. Just a few days before departure we happened to notice that our air tickets with Continental Airlines required non-American passengers to obtain a US visa, as we would be spending a few hours at Houston airport en route. Gnashing our teeth at this cruel setback, we rescheduled our flight, paying not only a rebooking fee but also for return train fares into London to the US embassy, where we were further horribly stung for an essential fast-processed visa. Ever conscious of our meagre resources, we had chosen the cheapest ticket available, so perhaps we shouldn't have been too surprised when we discovered that the airline left a great deal to be desired. We were very late indeed departing from London Heathrow – engine trouble we were told – and by the time we did the cabin crew were surly and unhelpful, bordering on offensive. Arriving in Houston, sleep-deprived and irritable ourselves, we were grilled at length by the immigration staff about our relationship with the USA and with any people we might know there. It was not the first time I had experienced naked animosity and aggression from officials whilst travelling, but it still came as quite a shock. It was many years, decades even, before I considered travelling to the country again. One winter's day I had woken up in Brighton and decided I simply had to see the Muir Redwoods and the Grand Canyon, but thankfully my second experience with US immigration staff, this time in San Francisco, couldn't have been more different – I was welcomed with a smile, and told to enjoy my stay. They do say that California is like a different country to the rest of the USA, and in my case this felt true.

Back in Houston, after the rude interrogation, we made our way to the transit desk to find out which gate our next plane was waiting at, only to be informed, in the most offhand manner, that there would be a three-hour delay – no apology, no food voucher, nothing. I am generally a fairly calm and patient person, unusually so according to some people, but my hackles were beginning to rise and I growled inwardly, vowing to write a fierce letter of complaint to the airline at the first opportunity. Finally, we arrived in LA, where once more we were obliged to change planes. Dragging ourselves along endless cold, carpeted corridors, feeling jaded and incredibly weary, it felt as though we had been travelling for days and what had started off as another adventure to be relished was steadily turning into more of an ordeal, if not a complete nightmare. It was a long walk to the transit desk and when we eventually found it, we were confronted with a notice informing us that our flight to Auckland would be delayed by six hours, possibly longer. On this occasion I decided to put on a display of controlled anger – to the surprised Continental ground staff I ranted and raved about the appalling journey we'd had so far, the inedible food and, not least, the shoddy treatment at the hands of the Continental cabin crew and Houston ground staff. It worked like magic. Within minutes we had both been issued with 'distressed passenger vouchers', which entitled us to a night at the five-star Viscount Hotel (pronounced Viss Count) just outside Los Angeles, with all our meals included, until the next flight to Auckland, twenty-four hours later. We accepted with grace and took a taxi a fairly short distance to the hotel, where the reception staff were no doubt trained to spot distressed passengers and treat them with extra consideration and kindness. The service, in any case, couldn't be faulted and if our room was a bit on the small side and there was a fair bit of noise from the freeway traffic outside, we thought it prudent on this occasion not to look our gift horse in the mouth.

After sleeping deeply in the king-sized bed with its luxurious midnight-blue, quilted bedspread, I remember waking with a slightly hazy memory of the events of the night before. We had taken full advantage of the wines and spirits offered on each flight. The food had been mainly unappetising, to put it mildly, but there's not a lot you can do to ruin a gin and tonic. We made ourselves some coffee and switched on the enormous TV on the wall opposite the bed. The first channel we hit on was displaying photographs of children, sometimes whole batches of siblings, who had gone missing. This was not just one or two isolated incidents; the sad little faces of suspected abduction victims, most of them Hispanic, kept on and on appearing until we must have seen thirty or more. In the end, we just had to switch the TV off – it seemed hardly credible that there were so many people out there beside themselves with worry about their children, and what of the children themselves? It was all most distressing.

Thankfully, the breakfast buffet helped to temporarily take our minds off the macabre news bulletin. I don't think I had ever witnessed anything approaching the variety and abundance of breakfast fare that was laid out before us on long buffet tables surrounding the vast hotel dining hall. Not having eaten properly for some time, we took full advantage of what was on offer: fresh Danish pastries, creamy blueberry yogurt and granola, tropical fruits, smoked salmon and cream cheese bagels, leek and herb sausages, crispy smoked bacon and golden hash browns – the last being a novelty for me, so perhaps the most appreciated of all. We ate heartily and drank several cups of surprisingly good coffee, coffee Agent Cooper, had he been there, would have described as 'Damn fine!'

The whole of our time in LA seemed to take place in a bit of a dream. We decided to head for Venice Beach and on leaving the hotel asked a passer-by if he knew where the bus station was. He pointed vaguely across the impossibly wide six-lane freeway to a small collection of buildings in the distance. Although we had an idea it might not be allowed, we decided the only thing for it was to simply cross this gigantic highway, which thankfully had very little traffic on it at this time of day. When we were just over halfway across, a flashy silver Buick sped by and, spotting two maniacs breaking the law in broad daylight by jaywalking, the driver looked back at us involuntarily over his shoulder, causing his car to swerve dramatically and narrowly miss the divider between north- and southbound traffic. Seeing a collection of buses with unrecognisable destinations, we asked a skateboarder if he knew which bus we should take to Venice Beach. Anyone would have thought we'd asked him to hand over his skateboard and baseball cap into the bargain, such was his reaction to being addressed this way in public. He stared at us for a few seconds as though we each had two heads then hurtled off on his skateboard in the same direction he had come in, whistling tunelessly and performing tricks, though there was no one around besides us to witness them. We managed to find our bus without his help, but had a similar reaction from the driver as we'd just had from the gangly youth. It was as though we had asked for tickets in a fun fair for a roundabout ride designed for tiny tots. Slightly unnerved, we took a seat on the sparsely populated bus, only to be sworn at by a hefty, red-faced woman in a purple sweatshirt and unlaced trainers. Were we sitting in a seat reserved for people with mobility issues? It didn't seem so. We smiled politely then proceeded to ignore her, pretending to enter into a deep, absorbing metaphysical discussion. The next odd bod we noticed was a balding, rheumy-eyed, senior citizen in a grey raincoat muttering to himself in the seat alongside ours. After a while, he rose to get off the bus and as we watched him step off onto the pavement, we noticed that his coat had somehow caught fire, goodness only knows how. He ambled slowly away from the bus along the sidewalk, in a world of his own, leaving a long, wispy trail of smoke behind him.

We finally arrived at Venice Beach and the first shop we saw gave us the feeling that time had stood still somewhere around 1967, the Summer of Love. It was a health food store of sorts called Psychedelia that also sold hippy beads, dope smoking paraphernalia, Crumb illustrated posters, incense, Indian clothes, patchouli oil and so on. A heavily tattooed, over-the-hill hipster with a feathered hat and a faded maroon corduroy jacket greeted us warmly as we entered, but by the time we departed, empty-handed, his smile had degenerated into a disagreeable sort of smirk – so much for love, peace and harmony, we thought. The first person we saw when we reached the boardwalk was the gormless skateboarder who had refused to help us at the bus station; this time he looked straight through us, tossed his hair back and sped off into the sun on his beloved skateboard. It was quite a mystery how he had made it to the beach before us, as he definitely wasn't on our bus, though he'd have fitted in well enough with the other passengers, and he looked too young to own a car. Astral projection we surmised.

Although the sun was out that day, there was a kind of orange haze hanging over the horizon and a muggy feeling to the air, which was not altogether pleasant. There weren't many people in the sea, which was a murky brownish colour and so, even if we had brought our swimmers, I doubt we'd have been tempted into the briny waters either. The bodybuilders were out in force, performing chin-ups, press-ups and chest-presses using various bits of multi-coloured apparatus planted in a giant sand pit, oiled up and pumping iron, as though their lives depended on it – for some it quite possibly did. We strolled along the seafront, bought sour cherry-flavoured ice creams and a second-hand book by one of the lesser-known Beat poets, Alex Trocchi, a friend of Rick's, as it happened. He'd been a most congenial host when Rick first arrived in London from New Zealand, after a year or so on the road in India and South East Asia. I had been looking forward to meeting Alex, partly as he shared my passion for stamp collecting, but very sadly he died before we were able to organise a rendezvous. My other recollection of Venice seafront is of the public conveniences. Possessing a bladder almost exactly a third the size of most normal adults, I need to be quite careful about when and how much I drink, especially if there's any uncertainty about where I might later find a lavatory. Having indulged in more than my usual one cup of coffee at breakfast, I'd reached the point at which I didn't have much choice in the matter – I would have to take a chance with the Venice Beach facilities. On entering, to my dismay, I found that none of the cubicles, which all faced the entrance, had doors. It was later explained to me that this was to deter illicit drug users, which is all very well, but one does feel awfully exposed compelled to relieve oneself in this way – I hadn't even brought my sunglasses, which might have afforded a degree of anonymity.

Arriving in Auckland in early January 1988, a perfect time weather-wise, we were made to feel very welcome by Rick's parents, Bob and Pauline, and I got introduced to the wide circle of mainly arty friends Rick had left behind some years previously. A small welcoming party with a mouth-watering homemade curry and gallons of wine was held for us by family friends, the Clarkes, a delightfully bohemian family of artists, writers and carpenters. The father, Nobby, was a great character, a small wiry man with strikingly dark, penetrating nut-brown eyes. Originally from Hull, he'd studied after the war at the *Grande Chaumiere* art school in Paris, lived in Bombay for five years working for the *Times of India* and had emigrated to New Zealand in 1952. Rick's brother Simon, a laid-back, jovial, lovable horticulturalist with a special interest in the marijuana plant, was very friendly with Nobby's son, another Simon, who had his father's eyes and artistic talent and taught art at Auckland Technical Institute. We spent many a happy evening with him and his wife Sue, who had a great sense of humour and ran a clothes shop in town. Nobby's other son, Marty, a carpenter, had built the most stunning and original house for himself and his family on a clifftop overlooking what was to become our favourite beach, Karekare, where horse races were held each year on the black volcanic sands beside the crashing west coast surf. The house was built of native timbers, kauri and rimu. It had an octagonal bathroom with stained glass windows, a mezzanine floor where all the children slept, antique brass taps at the huge double kitchen sink and an adjoining barn with surprisingly good acoustics, where some great all-night parties were held. I have only to hear a second or two of Paul Simon's *Graceland* and I am right back there in Marty and Margo's barn, where you didn't need to smoke a joint to get high, you just had to take a few deep breaths of the smoke-laden air. I was welcomed into the fold, called their English rose and christened Clarey – I think Nobby's sunny silvery-haired wife, Margaret, who had learned to make her inimitable curries when living in India, must have misheard when I was introduced, but I didn't mind and so Clarey I remained when among the Clarkes.

Rick's younger brother, Simon, after dropping out in India for a year or so, was running a successful garden centre in the trendy area of Ponsonby and had bought himself an unusual split-level house right in the heart of the bush at the foot of the Waitakere Ranges. He'd got Simon Clarke to paint a magnificent image of the Hindu elephant god, Lord Ganesh, the remover of obstacles, on his front door. We'd often visit him and his wild and wonderful wife Philippa at weekends, sharing a steaming hot tub and a magnum of champagne out under the stars and the cabbage trees, with the eerie cries of native birds reaching us from the depths of dark, primordial forest, as we languished half cut in the gently bubbling water. Philippa's mother, a rugged no-nonsense Northerner, owned a riding school outside Auckland and so Philippa had ridden horses since almost before she could walk. I'll never forget seeing her slip a halter over one of her mother's feistier horses, leap onto its back and gallop off like a streak of lightning, jumping bareback over hedges and fallen trees, hell for leather, like a Native American warrior. She rode with great panache and when I was next back home at my parents' I surprised our arthritic old horse, Brandy, by leaping onto his back à la Philippa and urging him to gallop across the field, which to my amazement he actually did and appeared to enjoy.

I quickly learned how cheap and palatable some of the local

wines were, and to this day my favourite white wine is New Zealand sauvignon blanc. According to the American wine connoisseur, Mark Oldman, this wine is like 'a child who inherits the best of both parents – exotic aromas found in the New World and the pungency and limy acidity of an Old World sauvignon blanc like *Sancerre*'. I was also greatly impressed by the variety of excellent ethnic restaurants and cafes around the city, where one could eat in style for a fraction of the cost of eating out in the UK. The one I came to love the most and still sometimes dream about today was called Guadalupe. It opened soon after we arrived in New Zealand and I believe we were amongst its first customers; we'd go there quite often to reward ourselves after a hard week's work. You entered through a nondescript door on the run-down but colourful Karangahape Road and as you ascended the steep wooden staircase and stepped onto the bare floorboards of the restaurant itself you would find magnolia and hibiscus petals strewn at your feet. The walls were covered with fascinating art, voodoo flags, skeletons, crucifixes and Caribbean artefacts. Playing through discreetly placed speakers there would be the coolest jazz, ethereal whispering wind instruments or rhythmic, desert blues, hauntingly beautiful and capable of elevating one's mood on the spot. The waiters and waitresses were madly hip and would not only recount the specials of the day as though reciting poetry but would entertain you, flatter you and flirt with you between courses. The food was out of this world, the dishes composed of exotic ingredients, many of which we'd never even heard of before, and decorated with tiny orange and purple edible petals. According to an old *New Zealand Herald* review, 'the clientele of musicians, artists and art students, poets and bohemian types made for a vibe inside those ruby red walls that few other venues in Auckland at that time managed to achieve'. So, I was not alone in my reverence for Guadalupe. I was beginning to see why Kiwi people called their country Godzone with such conviction, and why, however far afield they travelled, they would finally surrender to the magic, magnetic force that drew them back to their beloved homeland.

I soon understood too why the Māori name for the country is Aotearoa, land of the long white cloud. In my memory, the skies in New Zealand were almost always cerulean blue and the clouds, if there were any, were invariably long, white, slow-drifting fluffy ones. The magnificent pōhutukawa trees with their sparkling, vermilion bottlebrush blooms that grow right down to the edge of the beaches, along with the tall, swaying pampas grass, enchanted me, as did the sparsely populated, green-blanketed rolling hills of the countryside, dotted with sheep, twenty-five million of them at the last count. Jacaranda trees with their outrageous purple haze of blossom grew beside the roads along with other equally vividly coloured flowering trees. The climate of the North Island is sub-tropical, resulting in long growing seasons and high yields of crops. I loved to see lemon and other citrus trees in people's gardens and marvelled at the abundance of stone fruit, herbs and vegetables that grew ecstatically in the rich, dark, volcanic soil. It would not be an exaggeration to say I saw courgettes in Bob and Pauline's garden grow an inch or more overnight. Kiwi fruit was so plentiful that you would sometimes see great wooden boxes piled high with them at the side of the road with notices begging you to help yourself. Thick clumps of fragrant coriander grew like weeds and there were tart, orange physalis, or Aztec berries, from the nightshade family, with their delicate, golden, papery-lantern encasements, growing wild in the hedges.

It had been some time since Rick and I had earned an honest crust, and we knew that sooner or later we were going to have to face up to the work situation. As we gathered that there were fairly well-paid jobs to be had at both private language schools and the local tertiary colleges, we saw no harm in *applying* for jobs at least. After all, we didn't have to sign ten-year contracts, nothing was set in stone we told ourselves. The very first week we were in the country, we saw a post advertised for experienced language teachers at Languages International, one of the longest established and most reputable language schools in the city. We applied and were called up for an interview the next day. Languages International was housed in a fine, old, wooden colonial building in the centre of the city, just opposite Albert Park, with its luxuriant vegetation, luscious lilac, laburnum and purplish black magnolia, its fountains and quaint old rotunda standing forlornly empty in the centre. After being welcomed at the door by the school owners, Francis and Chris Woolcott, we were invited into their office to be interviewed together. Having worked with Americans for two years, some of their bravado and self-assurance must have rubbed off on us as we found ourselves taking it in turns to sell ourselves, offering to set up a self-study centre with new-fangled listening posts and recommending the best new commercial materials available on the market. We quietly took over the interview, but it didn't seem to do us any harm as by the end of it, Francis had decided to snap Rick up for her school while, to my amazement, Chris, then Supervisor of Languages at Manukau Polytechnic, offered me a full-time position at his college, setting up and running an off-campus ESL programme.

Chris Woolcott had apparently been approached by Lucy Taumoli, the influential and some might say formidable Samoan head of the Labour Department in Mangere, an area in the south of the city with a high percentage of Māori and Pacific Island inhabitants, to ask if a course could be set up to help new immigrants get to grips with the services and facilities in the area. Apart from assisting these newcomers to the country, the course also needed to be geared towards helping longer-term beneficiaries of unemployment benefits gain some interview skills in the hope of easing them off their benefits and into gainful employment. My first task was to interview potential 'trainees' at the Labour Department to select individuals whom I felt would take full advantage of the course and be willing to really make an effort to get a job on completion of the course. The fact that the participants on this course would be paid rather more than they would get from their benefits made it an attractive proposition and I guessed that many of the people I saw would have no real intention of giving up generous benefits to actually work, particularly if they had large families, which many of these people did.

The interview with the Woolcotts, at which we had accepted our respective job offers, was on a Friday. The following evening, we were invited to a party with some of Rick's oldest and dearest friends, Bruce and Kimmie, at their fabulous, old, rambling colonial house at the end of Dickens Street, overlooking Grey Lynn Park. These people really knew how to throw a party. The place simply buzzed with good music, amazing food, chilled vibes and an assortment of interesting people from all walks of life. It was the first of many legendary parties and the first time I was to witness Bruce devouring the worm at the bottom of the tequila bottle; he would gently tap me on the shoulder and as I turned around, he would grin at me with the evil worm protruding horrifically from between his lips. It was Bruce, I believe, who introduced me to Gary Larson's *The Far Side* and we would sit side by side on our sofa at weekends flicking through the pages, howling with laughter until the tears rolled down our faces. Of all Rick's old friends in Auckland, it was perhaps Bruce and Kimmie who accepted me most heartily into their midst when I arrived in the country and it was Kimmie who took time during that party to tell me she thought that I'd be great in the job, that I'd soon get to grips with the New Zealand system and be one step ahead of the 'trainees' when it came to showing them the ropes. Thanks to Kimmie's evident confidence in me, her encouragement and her infectious enthusiasm about this exciting opportunity I was being offered, I rolled up at Manukau Polytechnic that first Monday morning feeling I could tackle just about anything that was thrown at me.

I was amazed at how little guidance I received in those initial meetings – I was given pretty much free rein to set up and run the course however I thought fit. There was some mention of a course budget, though I don't recall ever being told just how much I had to play with. We touched on the idea of buying furniture and hiring a vehicle for student outings, but no suggestion of what type of vehicle or where I might hire one. As for course content, materials, outing destinations and so on – it was all left totally up to me. I found myself in the enviable position of having a clean slate to fill how I wished. My immediate superior at the polytechnic, Chris Woolcott, was always so sweet and tentative about anything we discussed, his hesitancy and unassuming air always had the effect of making me feel quite decisive and empowered, although I'm not sure if he intended this or not. If he did, he was a highly skilled and effective supervisor. I struck up a deal with Father Broekman, a Dutch Catholic priest, to rent what I thought to be a suitable venue, a spacious hall, mainly used for Pacific Islander events, with a kitchen and two smallish side rooms that I judged would be just large enough to accommodate two classes of six trainees each. At the back of the hall was a large wooden balcony that overlooked a small garden and beyond this were grassy fields, where friendly fantails swooped and horses grazed – a perfect spot for end-of-course barbecues.

It was only when I came to start interviewing prospective students for the first twelve-week course that I started to wonder if the classrooms would be big enough – some of the Pacific Islanders were simply enormous. Thankfully the South East

Asians, mainly refugees from Vietnam, but also a few from Laos and Cambodia, were mostly tiny, so aiming for a balance of the two seemed the best thing to aim for. On the first day of the course a man called Seti, a Samoan ex-boxer, punch-drunk we later surmised, failed to show up, so after the afternoon class I walked off into the housing estate opposite our hall in Bader Drive to find out what had happened to him. On knocking at the door, what sounded like a pack of ferocious dogs started barking and after a few minutes a large, heavily tattooed, bare-footed Samoan lady wearing a studded leather waistcoat and cut-off jeans appeared. She was highly suspicious when I asked if Seti was at home and, for a moment, I thought she might set the dogs on me. She was holding them back by their collars and they looked as though they were just aching to sink their teeth into the bare flesh of my skinny white calves. My explanation finally satisfied the lady of the house. She actually softened up and gave me a lop-sided, sparsely toothed smile, assuring me that her man would attend the course the next day – she would see to it that he did. When I later relayed this experience to Rick, he replied casually that I'd been taking quite a risk venturing alone onto that estate – that there was a very high crime rate, with theft, rape and murder stories appearing quite regularly in the local newspapers. I was advised not to make a habit of knocking on doors there unaccompanied.

Before Rick joined me on the course as my co-tutor, I worked with a few interesting people, two of whom became very good friends. Both Alison and Sharon were striking-looking, dynamic and highly intelligent New Zealanders – proud third-generation Kiwis with a great zest for life and a well-developed sense of humour. I had great fun working with both of them and I felt very fortunate to have them as my close colleagues. I would spend hours on the phone to Alison in particular in the evenings, discussing the quaint and lovable characters in the class we shared as well as a rather repulsive colleague we both had the misfortune to have occasional dealings with at the Polytechnic in Otara, a fifteen-minute drive away. Sharon was working on her master's degree at that time, and was on a bit of a tight budget. She would roll up minutes before the start of her class in a beaten-up old car, which hardly looked roadworthy, perform a few high karate kicks, if out of sight of the trainees (she had obtained her black belt whilst working in Japan), and march grinning into class, pony-tail swishing rakishly as she went.

When Rick came to work with me in Mangere he turned out to be brilliant at dealing with the various problems the trainees brought to class. Their benefit cheque hadn't arrived, their electricity had been cut off, there was a flea infestation in their home and so on. He would spend most of his breaks on the phone to the authorities, gently insisting until he achieved what he wanted, always remaining calm, reasonable and good-humoured. Rick once explained to me that the mastery of his emotions – no mean feat by anyone's standards – was a skill he had been taught whilst more or less an emotional prisoner at an ashram in Rishikesh a year or so before we met. In order to join the ashram, with its idyllic setting on a hillside overlooking the river Ganges, one needed first to be invited. Although life for devotees at the ashram was pleasant enough on the surface, one's days were governed by strict rules and regulations; complete humility and servitude were required at all times. If anyone ever left the ashram it was usually over the wall at night. I met Rick's former guru, Swarmi Balyogi Premvarni, in situ on our travels around India. He had undoubted charisma, however, and, after we'd drunk mint tea and exchanged pleasantries, he invited us to stay, offering to educate us in tantric yoga. Although I daresay it would have been an interesting experience, I can't say I was really tempted, particularly as I suspected my scepticism about the man and his methods would be an obstacle to any true spiritual growth.

My work in Mangere, apart from teaching, was taken up with general organisation, networking with useful people in the community along with report and materials writing, the last of which I have always had a great penchant for. Rick and I made a good team and, of course, were used to working together, as we had done ever since meeting at the Brighton vegetarian restaurant, five years earlier. I know of employers who are reluctant to take on couples in the EFL world, fearing domestic rows spilling over into the workplace, I suppose, but I think I can honestly say that in our ten years working together, not a single cross word was uttered, and remarkable though it may sound, the same more or less went for our home life. I have never understood those who say a good row clears the air, a bit of drama spices up a relationship and so on. I couldn't disagree more. Call me an old hippy, but I'm all for love, peace and harmony – you can keep your drama and histrionics.

One incident that occurred early on in my first course haunts me to this day. In order to transport the trainees on the weekly outings, I had hired a fourteen-seater vehicle. It was a bit like an old tank to drive; the gearbox was clunky and the wing mirrors juddered, making it hard to get a good clear image of what was going on behind. By the time the first outing came round, I really hadn't had enough practice driving the cumbersome machine, but I went ahead anyway. I'd decided to take the group to Auckland Museum to see something of the history of the island and attend what I'd heard was a spectacular Māori song and dance display. I had never driven this route before and the sky was looking ominously dark – it seemed to be brewing up for a storm. I'd studied the map well beforehand, and as I drove in what I felt to be the right direction, I wondered if the Māori haka tribal dance would frighten the newly arrived refugees, one of whom, a slight, nervy Cambodian lady who had Māori neighbours, had asked me anxiously if the Māoris were still cannibals. At one point on the journey there was a junction on a hill and just beyond the junction was a zebra crossing, which was only visible when one was practically upon it as there were no Belisha beacons. There were cars parked on either side of the road and the rain was just starting, so I was searching for the windscreen wipers. The trainees were in a state of high excitement and were all talking nineteen to the dozen in the back. All of a sudden there was a great thump, and to my horror, I realised I had hit something. A large Samoan woman had stepped out from behind a car right in front of us. She got up immediately and went to sit on a bench at the side of the road (someone later said, only half in jest, that it had been put there specifically for those knocked down on the zebra crossing to sit on to recover). The moment I had parked, all twelve of the trainees – a slightly odd-looking multi-ethnic troupe of all shapes and sizes – jumped out of the vehicle with me and piled onto the pavement. When a sour-faced, grey-haired old biddy with a stick who'd witnessed the incident started loudly berating me, they all leaped to my defence, outdoing her for belligerence and insisting it was not my fault, that I'd been driving very carefully and slowly and that she'd just stepped out in front of us. A traffic policeman came roaring up on his motorbike and more shouting ensued. The Samoan lady, meanwhile, appeared to be fine and assured me no damage had been done, but she was taken off in an ambulance for an x-ray, just in case, and the traffic cop took my details, telling me ominously that I would be contacted.

I'm not sure how I managed to get through the rest of the day, but, somehow, I did. I continued to escort my group to the museum, where even seeing the breathtaking *haka* performed for the very first time was not enough to distract me from my inner turmoil. That evening I managed to get the address of the Samoan lady from the police station and I went round with Rick bearing a huge bunch of flowers. We sat and talked with the composed rotund victim and her lightly built reticent husband for a little while in their simple sitting room with only a crucifix and a 3D picture of Jesus on the wall. My apologies were graciously accepted and I was implored as we departed not to worry anymore about it. Far easier said than done. As I lay in bed that night, hearing the thud as the body hit the bumper, struggling to still my turbulent thoughts, I imagined losing my licence, having to resign from my job and possibly even being given a prison sentence. In the end, I wrote a letter to the authorities explaining the mitigating circumstances and got off with a small fine. My confidence in driving, however, was badly shaken and when Rick joined me on the course as my co-tutor, whenever possible I got him to do the driving on the outings. We also exchanged the accursed vehicle for a Toyota Hiace van, which was very much easier to drive and had beautifully stable wing mirrors.

I spent a lot of time trying to dream up interesting and varied outings for the trainees and making phone calls to request guided tours of factories, etc. Someone had suggested a visit to a milk-bottling plant might be interesting, so I thumbed through the Yellow Pages searching for a suitably located one. There seemed to be an awful lot of dairies in the book, but then I told myself, Auckland is surrounded by farming country and thought of all that New Zealand butter that gets exported to each corner of the world. I picked one at random and when a gruff-sounding woman picked up, I explained who I was and why I felt a visit to her dairy might be a useful experience for my group of twelve trainees. 'Are you pulling my leg?' came a sharp reply. 'You couldn't even fit twelve people in here!' It turned out that a dairy in New Zealand is what they call a small corner shop or convenience store. I dined out on that little gaffe for some time. I was amused to learn various other common expressions in my early days in New Zealand. A park, for instance, is what they call a parking space, to be crank is to be sick, a smoko break is a tea break and 'good as gold' means 'right as rain'. (I learned this last one the day a woman fainted down by the harbour. 'Don't worry!' someone said to the rapidly assembling crowd. 'She's good as gold!')

The day I took the group to a milk-bottling plant (as opposed to a dairy) we all had to don white cotton coats and what looked like snazzy white shower caps. Our guide was a cordial PR lady, immaculately made-up and obviously keen to make a good impression. She went to great lengths to explain what went on in the factory and to speak slowly and intelligibly to the trainees. She gave a very comprehensive tour, during which Rick stayed quite close to her, asking questions at each stage of the milk-bottling process. At the end of the tour, we were all standing by the van about to take our leave when our guide discreetly indicated Rick and whispered to me: 'That one's English is really good, isn't it?' She had taken him to be one of the trainees and was so embarrassed when she realised her error, the poor woman blushed furiously. Bowling back to Mangere I relayed this exchange to trainees. They were tickled pink; for a moment I feared that Khahi, a highly strung, uncharacteristically plump Vietnamese gentleman, might burst a blood vessel.

Other successful tours included the Chelsea Sugar refinery in Birkenhead, where we saw great mountains of sugar in huge hangars with small birds trying and failing to fly as they were so drunk from gorging themselves on the fermenting sugar. We also visited the *New Zealand Herald* printing works, where our guide bore an uncanny resemblance to Steve McQueen, of which he quite possibly was aware, as he remained slightly aloof throughout the tour, as though to discourage scrutiny or overfamiliarity. We visited two fire stations, one right next door to our hall, where, to their delight, trainees were allowed to try on helmets and uniforms and practise operating the giant hose pipes. The other one was housed in a smaller building, quite close to the main runway at Auckland Airport. On this occasion, we had an animated, waggish fireman to show us around. He made a curious joke about some of the Māori firemen still being cannibals and how these ones would be the first to the scene if ever a plane crashed – he scanned the group with a devilish glint in his eye to see if anyone had taken him seriously. I do believe some had and I had to reassure them later on that it was just his little joke. Perhaps the most popular destination of all, though, was the Tip Top Ice Cream factory, where the tour always ended with the distribution of free ice creams.

What we actually did in the classroom was always negotiated with the trainees. I created files with a whole range of materials, many of them realia (maps, pamphlets, forms, etc.) dealing with a dozen or so areas of their lives – safety in the home and the workplace, telephoning skills, health (healthy living and dealing with sickness), form filling, complaining about faulty goods, interview skills and so on. Whatever I'd planned for the day I had to be prepared to shelve if a trainee came to class with a real, pressing problem, especially if I thought the rest of the class would benefit too from learning how to deal with it. Our afternoons tended to be a little more laid-back. We had a lot of fun performing sketches written by a brilliant group of EFL teachers with a love for theatre. The book was called *Off Stage* and was accompanied by a cassette tape with all twelve sketches recorded. I've used these materials in almost all my teaching jobs and have found the humour they contain seems to be timeless and universal. A favourite with my trainees in Mangere was called Superman and the Psychiatrist. The language focus in this sketch was on abilities, specifically can and can't. Various patients visit the psychiatrist and explain their particular problems – Superman can't fly or lift cars anymore; a librarian can't talk quietly, he can only shout, and so on. I've always found drama activities in the classroom to be particularly effective for shy students, as playing a role gives them a mask to hide behind. One of my trainees was a painfully shy Vietnamese fisherman, Nong, who spoke so quietly no one could hear much of what he said, even though our classroom was tiny. I decided to give him the part of the loud-voiced librarian, which he seemed quite comfortable with. Not only did Nong play his part brilliantly when we performed the sketch in front of the other class, but he continued to project his voice when speaking English even after the performance ended. If anything, he spoke a little too loudly, but as his confidence appeared to have grown, almost miraculously, since playing the part of the librarian, we tolerated it and were pleased for him, hoping his newfound self-esteem might even lead to success in the romantic arena.

Despite achieving excellent outcomes on our off-campus courses – almost all of our trainees went on to get jobs or places on further training courses – it was always a struggle to get funding to continue operating and the politics of the situation could be tedious. One day, after two and a half years, the battle was lost and I sadly found myself packing up and returning the keys to Father Broekman, whose parting words to me were 'Fight the good fight', an exhortation I'd heard many a time before and still hear sometimes in my head when faced with a thorny issue.

My next position was a temporary one at the Refugee Reception Centre, where unfortunately the highly likeable man who had run the programme for many years had just left and I found myself working for a rather prickly, supercilious woman, who seemed to favour paper qualifications over skill, aptitude and experience. On arrival she had ruthlessly disposed of all the teaching resources that had accumulated over the years – a drastic act that had given rise to many a furtive comment about the baby being thrown out with the bathwater. When I arrived at the centre, therefore, there were very few teaching materials in the files, which was not really a problem as I was getting quite used to creating my own. A few weeks after I'd started teaching, a permanent position came up, for which I applied, but was told, not too unkindly, that they were really looking for someone with a master's degree, which I didn't have at that stage, so that was that. I don't think I'd have enjoyed working for this particular woman in any case. There was something rather off-putting about her. She tended to fix you with a cold, patronising stare and when she spoke her lip would curl disparagingly. As a result, she failed to establish rapport with her colleagues, and I don't think that's just sour grapes on my part. The atmosphere in the open-plan office was not one conducive to a relaxed sharing of ideas and resources, so in that respect she was failing too and, though I'd enjoyed my time in the classroom, I was not sorry to take my leave when I came to the end of my short contract.

I was invited the following week to work with Rick at a highly regarded private language school in the city, Crown English. The director of studies, Julia Walton, and the staff room ambiance were everything that my previous employer and working atmosphere had not been. I became almost instant friends with Julia and loved her modus operandi. At least once a week there would be an informal meeting in the staff room, where Julia would convey any bits of news about the school that she thought might be of interest to us. Her desk was right there in the corner of the staff room and there was no obvious feeling of us (the teachers) and them (the management). The director of the school, Alan Chisolm, was every bit as personable and approachable as Julia – how could one not appreciate working for someone whose favourite writer was that wonderfully manic, deceptively serious Gonzo journalist Hunter S Thompson, author of one of my all-time favourite books, *Fear and Loathing in Las Vegas*? I felt I was among family.

My first class at Crown was made up almost entirely of young Japanese students, a nationality I'd had virtually no experience of teaching up until then. On my first day with them I bounded into the room, greeting the class warmly, briefly introducing myself then launching into the first of my 'getting to know each other' activities. Something was wrong, I was being eyed up with deep suspicion and individual students were not responding when I asked them simple personal questions. I persevered with a range of lively communicative activities, including my 'tried and true' ones that previously had never failed to get students involved, chatting and exchanging information. By the end of the class, I had the most awful feeling that I had lost my touch and that my days as an EFL teacher were numbered. I had heard it said that younger students really preferred young teachers, so perhaps at thirty-six I was simply past it – in their eyes at least. I had learned the hard way that Japanese students don't normally like to speak out in front of their peers; they are far more comfortable working quietly in pairs for speaking practice, or sometimes in small groups with carefully chosen leaders (older class members if there are any). I gradually learned by trial and error how to get my Japanese students to talk, but I must say, working with these mainly Japanese classes was not a lot of fun and it made me thankful we hadn't rushed off to Japan in our early days on the EFL road, as I don't think we'd have enjoyed ourselves nearly as much as we did working in Bangkok and Taipei.

I had only been working for Julia for a few weeks when, to my astonishment, she called me aside and asked if I would step into her shoes for a week while she was away on a business trip. Not only did I accept, but I also stipulated one condition – that while I was acting DOS I would not be required to teach as well. I can't believe my audacity in making such a request, but Julia calmly accepted and the week went by without mishap, although one rather frosty and ambitious female teacher, who had been at Crown English for some time, did give me some oddly penetrating looks on her way to class.

During this time in New Zealand, the late eighties, the number of students from East Asia, notably Japan, Taiwan and Mainland China, wanting to come and learn English was increasing steadily and new language schools were mushrooming all over the country, particularly in Auckland. An advertisement for Director of Studies at one of these new enterprises caught my eye and, encouraged by various friends and colleagues, I went along for an interview. The name of the school was a slightly absurd one, the English Language Development Centre (ELDC) and the investors were all from Mainland China – York, Freddie, Mike and, the brightest of the bunch, a stunning-looking, vampish young woman with cheekbones to die for, Fuchsia Wen – 'the gang of four', as I came to call them. I believe they all had Bolivian passports, degrees in computer science or engineering, and, like so many Chinese, strong entrepreneurial instincts and acumen. They were looking for someone to set up and run the language teaching side of the business and I managed not only to convince them that I was the one to do it, but also to negotiate a very good salary and conditions. Julia didn't bat an eyelid when I told her I'd found another job, and wrote me not only a great reference for my short spell at Crown, but also an excellent letter to support my application for the MA TEFL at Reading University a few years later.

The first few weeks at ELDC, which was housed in a distinctive modern building of glass and red metal in the city centre, I worked on half salary designing a curriculum and syllabi for various levels as well as ordering resources and equipment. One morning I went into the office and saw the Chinese directors standing around the fax machine, with faces like thunder. As they failed to greet me in their normal friendly fashion, I knew something was very wrong. I was stiffly handed a fax addressed to me that had evidently just come through and been read by all four of them. It was from my old colleague Patrick O'Reilly, in Taipei. He was writing to congratulate me on landing the new job and to say how delighted he was that I had managed to get my life back together after my dark years of heroin addiction, working in sleazy strip joints in Asian cities to fund my habit. He went on to say he hoped the needle marks had faded and asked if I was able to wear short-sleeved blouses again – he really hoped so. It was a very clever trick, but a diabolical one, and I had quite a job convincing the gang of four that this was just my old Irish joker friend Patrick having a wicked laugh at my expense.

Before the students started arriving, I was asked, slightly to my alarm, to give a demo class, with the gang of four as guinea pig students. The night before this class there had been a rare emotional upset at home and I came into work the following morning sleep-deprived and still feeling fragile and weepy. Strangely enough, the demo class couldn't have gone better. I was articulate, dynamic and amusing and got them all communicating 'meaningfully' in the target language, picking up new idioms and clearly enjoying themselves. I went home exhausted but elated that I had pulled it off. On various other occasions after sleepless nights, either through illness or domestic dramas, I have surprised myself by switching into a gear I didn't even know I had the moment I entered the classroom. The curious thing is, I'm fairly sure I have given some of my best lessons ever on the odd occasion when I have been seriously under the weather or have gone in to teach totally unprepared.

My first teacher, Dora, a Greek Cypriot, was recommended by my old colleague, the boisterous black-belted Sharon, and what a great recommendation it was. Dora was just perfect for the new school, so cheery, comradely and conscientious. Nothing was too much trouble for her. We hit it off instantly and would pop out for jolly *dim sum* lunches, whenever we had time, at the Chinese restaurant next door. She and her husband Simon, a highly personable news presenter for TVNZ, gave the most wonderful parties, and if ever we dropped in to see them at the weekend, we would be treated to the most cordial Greek/Kiwi hospitality. I had my own office next to the staff room with an enormous old desk, which was always covered with piles of books, papers, folders, etc. I must have given the impression of being a bit of a perfectionist, as Dora would tease me saying she was sure my first job in the morning was to measure the distance between each item on the desk so that everything was arranged perfectly symmetrically. I remember once having to coach dear Dora in office telephone language. I'd just popped downstairs to the bathroom and on returning to my room I caught Dora, answering my phone, saying, 'No, sorry, Carrie's not here at the moment. She's on the toilet!'

As the school grew, I steadily took on more teachers and the job, perhaps inevitably, became increasingly stressful. I was mostly very happy with the teachers who came to work for us, with just the odd exception. One teacher took a shine to some of our new resources and started secretly photocopying whole books on our photocopier to add to her personal library. I found a discreet way of letting her know she'd been rumbled, and to my relief she left of her own accord soon afterwards. I believe the law at that time required employers to give members of staff they wanted to get rid of a verbal, then a written warning, and I hadn't wanted to start this process if I could possibly help it. The other problematic teacher, Jane, was a small terrier of a woman with a pronounced gap between her front teeth and short, tufty, blonde hair. I'd been warned about taking her on by my friend Julia, but I was desperate for teachers at the time and thought

I could handle her. To begin with, everything went fine; her students were happy and I remember being impressed at how she would stay on after class each day filling out the daily lesson record in great detail in beautiful neat handwriting. She was always very polite to me – perhaps suspiciously so – and was clearly on her best behaviour. One Friday afternoon she had a small advanced group of mainly young Taiwanese students for a conversation class. Somehow the discussion had got around to attitudes towards gay people in the students' own countries and one of the group said that in his country gay people were regarded as 'hooligans' and were punished. Poor Jane, being gay herself, must have just seen red and I gather proceeded to press each other member of the class to not only say what the situation was in their home country but also what their personal view was. The first I heard of all this was sometime after the end of the last class when the whole group, minus Jane, trooped into my office to tell me that they'd come to a unanimous decision that they didn't want Jane as their teacher anymore. I defended Jane, telling them they were fortunate to have such a well-qualified, experienced teacher and that I was sure they could sort it all out on Monday. I rang Jane at home a little later to ask for her side of the story, but apparently her parents were paying her a rare visit and she was livid that I should have rung while they were there, though goodness knows, all she needed to do was tell me she'd ring me back later or over the weekend. I don't even remember exactly what happened on Monday, except that Jane arrived with a shaven head, surly and unrepentant. Unfortunately, despite some effort on my part, my relationship with Jane never recovered, which upset me greatly. I remember thinking at the time that I was clearly too thin-skinned to be an effective manager and wishing I could return to just being one of the gang, enjoying the camaraderie in the staffroom and simply concentrating on my teaching and materials development.

As the months went by and the seasons changed, I would put in long hours during the week and would regularly go into the school to work at weekends too. I was in danger of becoming a workaholic and I suspect this was not doing my relationship any good. Thankfully, the year was broken up by occasional marketing trips to Thailand, Korea and Japan. This work included setting up stands and representing the school at educational fairs, which was fun as one met all sorts of interesting people. Whilst I was in Japan, I ran into Chris Woolcott, who was there promoting his own school, Languages International. He was as warm and cordial as usual, but after a few minutes his face clouded over and he told me it was a pity that I had got involved with the gang of four as they were not wholly to be trusted. I didn't allow myself to get drawn into a discussion, but the fact was I had already strongly suspected that many of our Mainland Chinese students had signed up for courses in order to get study visas, but had no real interest in studying – it was just a way of getting into the country. I had been told that during the troubled days following the Tiananmen Square massacre Beijing taxi drivers had made a small fortune ferrying people to the airport. A few of those taxi drivers, who were friendly enough but totally uneducated, ended up at our school. They attended classes for a week or two, were attentive, courteous and always quick to laugh if they thought the teacher was attempting to use humour during the lessons, but then quietly slipped away, never to be seen or heard of again. I sometimes wonder what became of them, whether they achieved any sort of command of the language and if they found work that gave them the same sort of independence that taxi driving had done.

The academic side of the school was, though I say it myself, quite impressive – I'd ordered all the latest teaching resources from Oxford and Cambridge University press amongst other publishers and had even been on a book-buying trip to Sydney, having convinced the directors that it would be much better for me to go there in person, so I could have a proper look at the books before buying them. The directors knew I loved travelling and were generous about paying for air tickets and good hotels while I was away. Part of the reason they were prepared to pay for prestigious hotels, the Hilton in Seoul for example, was that they thought prospective agents would be impressed. I was under strict instructions on the Korean leg of one marketing trip not to eat at the hotel, but to venture out to cheaper places for my meals. This was all very well in Thailand, where I knew the ropes and could eat like a queen for next to nothing, but Seoul was a new city to me and, not having the internet at that point with instant information about places to go and how to get there, it was very hit and miss. My most vivid recollection is of sitting in a backstreet hole-in-the-wall eatery advertising Korean barbecue, being served charred lumps of what looked like pure pork fat, my eyes stinging with smoke, and being stared at as though I was an extra-terrestrial.

About halfway through my two years at ELDC, all the language schools in NZ had to undergo a rigorous government inspection. Mountains of paperwork were required – everything from mission statements to details on the curriculum, on syllabi for each level, lists of resources and so on. Again, my weekends were often taken up with this documentation but, to my delight, as a result of many months' hard graft, we were one of the first private schools in Auckland, if not in the whole country, to receive NZ government approval. The directors were suitably impressed and by way of thanks, Rick and I were invited to a truly sumptuous Chinese banquet at the best Chinese restaurant in the city. I was also sent on a second marketing trip to South East Asia, and, as I was due some paid leave, I stayed on for an extra couple of weeks in Thailand, knowing that Dora would hold the fort while I was away. In retrospect, that second marketing trip may possibly have been something akin to a golden handshake, as the directors all knew how very attached I was to that part of the world. On the other hand, it could have been a last-ditch attempt to recruit more students. I think the latter explanation is probably the more likely, as I don't think any of my employers ever allowed sentimentality to cloud their business judgement.

Although I suspected that the school had problems, I don't think I'd realised that things were going quite so rapidly downhill financially. The truth is, the school had been under-capitalised from the start – and by the time I returned from my extended overseas trip, the gang of four had decided drastic measures would have to be taken. I was asked over the phone by York the night I arrived back if I would increase my contact hours and accept a significant pay cut as they could no longer afford to pay my salary. I refused and the next thing I knew I was being confronted in my office at the end of the following day's work by York accompanied by his slimy Malaysian lawyer and told I was being fired – to take my stuff and leave. The reason I was given was quite absurd – my partner was working for a rival school and I was a security risk. The fact of the matter was that Rick had helped us all no end with ongoing advice, which ELDC had only benefited from. I rang Rick and he came straight over from Crown English. I remember York's face when Rick asked him if anyone could possibly have worked harder for them than I had over a period of two years. I believe York blushed and mumbled something that may have been no, but certainly wasn't yes.

For the rest of that day, I was in a state of shock and remember my hands shaking as I made my way out to the car, which Rick had parked hastily and illegally on the pavement. The following day I made some phone calls to enquire about the procedure for unfair dismissal claims and was told I had a very strong case. My contract had included a generous severance payment and I was told I should get this plus some extra for the way I'd been treated. It was just a few days later that it was announced on television that ELDC had gone bankrupt, so no more money was to come my way from that source. My time working with the gang of four had been interesting, challenging at times, but by no means all bad. I'd had a lot of fun with York, particularly on the first marketing trip to Japan, where he'd surprised me one evening after work by giving me a wonderful, relaxing face massage using an exclusive Chinese face cream, doubtless containing dubious ingredients. Fuchsia, too, a top-notch engineer who earned herself the title 'queen of the New Zealand railways' moonlighting at the same time as a humble vendor of fast food in a mobile kitchen she'd acquired, had always been respectful and pleasant in my dealings with her. Our conversations in my office generally revolved more around gossip and her knotty love life than it did around work matters. Freddie and Mike I'd seen much less of – they both kept their distance but I had no trouble from them. It was just a pity it all ended the way it did. I'm sure it could have been done more humanely, but then the situation had become critical and business is business, I kept telling myself. I should have known better than to take it all personally. I'd be very interested to know what became of my former employers. Like many Chinese people I know, they were all hard-working, resourceful and highly enterprising and I strongly suspect that by now they will all be living very comfortably in their retirement, wherever that might be.

After five years I decided to leave Godzone, ironically just at the point where I had applied for and gained New Zealand citizenship, giving me dual nationality. My reasons for leaving were varied and complex, perhaps to be explored another time. Suffice it to say, it was a terrific wrench – I cried every day for a month before leaving. My job had been snatched rudely from me and I was about to forsake my lovely Mount Eden home with its west-facing balcony, its magnificent view, sublime sunsets and treasured hebe collection. I was also about to leave an extremely close ten-year relationship and venture out into the windy desert once more – for better or worse, it was the end of an era.

Chapter 11

From Cymru to Croatia
via Rio and Reading

'Born to travel!' – these were Rick's last words as he saw me off at Auckland Airport, and perhaps it was true; nothing in those days seemed to excite me more than boarding a plane bound for distant shores with a dream and a mission. I was stepping away from five years of relative stability in New Zealand, and in many ways from an idyllic existence, out into the unknown once more. I started off in Japan, looking into some work possibilities, at one point drinking *sake* with university professors, who grilled me on my knowledge of Jane Austen and asked what I had published to date, which was precisely nothing, besides a partially plagiarised review of *Cider with Rosie* in the school magazine aged around thirteen. I was complimented on my ability to keep up with the *sake* drinkers, but my literary awareness, it seemed, was not so impressive and, as I didn't fancy teaching children or reporting to the infamous Illingworth, the arresting yet cool and business-like new director of the British Council, I winged my way back to the UK just in time for my cousin's wedding in North Wales.

It was a fabulous affair, with a marquee full of spring flowers on the banks of the River Mawddach, which flows down from the snow-capped mountains of Snowdonia through some of the most scenic countryside in the UK. For centuries the Mawddach was known not only for its abundance of trout and salmon, but also for its gold panning and shipbuilding industries, though it would be hard to find any evidence of these today. I have a photograph of the newly married couple, Michael and Clare, being showered with confetti outside the little stone church in Dolgellau. The bride, clad in a becoming, figure-hugging, ivory lace dress, appears a little flushed yet clearly immensely happy, while my cousin, normally a tad reserved and unassuming, looks vaguely surprised to find himself the centre of attention, yet self-possessed and exceedingly dapper, sporting a spotless, dark suit he'd splashed out on for the occasion and a red silk tie, whose threads glinted in the Welsh morning sun. Standing just to the right of them on the cobblestones is my uncle Crawfurd's magnificent vintage bottle-green Aston Martin, lovingly restored for the second time for the event. I have a distinct childhood memory of clambering into a rusting open-top sports car in the long grass at the bottom of their garden in Cheshire. In my mind's eye, it has become home to spiders, woodlice and roosting hens, who occasionally lay a speckled egg or two on the soft mossy floor. According to Mum, her older brother Crawfurd bought the car as a write-off for next to nothing just after the war. The first restoration project, during which my uncle spent every waking hour supine under the adored vehicle in his parents' garage in Hollingworth, overlapped with his wooing of my aunt Rosemary, a serious, scientifically minded girl from Mum's boarding school, who went on to become a high-flying orthodontist. His prospective mother-in-law was not amused when she went to meet him for the first time at the Red House and he emerged from under the car to greet her in grubby overalls with blackened fingernails and smears of oil across his flushed and beaming face.

After stripping the car down, he sent off the bent chassis to be straightened, then built it up again, lavishing enormous attention on engine and body alike, until it was virtually as good as new and ready to participate in rallies, which it did and occasionally won with Crawfurd at the wheel and Mum as map reader. There's a dog-eared black and white photo of me aged around six months standing on the driver's seat, rosy-cheeked with blonde corkscrew curls, clutching the steering wheel and laughing sideways at the camera. The second restoration took place after my uncle died in the nineties, presided over by my cousins, Michael and Peter. The old girl now lives in California, at Michael and Clare's San Diego home, as it was decided that the climate there was far more suitable for flamboyant open-top driving than the scenic yet often rain-sodden hills of North Wales.

Back at the wedding, with Clare's family hailing from the Emerald Isle, there was an Irish *céilidh* band and dancing until the early hours of the morning, though I flagged well before the music ended as I was jet-lagged and liable to become emotional whenever I allowed my mind to dwell more than momentarily on all I'd left behind on the other side of the globe. My dear mother must have known I was wrestling internally over my decision to uproot myself from my Auckland home and, as we crossed the little bridge over the river on our homeward journey the following day, she tried to cheer me up with a topical anecdote about my great grandparents, Christina and Harry Costobadie.

Harry, like most of the male ancestors on my mother's side, was a very keen fly fisherman and was out with his fly rod one day on that very bridge that leads into the small town of Dolgellau. All of a sudden there was a sharp tug on the line, and to his amazement, he realised he'd hooked not a trout as he'd expected but an exceptionally large and lively salmon. Possessing only a standard fishing licence, rather than one for salmon fishing, and being notoriously scrupulous, he sent his wife Christina speeding off to the post office in town to buy the correct document before landing the poor writhing salmon. My great grandmother was every bit as honest and upright as her spouse; it was she who had once insisted on April Fool's Day that a clothes horse be placed in the garden at the family home, Overdale, before my grandmother, Laura, could play a trick on her father by telling him that there was an escaped horse grazing on his precious lawn.

Having reserved a place on the highly recommended MA TEFL course at Reading University, I set about planning a trip around South America with my old friend Jude, whom I'd met in Cambridge on our introductory TEFL course. We'd talked of doing this trip practically since the day we'd met, but had never been ready to actually get up and go at precisely the same time. Vaccinated against every single item on the long menu at Thomas Cook's London travel shop, we set off on New Year's Eve, 1991, armed with pepper spray, to use against potential molesters, and lurid pink mosquito nets, which we'd soaked in an expensive solution that guaranteed to transform the nets into 'impenetrable shields against all known biting insects'. It was hard to say if our money had been well spent or not. The fact was, we barely saw a single mosquito on the whole two-month tour, including in our camp deep within the Amazon jungle – either the solution was so effective that it deterred all insects within a very wide radius, or there simply weren't any biting insects in existence along the whole of our Latin American trail. Actually, Jude hadn't had all the vaccinations on offer at Thomas Cook's; she'd decided against the rabies jab as it was unusually expensive. As I'd already been injected in each arm and each buttock that day, I had to take my rabies vaccine home in my handbag to be administered at my GP's at a later date. It was all we could do to clamber onto a London bus after being spiked all over; the whole of my right side seemed to be seizing up rather alarmingly. The pain, however, was bizarrely enjoyable, Jude and I agreed, as it was the first step in our thrilling and long-awaited adventure. Whenever we encountered stray dogs or shifty-looking monkeys along our path, whether in the Brazilian Pantanal or the Bolivian Altiplano, Jude would make sure I led the way, wisely using me as a human shield against mangy biting animals. Poring for hours over travel guides and a huge map that almost covered my parents' dining table, I'd planned our route as a giant circle, starting in Rio, travelling down through Brazil, over to Bolivia and Peru, and arriving back on the Brazilian coast in Recife in time for the annual carnival. It was a successful and highly enjoyable trip in many ways, but I'm not going to embark on a detailed account at this point. Let's just say, the expedition satisfied my wanderlust for a little while, long enough to enable me to apply myself to the rigours of the MA course, which I'd been told was an essential step to take if I was in any way serious about my teaching career.

It was a little strange being a student once again after a gap of seventeen-odd years. I still had the sound of panpipes playing in my head and touching down at Heathrow a few days earlier in a chill February fog had brought me back to earth with a disagreeable thump. I think I'd have enjoyed the MA experience considerably more if I'd been living on campus in one of the halls of residence, as most of the others on my course did. I was staying with my parents for financial reasons – I'd just spent two months travelling and the course alone was costing me a small fortune. On top of this, there was the cost of books, petrol and a fat dissertation fee. We'd been given a pre-course assignment on setting up a self-study centre, something I happened to have already done, so in a way, I was broken into post-graduate work quite easily. In the feedback session with my warm and jolly personal tutor and testing guru, the late Cyril Weir, I was told my academic writing was fine but that my referencing technique was 'rather idiosyncratic' – nothing that couldn't be rectified with a little guidance.

Although I enjoyed some of the course reading, sociolinguistics in particular, as well as the mental exercise of doing assignments, I found the taught part of the course rather disappointing overall, as I failed to see how most of it would ever improve my teaching in any way – it was all so terribly academic. Who cares, I sometimes asked myself, what various grammarians each thought the function of a certain noun or verb phrase in a particular sentence was. Having said that, I must admit I found the sentence parsing we were required to do on the grammar course rather fun and was reminded of the basic parsing we had done once upon a time in English classes at grammar school. The only difference was that the sentences we were given to parse on our MA course were far more complex and extraordinarily long – sometimes filling half a page or more. The Testing and Management components of the course seemed rather more practical and useful, and it was in these two that I got my best grades. I probably should have chosen Testing for my dissertation and done a straightforward piece of quantitative research, as strongly advised to do. As it was, I ended up doing an unusual piece of qualitative research and getting rather bogged down in an overly lengthy discussion of affective factors. The original impetus for this was my interest in the creation of an optimum environment for second language acquisition, an environment where there is a sufficient amount of pressure to stimulate learners but not so much that the pressure becomes debilitating. I was told my study would need to use 'triangulation' of data if it was to be taken seriously. I forged ahead with some trepidation, struggling particularly with statistics and the technology required to create professional-looking graphs, weeping in despair onto my keyboard one evening at the university library, being comforted and assisted by a kind young undergrad, who achieved in a couple of minutes what I had been trying to do for an hour or more.

At one point during the second module, I was required to give a seminar on an academic paper for the Spoken English component. As the time approached, I became more and more anxious and ended up going to talk to the university counsellor. Before I even opened my mouth, she had guessed which course I was taking – she had more patients, I learned, from CALS (the Centre for Applied Linguistics) than from any other department. I was by no means alone, I realised, in finding it all increasingly nerve-racking. For insomnia and loss of appetite, I was advised to drink hot milk laced with brandy before bed and, if not hungry enough to eat proper meals, to keep eating bananas. The poor woman looked so careworn and undernourished herself I felt tempted to offer her a few words of advice of my own. I emerged from her office feeling my problems were not so bad after all. I did, however, visit a GP a week or so later at my mother's surgery. Doctor Corfield must have had a quiet afternoon as he took the time to question me at great length about my life and commented on my peripatetic lifestyle – I didn't reply as I was not sure of the meaning of peripatetic and didn't want to appear dense. I was still worried about not being able to sleep and told him how one of my friends' breakdowns had occurred after a similar period of insomnia. 'I wouldn't worry,' he said. 'If you were going to crack, I believe you would have done so by now. When some people are under prolonged stress, they tend to become psychotic. When you are under stress,' he went on, evidently trying to reassure me, 'you tend to become neurotic and the worst that will happen to you is that you'll just become a gibbering wreck.' Whenever I think I'm not coping with life and might be brewing up for a spell in a psychiatric ward, I remind myself of the doctor's words that day and immediately feel calmer. He prescribed some beta blockers for the day of the seminar and told me how they'd worked a treat for him the day of his medical practical exam. On the train journey up to Glasgow from London he'd realised that he'd left his stethoscope behind. Instead of panicking he'd laughed out loud, resolving to borrow one from a doctor in the corridor at the teaching hospital where his exam was to be, which he did, and from then on everything went like a dream. My seminar went like a dream too, so much so that I barely remember a thing about it.

Towards the end of the second taught module, we started to look at research techniques and were encouraged to start thinking about a suitable area for our own piece of research. Our dissertation, we learned, should be no more than 25,000 words. I realised to my dismay that many of my peers knew exactly what they wanted to do and could be seen combing the library shelves for specific publications and leafing purposefully through journals, speaking nonchalantly of 'getting it done' in a matter of months. After much procrastination, I finally settled on affective factors in the language class, specifically on anxiety in the adult EFL class, but I found it incredibly difficult to get into a steady rhythm of work. I was not very happy living with my parents in Wokingham, as, much as I adored my mother, I had never seen eye to eye with my stepfather. I moved back to my dear little patio flat in Brighton, but Henrik, the Dane, who lived above me, was in the process of converting his dwelling into a Scandinavian paradise with timber-lined walls, floors and, by the sound of it, ceilings too throughout. The banging and drilling went on seven days a week and was quite simply intolerable, so in the end I had no choice but to rent my flat out and rethink things.

I spent a few months working for the British Council in Bahrain and after this set sail for Hamburg, where I had managed to line up a job at the language school Inlingua, hoping not only to start doing research into the effectiveness of the controversial teaching method Suggestopedia for my dissertation but also to revive a romance with an old flame I'd met in Greece in my early twenties. The whole German episode was disastrous on every count, and so once more I returned to Wokingham to regroup and recharge my batteries. Back I came to Brighton (thankfully the Dane had completed his renovations) and this time I got an interesting job offer at one of the best language schools in the area, if not in the whole of the UK – the English Language Centre (ELC). I was interviewed by one of the most amiable and thoroughly good-humoured people I have ever had the pleasure of working with, the one and only Peter Tamkin. I was gently quizzed that day on my knowledge of current EFL publications and as I had always taken a great interest in innovative methods and effective teaching materials, my enthusiasm was picked up on – and to my delight, I was in!

I'd been given three years to complete my dissertation from the end of the second taught module and I confess I used every second of it. Apart from the spells in Bahrain and Hamburg, I divided my time over those three years between Wokingham and Brighton, with visits to Thailand to break up the winter. For most of that time, I worked happily at ELC, returning to my parents whenever I needed to use the library at Reading University or see my genial tutor, Cyril. For the big push towards the end, I spent several weeks at my parents', working flat out. I was still tweaking the text and rearranging paragraphs, hammering away on my little daisy-wheel typewriter right up until midnight on the last evening before submission. On the morning itself, just as I was retyping the final paragraph, there was a power cut, so I had to wait until the afternoon, pacing up and down like a caged animal, for the power to come back on – I couldn't bear to hand my document in with errors in the conclusion. Driving into Reading that afternoon I couldn't believe my bad luck – to be held up by roadworks and interminably long traffic lights on a stretch of road where normally I would have put my foot down hard on the accelerator. As luck would have it, there were no parking spaces in the CALS car park, and, as there was a warden lurking about, I had to look for a space over on the other side of campus, which seemed to take an age. Sprinting across the grass at one minute to four, I saw two other red-faced people running for their lives from two other directions. We all arrived outside the door of the CALS building at 4 pm on the dot, panting and slightly dishevelled but laughing to realise we were not the only ones to be cutting things so fine. Needless to say, after handing over our papers, we all headed straight for the nearest pub and spent a wonderful hour or so exchanging stories and plans for the future. When the results came through a couple of months later, I happened to be at my parents' for the weekend and alone in the house. Overjoyed at the result, I skipped, happy as a sand boy, down the country road to the field where our old horse stood by the gate in a patch of mud and shared my news. At the time, it felt like a tremendous achievement, particularly sticking at it when I'd so often been tempted to pack it all in. I still have dreams that I haven't finished my dissertation, along with dreams that I haven't done any swotting for O levels – I very much suspect that I always will.

Being taken on by ELC was another achievement and applying there for work was probably one of the best moves of my life. I made lifelong friends there, especially dear Zoe, without whom this memoir quite possibly might not have been completed, and ultimately, of course, I met my husband, Simon, there. The work was seasonal so I'd normally be as busy as I wanted to be from Easter through until the end of the summer, then student numbers dropped off and the work would be more sporadic, so I'd have to supplement my income with other work. The easiest temporary work to pick up was silver service waitressing for agencies, a job I always used to enjoy in the olden days, before my tolerance of officious young catering managers lessened to the point where I would tend to get into arguments with them. I once stood up for two younger temps who'd just been told that as they had only worked until 11.50 pm they didn't qualify for a free taxi home (you had to work up until midnight to qualify). This was at a five-star seafront hotel and the duty manager in question should never have been working at all that evening, as he was clearly ill and kept sneezing all over the food about to be served. I gave the snivelling, pasty-faced duffer such a piece of my mind he got worked up into quite a frenzy. 'I'll see to it that you never work in a hotel or restaurant in this town again as long as you *live*!' he spluttered, positively incandescent with rage. I smiled indulgently at him, telling him I was 'terrified' and had a good laugh at the agency the following day, where I was assured that there would always be work for me wielding a fork and spoon when I wanted it.

On two occasions, the first in autumn and the second in winter, I was asked by ELC to do short work stints in Zagreb, Croatia. The first time the country was officially a war zone, so before leaving I was told by the cheery director, Charles, not to take any chances. If I felt I was in danger, I was to leap into a taxi and tell the driver to head immediately for the border with Slovenia. I was not to worry about the cost – my safety came first. I remember lying there wide awake my first night in Zagreb, hearing helicopters and planes flying overhead, wondering if they were about to blow us to smithereens. There were buildings riddled with bullet holes around the city and much talk of the war in the news, but people went about their own business as usual and I didn't really feel unsafe while I was there. My main worry that first Sunday night was what I was going to wear to teach my first class at a city bank the following afternoon, as my luggage had gone missing and I only had the very casual clothes

I had travelled in. Fortunately, our agent in Zagreb, Yazna, a rather mournful-looking, pouty but pleasant enough Croatian woman, and her initially silent, circumspect Serbian spouse, Mirko, had a daughter with a similar build to me, though she was quite a bit younger. One of her outfits – a rather loud orange and black one – was picked out on Monday morning and I was made to stand to attention in it while Yazna's elderly mother created a few darts and sewed them deftly into place. The style was not mine at all; it was very much that of a teenage girl, which I certainly was not. I was a little unsure about the initial impression I might give at the bank – mutton dressed as lamb, I could imagine them whispering – but as Mirko entertained me whilst driving there the following morning, I wasn't given much chance to brood about it. He was very keen to teach me a few words of Serbo-Croat and I must say he did rather a good job. As we were waiting at a red traffic light he pointed to a large pile of cabbages on the pavement beside us, looked me in the eye with great earnestness and pronounced, as though articulating a command to a special needs child, '*Kupus*!' He did exactly the same thing with the traffic lights: '*Semafor*!' These two words, along with the words for 'trip up' – '*da se spotakne*' – and 'fine view' – '*Dobro pogled*' – taught in a similarly indelible fashion by students during a business English class, will remain with me, I am quite certain, until my dying day. I have been waiting patiently for the opportunity to tell someone to be careful not to trip up over the cabbages whilst admiring the fine view beside the traffic lights, just as I've been waiting to use the first phrase I learned in Spanish: 'The vultures are eating olives.'

Despite a dearth of interesting materials, I managed to cobble together suitable lessons with various groups in Zagreb, and by and large I believe my students were happy, though one university lecturer did once ask me whether I was a 'professional teacher', which he later claimed had been a joke. I imagine he was expecting more of a lecture-type experience rather than being asked to participate in the student-centred activities I devised, involving the imagination, revelation of feelings, aspirations, etc. Possibly he was a little uncomfortable with my style of teaching at first, but thankfully there were no complaints. There was one other occasion when a very confident young German businesswoman in one of my UK business mini-groups asked me directly what my normal job was. I don't think her intention was to insult me. She had thought that I was doing a temporary summer job at the school during their peak period, and that I had another proper job for the rest of the year. My wounded pride must have been written all over my face as I had a particularly warm thank you from the class at the end of the course and I was ceremoniously presented with a bottle of *Veuve Clicquot*. It's hard to say if this gesture was sufficient compensation, but I accepted the champagne as graciously as I was able to. I foolishly saved the bottle for a special occasion and one of my brothers – you know who you are – found and drank it with his new girlfriend before I had a chance to do so myself.

My time in Croatia, on both occasions, was quite special in a number of ways. The work was challenging as I had to create my own materials to suit various types of student, from politicians to poets, working in a number of locations around the city. More often than not I would be teaching in the evening in a dilapidated university building in a vast, cavernous room with rickety old furniture and a squeaky old blackboard, which would invariably be covered in chemistry symbols when I arrived, and ancient oil radiators that did nothing whatsoever to heat the place, so the temperature of our room during my winter stint remained sub-zero. Some of the more affluent students would keep their mink coats on throughout the lesson. Yazna had asked me to give private lessons to a close friend of hers, a professor at the university, twice a week. He was a decade or so older than me, an aloof and egotistical academic, with pitted skin and black beetling eyebrows. He appeared to like my teaching style and steadily developed something of a crush on me, surprising me one evening by begging me to accompany him on a mini skiing holiday at an exclusive Slovenian resort. Having no desire to spend any more time than I had to with the professor, I tactfully declined, thus in effect ending the private lessons and putting some strain on my relationship with Yazna.

During my free time in Zagreb, I was fortunate enough to have a wonderful friend and chaperone, Darko, a debonair, middle-aged marketing professional, who had been in one of my General English classes in Hove. Before returning to Croatia, Darko had insisted that if ever I came to his city, I should contact him as he would like to show me his country. He and his convivial wife, whom I met one night at the opera, had a comfortable arrangement whereby each led their own lives but continued to cohabit peacefully until the teenage children had left home. As Darko was a little heartbroken, when I arrived, from an affair that had just ended, he threw himself into his role of escorting me after work and at weekends to all the best restaurants and local places of interest, of which there were many. I think back on that time as one of the most cultural periods of my life – I was taken to ballets, operas, concerts, plays, jazz clubs and exhibitions of every description. At weekends we'd drive through glorious, golden autumnal landscapes, past hillside vineyards and fat cobs of yellow corn hanging in rows or stacked beside simple rural dwellings with livestock milling around alongside. We'd visit castles, cathedrals and historic buildings, including President Tito's birthplace, where I swear a reincarnation of the ruler himself, in the form of a black and white sheepdog, sat disdainful and alert, ears cocked on the threshold of the quaint, thatched-roofed abode. At times we'd drive quite far afield – Varaždin was right up in the north of the country on the Drava River, a magnificent city with baroque and rococo architecture and a seventeenth-century palace, Sermage, with its fine collection of old masters. As we sped by tractors and old folk in ancient cars bumbling along in third gear, overtaking everything in sight with only seconds to spare before colliding with approaching vehicles on the narrow two-lane road, I commented on Darko's reckless driving, to which he replied indignantly and clearly hurt that he was driving extra slowly and carefully on my account. I refrained from further comment that day and kept my eyes firmly shut when overtaking.

Another weekend, I was taken to magical Istria, the largest peninsular in the Adriatic Sea, up near the Italian border. We spent the night in majestic Opatija, with its grand, turreted seaside residences, its monkey puzzle trees and all its old-world charm – it had been a fashionable resort in the 19th century before the land was taken from Italy and given to Croatia. Our hotel overlooked the marina with its sleek Sea Ray schooners, catamarans and jazzy jet boats, where millionaires rubbed shoulders with film stars, mafia and business tycoons. The town is dotted with fine old villas from the Habsburg era, their gardens a riot of exotic plants, about which Darko was impressively knowledgeable. We strolled in the October sun along the *lungomare* promenade that snakes along the coastline, stopping now and then in the shade of a cypress tree, musing about setting up our own language school with some of the classes held on our school pleasure cruiser. Standing high above the glistening sea in the semi-ruined, thirteenth-century fortress of Gravina, we gazed down from the ramparts over the Rjecina river valley to the docks, the Adriatic and the distant island of Krk. Pula, my favourite of all, enchanted me with its cobbled streets, triumphal arches and magnificent first-century amphitheatre, a perfect miniature version of the one in Rome, and we feasted on the most succulent oysters I have ever eaten.

On my birthday, at the end of November, we drove up the forested mountain of Sljeme just outside Zagreb, to a restaurant Darko knew, where we sat in the sun on a tranquil geranium-filled terrace, looking down towards the capital trying to pick out the city landmarks. We had wild boar cooked in red wine followed by cherry strudel, lingering over the last of our ice wine, comfortable in companionable, contemplative silence. We knew our days were numbered and that occasions like this were rare and precious. As Darko was a keen photographer and I was regularly coerced into having my photo taken, I have a good pictorial record of our many pleasurable peregrinations, the only blight for me being that I happened to be sporting my one and only perm and looked for all the world like a beaming blonde sheep, peeping out from behind rhododendron bushes, Roman pillars and dusty wooden ploughs.

I did, in fact, return to Zagreb almost exactly a year later. There was a lot of snow that winter and there was vague talk of being taken skiing on Sljeme mountain, though perhaps it was just as well the plan never came to fruition. I was living at this time on the outskirts of the city, in a bleak fifties apartment block opposite a chocolate factory, whose noisy clanking machinery started up long before daybreak, causing me some loss of precious sleep. I had a long tedious tram ride into town each day, fighting all the way not to fall asleep sitting bundled up in woollies on my heated seat. These heated seats were an unusual and much-appreciated luxury in a previously communist country. On some of these journeys the seats were not only heated but seemed to vibrate too, a fact that led to much hilarity when our Hove school marketing manager came to town. 'Aha!' he exclaimed over pizza and wine one lunchtime, 'so *that's* why some of these dour tram passengers break into sudden smiles for no apparent reason in this country – it's the vibrating seats!'

On this second sojourn, I saw less of Darko, as I had entered into a romantic liaison with another Zagreb resident, which I thought prudent to keep secret from him. My new companion was if anything an even worse driver than Darko and, as his car was a great deal smaller, our drives to outlying beauty spots at weekends were considerably more hazardous. One Saturday morning our destination was an ancient church in a somewhat remote location. The heating in the old Skoda was not working and I had foolishly decided against putting on my thermal underwear that day. By the time we arrived at the rather sad-looking little church, I was chilled to the bone and beginning to wish I had stayed in bed with a good book. Although the sun was out, it was desperately cold inside the church and as each picture and carving of note was pointed out and its history relayed, I tried my utmost to be an appreciative and attentive companion but found myself stifling yawns and longing to be anywhere but there. Unfortunately, I had arranged to meet Darko that afternoon too and hoped I might be taken to a nice warm Zagreb tea house for afternoon tea with Croatian pastries. To my disappointment, I was told I was being taken to a very important historical place outside the city. After a little while, I started to recognise the route and it started to sink in that we were heading for the very same place I'd been that morning. Thankfully I'd had time to change into warmer clothes, but Darko knew his history and liked to hold forth when given a chance, which he did on this occasion at great length. I was a captive audience and totally dependent on the kindness of my friend for a lift back to civilisation, so once more my thespian skills were put to the test and I told myself that this double ordeal was not such a very high price to pay for being driven around a beautiful country on my days off with adorable erudite Croatian gentlemen.

I'd been rather taken aback and more than a little peeved to learn that on this second Croatian trip I was to share a flat with a colleague from the school in Hove, who had actually become a friend. She too had a boyfriend in town and to my amazement one Sunday morning soon after arrival I found myself getting togged up to go traipsing around in the deep snow, to give her some privacy while she received her lover. I'll do the same for you one day, I was promised. My friend's beau was an affable academic working in the faculty of agriculture, a good friend of Darko's and a former private student of mine. His English was not as good as Darko's, though he made a valiant effort to respond to my questions during the lessons. On one occasion we were working on past tenses and I asked him if, basically, he'd had a happy childhood. Frané embarked on a very long-winded account of a time he'd stolen a bicycle and had got lost out in the country. It was an entertaining tale but hadn't answered my question at all. It was only that evening as I was reflecting on the day that it occurred to me that my 'basically' had been heard as 'bicycling', hence the anecdote involving a bicycle.

One evening Shirley and I were invited on a double date with Darko and Frané for a very special gourmet meal at a farmhouse belonging to the agricultural college. Darko had intimated that it was going to be a feast fit for royalty, as they were employing the best chef in the city, if not in the whole country, to cook for us at the farmhouse. The whole occasion reminded Shirley and me a little of *Babette's Feast*. Each course was lovingly prepared and served by the huge and humorous master chef himself, clad in whites and flamboyant chef's hat. For each dish, there would be a carefully chosen wine to accompany it and the courses were thoughtfully spaced out to give us time to talk and savour the homely ambiance. By the time we'd finished our dessert, coffee and liqueurs, we were wonderfully replete and the men were both steaming drunk. This posed a problem as the farmhouse was a few miles out of the city and there was no public transport at this hour. There were, however, some carthorses grazing in a paddock nearby and we spotted some old carriages and tack in a farm building. So anxious were we not to end up maimed in a nasty traffic accident, we seriously considered trying to catch and harness the horses to transport us home. It seems so absurd in retrospect, I think we must have been at least two sheets to the wind ourselves, though we thought we had been pacing ourselves commendably. There was nothing for it but to let the men drive us home in their cars, which were, fortunately, both large and robust. At one point, Darko's car mounted the pavement outside a city department store as he waxed lyrical about the architecture of old Zagreb and I had to yank the steering wheel swiftly to get the vehicle back on track. Arriving outside our flat, we said our farewells and for the one and only time Darko broke our code of decorum, begging me, 'Caroline, pleeese, just a leeetle keees.' I kissed him fondly on the cheek and, though I'm not really religious, I silently prayed that he would get back to his home in one piece.

Apart from our chivalrous chaperones, the other thing that compensated for the harsh physical conditions during my time in Zagreb was my so-called Business English class, composed as it was of rather high-flying business people and distinguished professionals from diverse fields. There was an English schoolteacher, a university lecturer, a trade union leader, a woman with a high position in the police force, a politician, a gynaecologist and a poet, who was also the editor of a well-known literary magazine. It was quite hard to think of language to teach that would be of use to all of them, and as it was evident from the start that they were a lively bunch who really appreciated a joke and a bit of fun, I ended up supplementing the Business English course book with various activities of my own devising that I hoped would amuse them. Early on in the course, it became clear to me that each and every one of this group seemed to have sex on the brain, as innuendo was seen in almost everything I presented and even the soberest of discussions risked becoming risqué, if not downright lewd, if the students were given free rein.

On one occasion, we were on a chapter in the book dealing with marketing and the students were asked to work in two groups designing a new soap and drawing up a marketing plan. One group chose the form of a tennis ball for their soap, exactly the same size, they emphasised, as the part of the male anatomy it resembled. This soap, they proclaimed, would improve people's game no end, both on the tennis court *and* between the sheets after the match. Fired up with the subject, the gynaecologist confided in the class that he had recently exchanged his wife of many decades for a much younger model and how this too had improved his game enormously. His laughter was so infectious it was impossible not to join in, and from that point on I felt I should go with the flow and steer the conversation around to memories of first loves, learning about the birds and the bees and so on. Everyone went home that evening in high spirits, throwing their imaginary tennis balls into the air and swinging their tennis rackets with panache. The end of this course coincided with my departure from the country, by which time I'd come down with an atrocious cold. I was not only presented by my boisterous business brigade with flowers, cards and gifts but was also given such a touching speech of thanks for my efforts that I was moved to tears, not just one or two, but a veritable river of them. It was most embarrassing, but I think they all knew I was in the throes of some nasty debilitating bug and that I was really not quite myself. Knowing them to be people of the heart themselves, I felt they probably understood my excess of emotion that evening and was fairly sure they wouldn't hold it against me. As I surged forwards on the runway the following day, in my cramped economy Croatia Airlines window seat, rising steadily above the fog-enshrouded airport of Zagreb and spires of the ancient city, I experienced a bittersweet medley of emotions. Regret that I had unwittingly caused dear Darko the pain of unrequited love and even some justified jealousy, regret that it somehow seemed unlikely that I would tread the charming cobbled streets of Zagreb again and enjoy the many cultural delights it had to offer, but at the same time immense gratitude that I had been singled out by my dear colleague Jeff at ELC to represent the school in this lonely outpost and that I'd been given the chance to get to know so many admirable people who had lived through war, political upheavals, personal loss and uncertainty, yet who had maintained a fierce conviction that life was there to be embraced, for enjoying and for living to the full. If only temporarily, it would seem a little of the stoical Croatians' resilience and good humour rubbed off on me. I returned to my parents' home in Berkshire for Christmas and astounded the rest of the family, used to my pathetic wimpishness when it came to winter temperatures, by breezing around the place in T-shirts, brewing up and distributing potent steaming concoctions laced with *sljivovica* (plum brandy) and waxing lyrical about the Croatian culture and countryside, showing a warmth and benevolence towards my stepfather he'd rarely witnessed before.

Chapter 12

Thailand Revisited

One Friday afternoon halfway through the glorious summer of 1997, I was called into the slightly cramped, paper-filled DOS's office at the English Language Centre and asked if I'd mind coming into work half an hour early on Monday morning to show the new boy the ropes – explaining the quirks of the photocopier, showing him where the teaching resources were kept and so on. As I was not then working at the main school in Palmeira Square but at the Summer School, Loxsdale, just down the coast in Portslade, I had to set out for work quite a bit earlier in the morning as it was and, being a great lover of my bed, I must admit I was none too pleased. Smiling ruefully and saying I'd be delighted to oblige, I left the room muttering softly to myself. The new boy was none other than sunny-faced Simon, the man I was to marry three years later in a simple ceremony in Dubai. The tall, blonde, well-built young man had just returned from the Glastonbury music festival (with trench foot, so he told me, from keeping his boots on in the mud for days on end) and, as I had just returned from California, where I'd revived my interest in the music of the Grateful Dead and other West

Coast bands, our early conversations revolved more around music than academic matters. As neither of us was attached at that time and we appeared to have a great deal in common, it was not long before we became 'an item' and were making plans to move somewhere warmer together for the winter, when the teaching work at ELC slackened off.

I was quite keen to return to Thailand and felt it might be a good place for Simon to cut his teaching teeth, as I had done fourteen years earlier. The only problem was that Simon loathed flying, so, after a fruitless attempt to persuade him to brave the journey with a good airline, I started to come round to Simon's idea of heading to Prague instead. Through a personable hippy capitalist friend of Simon's who owned a few properties here and there, we managed to line up some rather basic sounding accommodation in the suburbs and started following up leads to possible teaching work. I was a little concerned to hear that it could be hard to get fresh vegetables in the city in winter and even more so to hear that the ubiquitous icy cobblestones were quite treacherous and led to many a broken ankle. Still, the planning continued and we were about to buy air tickets when to my astonishment and delight Simon announced one morning that he was prepared to endure the long-haul flight to Thailand after all, so out we went that very day and bought one-year open return tickets to Bangkok leaving seven days hence. Various friends with whom we were not in regular contact had envisaged us marching off to work, fur-clad and hunched against the central European cold, through the frosty, history-soaked streets of Prague, and were surprised some weeks later to receive postcards from northern Thailand, waxing lyrical about the balmy tropical evenings, the sound of monks chanting in a nearby temple and the fragrant frangipani blossom in our back garden.

We'd managed to get reasonably priced air tickets with

Emirates, one of the few airlines operating on our route that had a good enough safety record to satisfy my anxious co-passenger. Having no faith in hypnotherapy, which I'd generously offered to pay for, Simon decided to make the journey instead on drugs. His GP prescribed twenty milligrams of Valium, advising him not to mix the muscle relaxant with alcohol as this could increase the effect significantly and quite possibly make him fall over. As soon as we arrived at the airport, Simon made a beeline for the departure lounge bar, and proceeded to drink four pints of Old Speckled Hen, timing the taking of the Valium so that it would kick in around take-off. As we boarded the aircraft, I whispered confidentially to the most senior-looking member of the cabin crew that my partner had a severe phobia about flying and that I wasn't at all sure how he'd react during take-off. She assured me that he would be very well looked after, adding rather puzzlingly that she was actually a pilot herself, and indeed almost as soon as we got ourselves settled in our seats an engaging young cabin attendant came over and introduced herself as Polly. She told Simon that she would be personally responsible for him on the first leg of the journey to Dubai, and asked if we'd like a drink before take-off. Simon readily accepted, and as I thought it polite to keep him company, so did I, and only felt mildly embarrassed at the indignant looks from the passengers sitting alongside us. As we lifted off into the air, Polly sat in a little fold-up chair just opposite us, maintaining steady eye contact with Simon the whole time. It was clear to me that the poor man was experiencing some indescribable torment, but I refrained from saying or doing anything as he seemed to be dealing with it quite well himself, and anyhow Polly was very much on the case. The minute the seat belt light went off, the drinks trolley came bowling up the aisle straight to us and once more we stocked up on miniature bottles, my tipple that day being a good spicy Bloody Mary. After the drinks had been served, Polly came and knelt in the aisle beside Simon and gazed affectionately up at him. 'Just what is it that frightens you, Simon?' she asked, appearing to want very much to understand his emotions. 'Basically,' he answered, 'just crashing and dying a really nasty death.' Experienced though Polly was at reassuring nervous passengers, in several different languages even, she had no ready answer to this, and even if she had, I doubt very much it would have affected Simon's state of mind at this point in the proceedings.

After an hour or so, I made my way to the loo, leaving Simon in Polly's tender care and thinking everything seemed to be going as well as could be expected. The next thing I knew, I was lying on my back on the floor of the galley with a small flurry of cabin crew peering anxiously down at me. Quickly closing my eyes, I listened to them discussing me in hushed tones and heard one of them drawing the curtain to give us all a bit of privacy. An ice pack was mentioned and was about to be applied when I decided I'd had enough. 'I'm absolutely fine,' I assured them, sitting up and smiling, 'I must have drunk my drinks too quickly, that's all.' 'Oh no, Madame,' I was told, 'it will be the pressure' – they seemed keen to assuage any embarrassment I might have been feeling about getting drunk and disorderly on board their aircraft. The rest of the flight, thankfully, passed without further incident. The drinks kept coming and Simon kept drinking, leaving his inflight lunch untouched, claiming to be far too frazzled to consider food. On leaving the plane in Dubai, I found one of the cabin crew at my elbow steering me towards a tall, eager-looking young Emirati man with a wheelchair – I was strongly advised to use it 'just in case' – of what I'm not quite sure. I think they were concerned that the slight bump I'd had on my head as I fell against one of the seats during my swoon might later have repercussions, namely a lawsuit, and they were bending over backwards to do all they possibly could to be helpful. I have to admit I only really went along with it to see how it felt to be without the use of my legs for an hour or so, totally dependent upon another for getting around the airport.

I left Simon sitting on the floor in a passage near the gate, completely uninterested in accompanying me and my carer, Mohammed, around the duty-free shops, but encouraging me to kill an hour or so doing this if I liked. Dubai duty-free shopping is supposed to be paradise for lovers of luxury goods, and I confess I did get briefly distracted amongst the daring designer garments, the impossibly chic, bejewelled sunglasses and the plethora of new beauty products, perfumes and potions, many of which I desired but none of which I needed. I was sitting gazing up in wonder at an aquarium filled with angelfish, butterflyfish and other dazzling beauties, part of the display for the fantastically priced La Mer beauty products, when I happened to glance at my watch. To my horror, I saw that it was a matter of minutes before the plane took off again – I had become so relaxed in the care of my young man I had foolishly thought he would take responsibility for getting me back on time. I was tempted to leap up and make a dash for it, but thought we might stand a better chance of getting through the crowds with me still in the wheelchair. I urged Mohammed to go as fast as humanly possible, and we careered along until we got to a lift taking us down to the correct level to enter the specialised vehicle that would transport us across the tarmac to the plane. To my great relief, sitting there beside me were two other, older, people in wheelchairs, who I quickly ascertained were also Bangkok bound. I smiled broadly at them, suddenly feeling the most awful phony to be posing in this way as a disabled person. On reaching the seat indicated on my boarding pass, I was appalled to find that Simon was not there. There I'd been gadding about in the airport enjoying myself, while my poor Simon had been going through who knows what solitary horrors, had reached crisis point and had chickened out of the second flight! What would become of him? The Emirati authorities were not known for their tolerance of foreigners who were found to be full of pills and alcohol. Wild with panic I rushed to the door, which one of the cabin crew was in the process of shutting. 'Wait, wait!' I pleaded, creating a welcome spot of drama for the seated passengers. 'My husband's still in the airport!' It turned out that Simon had, in fact, boarded the plane in plenty of time – I don't think he's ever been late for anything in his life, a fact I've always put down to his German ancestry. I was gently informed that we'd been upgraded to business class for the second and longer leg of the journey. My joy at hearing this was twofold – I was thrilled both for myself and for my man – but sadly the champagne, crystal glasses, superior food, seats and service didn't make a jot of difference to Simon's enjoyment of the rest of the time aboard the Emirates flight. He did smile fleetingly, however, when presented with a small ceramic model of a mosque, a token of Emirates' gratitude for our choosing to fly with them. To this day we've never really decided whether the upgrade was on account of my fainting fit or of Simon's extreme phobia about flying.

By the time of this visit to Thailand with Simon, I had been to the country so many times before, the dramatic onslaught to the senses as one entered the capital was wonderfully familiar. For Simon, however, never having been further afield than Florence, it was a dazzlingly fresh experience and it gave me great pleasure to observe someone who had never been to the tropics before. Our backpackers' guest house room that first night was pretty dismal, with dark cement walls, and a few sticks of furniture that wouldn't have looked out of place in a prison cell. Not knowing how long it would take to find suitable work, we were starting off on a low budget and my favourite Khao San Road guest houses were all full. Still, Simon's joy to be there was written all over his face, only slightly enhanced by the after-effects of the hefty dose of Valium his doctor had prescribed for the flight washed down by rather more than the recommended daily number of units of alcohol.

After a couple of days sightseeing and revisiting some of my old haunts, we caught a night train to Chiang Mai, as I thought it would be more interesting a second time round to be working in a different city. We shared a top bunk with crisp white sheets, leaving the window open to allow a cool breeze to wash over us. What with the residue of jet lag and the excitement of the train journey, hurtling through the night, shimmering outlines of gilded temples flashing by, water buffalo in the fields, coconut palms and tangled jungle all around us, we didn't sleep a great deal. At one point I must have dozed off and awoke a little surprised to find Simon gone. Peering out through the curtain that enclosed our bunk, I caught sight of him in the area between carriages, beer in hand, chatting to the train guard as though they were old friends. I believe this is one of Simon's happiest memories of his time in South East Asia. As the sun rose over the paddy fields and the temperature steadily climbed, the water started to evaporate, creating a curious haze that enhanced the dreamlike state we were already both in.

To my mind, Chiang Mai is rather a strange city, as it is surrounded by a dry moat yet doesn't really have a centre or any discernible planned layout. There's no proper transport system; local people get across town in tinny little trucks with cramped metal benches in the back, for which there's no fixed price – they operate like communal taxis and you just have to barter until you feel a fair amount is being asked, banging on the driver's window when you recognise your destination. Although I'd heard that it was cooler in the north of the country and we'd decided on Chiang Mai partly on this account, if anything I found it to be hotter than Bangkok, as there was very little breeze, and I later heard that the summer we spent there was a particularly hot one. We soon found what we thought to be a perfect place to live – a large, airy furnished room with balcony, air conditioning and its own en suite bathroom in a quiet, almost-posh hotel on the western edge of town. Our new address was Room 309, *Pornphun* Court, *Phra Pok Klao* Road, Chiang Mai – we liked the sound of it. The room came with a TV and fridge but no kettle, so out we went our first day there to search for one. Having scoured the city but failed to find a single kettle for sale, we decided on a crafty and in fact preferable alternative – a snazzy pink and white vessel, vaguely resembling a dalek, with a plug and a pump that produced boiling water whenever required and only needed to be filled once a day in the morning. We bought fruit, yogurt, muesli and coffee for breakfast and ate our other meals out, as it was cheaper and the range of food more than adequate. I became adept at choosing the juiciest limes and the best papayas – bizarrely, the more battered and mouldy-looking the papaya, the sweeter and more delicious it was. Papaya, best eaten I found with lime juice, has the added benefit of containing an enzyme that helps digestion and even tenderises meat, which is why you sometimes see skewered meat in Thai food stalls being coated with papaya juice before being barbecued. Simon bought a crate of Chang (elephant) beer, which he smuggled past the beady-eyed old battle-axe on the reception desk, and I bought the wherewithal to make margaritas in the evening, so we were all set as regards a modest home, all we needed now – Simon in particular – was some paid employment.

I had already spoken on the phone from the UK to the DOS at the British Council in Chang Mai. He'd sounded encouraging and had said he could well have work for us, to trot over and see him when we arrived in town. Unlike the arrogant Illingworth, the DOS I'd first met at the British Council in Bangkok and again some years later in Tokyo, the younger DOS of the Chiang Mai school was welcoming, down-to-earth and extremely personable. As he only had children's classes just then on offer, however, we reluctantly but fairly swiftly declined, cursing as we left the fine old building with its nicely kept grounds, as we knew we would have been far better paid there than just about anywhere else in town. Fortunately, Simon found work soon after this at an American school, American Universities Alumni Association (AUA), where the DOS, John Gunter, a kindly older American, took him under his wing and a comfortable working relationship was quickly established. I considered working for AUA myself and even gave the required demo lesson observed by Gunter's skinny sidekick, Louisa, who seemed overly concerned about my ability to stick to the textbook when my overwhelming desire was to create some fun by deviating from the blasted thing. Besides my natural antipathy towards Louisa, I didn't especially like the idea of 'pop-ins'. This open-door policy in effect meant that any of the supervisors could just barge into one's class whenever it suited them to make sure one was adhering to the prescribed course and not waltzing off into frivolous realms of fantasy.

Fortunately, I had rented out my little mortgage-free flat in Brighton and was planning to use the accumulating funds to live on if necessary and to travel to Vietnam and Cambodia at the end of our year in Thailand. For this reason, I was in no hurry to get back to the classroom myself. We had discovered a tiny second-hand bookshop near our hotel run by a slightly disreputable-looking, middle-aged British gent, who, in his own words, 'didn't stock rubbish'. He did as it happened, but if you hunted around a bit, there was plenty of good stuff there too between the whodunits, the self-help and the beach literature, so I decided my time would be well spent in Chiang Mai reading all the books I had not got round to reading in the past, starting with *War and Peace*. I'd happened to mention my intention of reading this book to my stepfather just before we left Blighty and to my surprise, he'd promptly gone to the bookcase and taken out his own compact, lightweight copy printed on bible paper, which he'd touchingly offered up as a parting gift. One of the highlights of our week in Chiang Mai was a visit to this dusty little shop to trade in the books we'd read and pick out a fresh new batch.

Seeing we'd pushed the single beds together on our first night at *Pornphun* Court, the chambermaids, who cleaned our room and changed the bed linen and towels twice a week, must have taken us for newly-weds, as they gave us coy, knowing looks when we passed them in the corridor, probably thinking to themselves what fun we two must be having. They put extra undercovers on our bed to smooth out the bit where the mattresses joined, making it a lot more comfortable, and sometimes even exchanged our white sheets for pink ones. Our balcony overlooked a leafy private garden, full of flowering trees and plants that attracted huge butterflies and some interesting tropical birds. As the skies were invariably clear, we got a good view of the moon and stars in the evening as we were philosophising over our aperitifs. There was just one drawback to our new home and that was that the garden below was inhabited by ten assorted pet dogs, which barked, bickered and howled intermittently day and night. We spent a fair bit of time discussing ways of silencing the hounds and punishing the owners. One evening early on in our stay we had a bit of a set-to with our neighbours. At my coaxing, Simon had gone out and bellowed at the loathsome creatures, which had had little effect on them but had brought the man of the house and his two daughters rushing out to investigate. A fairly heated and unsatisfactory interchange ensued and thereafter one of the daughters took to patrolling the garden in the daytime with a large stick, shouting and swiping at the animals, generally stirring them up more than ever. In exasperation, one night, unable to sleep on account of the racket, we made a water bomb out of a plastic bag and threw it at the rabid-looking cur we took to be the main culprit, which did nothing whatsoever to stop the barking; if anything it made the dogs worse, and as we are animal lovers, it just made us feel guilty. In the end, we decided to forfeit the room we'd come to be fond of for a darker front room overlooking the main road and a Shell garage. Though not as pleasant as our first room, it was undeniably a great deal quieter and the view of the mountains along the skyline went some way towards compensating for the flora and fauna our initial room had looked out on.

From our new balcony, we got a clear view of the noodle soup shop opposite, where a scrawny young member of staff in a white hat and overalls could be seen at the front vigorously dunking noodles in and out of a large vat of stock before pouring them into bowls and adding beansprouts, coriander, shreds of meat and so on. We only ate occasionally at this place, as we normally had soup at lunchtime at a different shop run by a composed and motherly older woman, who simply radiated well-being – Mrs Soup. Her food was prepared and served with such love and care that we felt we were getting a lot more than straightforward nutrition at her shop – we were getting food for the heart and soul too, there was no doubt about it, even to Simon, who has never been spiritually inclined. She would feed us as though she was feeding her long-lost children returning from the war, and her homemade crispy wontons were simply out of this world. Just a little further on from Mrs Soup's shop was a popular and bustling open-air food market. To get there we had to first cross the moat, which encircled the town, and then choose our moment to scuttle across a very busy wide road. The array of foods, once we got there, was almost overwhelming at first, but we gradually made our way through the various types of cuisine until we'd established half a dozen or so firm favourites. At least once a week, we'd go to Mrs Beef's stand. She was an enormous, dignified woman, almost totally spherical in shape, with smooth skin stretched across her ample cheeks, which were rosy and polished-looking. Her hair was tied back into rather a severe bun and her expression was pleasant yet enigmatic. She didn't register when she saw us sit down at one of the little tin tables, but she knew we were there and what our preferences were – no fat and extra pickled mustard leaves – so as soon as she'd prepared her previous orders, she set about making ours, slamming her meat cleaver down on the wooden board, making neat diagonal cuts across the meat before arranging it meticulously on a neat mound of rice, pouring a small ladle of gravy over it and adding the pickled greens deftly at the side. Although I've never been a great meat eater – I used to prefer cheese and biscuits to our Sunday roasts when I was growing up – Mrs Beef knew a thing or two about cooking meat and I became something of a convert living in Chiang Mai. The funny thing was, we'd been eating at her stall for some time before it was pointed out to us that it wasn't beef we were eating at all, but pork. It was much too late to change the name of our hostess, however, so Mrs Beef she remained.

For special occasions, at the end of the week or when we were feeling a little flush, we'd go to Mr Fish. He was as jovial and friendly as Mrs Beef was reserved. The moment he spotted us in the crowd he'd wave a cheery *Sawatdee krap!* and hold up his most impressive fish, assuring us it was 'very fresh, very good and not expensive' – '*pla sud, di maak, mai peng!*' We were never disappointed; his fish was so succulent and beautifully prepared (usually with chilli, lime, ginger and coriander) it sometimes seemed odd to be sitting on wobbly metal stools in a dusty street market amidst a bustling throng of simple working folk and not among formally dressed diners in the hushed reverence of a Michelin-starred restaurant. If Mr Fish was a tiny bit on the pricey side, for those on Thai wages at least, the Buddhist vegetarian restaurant a ten-minute walk in the opposite direction was so cheap as to be positively laughable – we simply couldn't understand how the magnificent cook cum overseer, Mr Vegetarian, could buy all the many ingredients to make a dozen or more huge pots full of appetising food, pay serving staff and cleaners as well as rent and power bills and make any profit whatsoever. You would queue up with an empty plate and servers would dish out rice topped with whatever delicate concoctions you fancied – just a modest amount of each, so you wouldn't feel greedy if you tried four or five different ones, which we usually did. Iced water or tea in metal beakers would be served free of charge and the little restaurant, though always crowded, had an air of serenity as people ate silently, eyes downcast under the whirring ceiling fans, and left quietly when they'd finished. As we left each time, invariably replete and content, we'd convert the Thai baht we'd just spent into sterling and would look at each other in amazement, as it never came to more than fifty pence a head, and was usually nearer thirty. One day we calculated what our average weekly expenditure was – if we were extra careful and resisted buying any luxuries, we could manage on approximately fifteen pounds a week all-in per person. I was not unaware that during this period in Chiang Mai, perhaps due to the lack of challenging occupation in my life, I might have been fostering an unnatural interest in culinary matters.

One day, on my way back from the central post office, where I would always go hopeful of getting mail and news from back home, but was often disappointed, I stumbled across a small nondescript language school with dusty windows on the main road, just beside the cock fighting field. I stopped for a few minutes to watch two particularly fine cocks strutting grandly about the enclosure, their iridescent tail feathers glinting in the sun. I was reminded of our first week or so in town staying at the Top North Guest House, with its beautiful leafy garden and crystal-clear turquoise pool, being woken up at the crack of dawn by an over-zealous rooster, that continued to crow for all it was worth throughout the day. Seeing someone the other side of the window, I knocked at the door and got into conversation with the owner, a seemingly warm and cheery woman, who resembled a shiny-eyed hamster with a frilly ruff-like collar around her short, plump neck. Possibly against my better judgement, I agreed to do a little teaching for her at a rather low rate of pay. Unfortunately, the students were solely young learners, which I knew would mean a lot more time spent on materials preparation and almost certainly more blood, sweat and tears than generally experienced with adults. As previously relayed, I'd taught Thai children once before, during my year in Bangkok, and had found some of the boys especially hard to handle. I seemed to lack the natural authority required to instill respect and achieve the law and order so essential in classes of young learners.

As I sauntered back across town to *Pornphun* Court, I wondered if I'd done the right thing and thought back to my experience fourteen years earlier giving private lessons to a couple of very privileged children in the capital at weekends. The girl, Alison, was bright, cheerful and a delight to teach, but her younger brother, Albert, was impossible. Their mother was an academic doing research on chimpanzees at one of the city's universities. She actually admitted to me on one occasion that she found this work infinitely more rewarding than motherhood and so had employed me to get both Albert and his sister Alison's English up to scratch so that they could attend a boarding school in the UK; this would then enable her to devote herself to what she considered her real work. The trouble was Albert was hyperactive and had no interest whatsoever in learning English vocabulary, even if it was taught through carefully devised games such as Animal Pelmanism and Fruit and Vegetable Bingo, which I'd spent all the previous evening toiling away to create on the bed in our one-room abode. Even when they came to visit me in hospital the time I had food poisoning, Albert had rampaged around the room, putting up the bars on the side of my bed and playing with tubes and bottles and anything he could get his hands on. The only time he actually behaved was on the occasion I took them to Bangkok Zoo. The transformation was incredible – that day he became malleable and courteous and actually tried to learn the names of some of the animals, including my favourite New World monkey, the cotton-top tamarin. I wouldn't mind betting that Albert went on to become a zoologist like his mother – either that or a zoo keeper. There was no doubt he had an affinity with animals and in his utter joy at being allowed to give the old rhinoceros a bread bun I saw another side to the manic monster he'd been up until that day.

I had given my word to Ms Hamster, however, and so that night I knuckled down and prepared what I thought would be some interesting activities to keep my new young students entertained. I launched into my first lesson with a small class of eight and to my horror I realised I had another overactive and almost unmanageable boy to deal with, horribly reminiscent of Albert in Bangkok. His name was Don and he too happened to have a sweet, angelic older sister. If Albert and Alison's mother had been overly preoccupied with academia, Don and Dang's was considerably younger and appeared far more concerned with fashion and appearances than the education and well-being of her children. She seemed, in fact, to be so young and frivolous I rather doubted her suitability for motherhood altogether. I envied my co-teacher Hannah, who had taught classes of fifty children in Hong Kong and seemed to have the knack of keeping them all under control and on task. I found the discipline required to teach this relatively small class of young

Chiang Mai residents, particularly the job of keeping Don in check, exhausting and far from enjoyable.

One afternoon, Don had been if anything worse than usual and he could see he was getting to me. I was enjoying a few moments respite in the break and was sitting – I hesitate to give such a graphic description, but I'm afraid it is necessary to convey the urgency of the moment – on the lavatory in a tiny shed in the back garden, which had no light and no lock on the door, so I'd left the door slightly ajar. All of a sudden, I heard the thundering of tiny footsteps approaching my refuge and, as I flung out my arms to prevent the door from being thrust open, revealing 'Teacher' in such a compromising position, I felt an almighty force that seemed for a moment even stronger than my own, despite the fact that I probably weighed about four times more than my juvenile assailant. I naturally assumed that this could be none other than the diabolical Don, tormenting me even now, in my fifteen-minute break, trying to push me once and for all right over the edge. After what felt like a long time, but in actuality could only have been a minute at the most, the pushing stopped and there was a moment's silence. I then heard a plaintive little voice saying, 'Miss *Calleee?... I'm solleee!'* and I realised it wasn't Don at all but Titi, one of the sweetest, most obliging and well-behaved children I have ever had the pleasure of teaching. The poor boy was mortified when we came face to face in the classroom a few minutes later. I have fond memories of teaching this adorable child, and would have adopted him in a flash if given the chance, but I will never forget the reproach with which his stern, grey-haired mother told me that it was a pity there was no continuity for the children in this school, that the teachers were forever upping and leaving – which was hardly surprising when one considered that the resources were pitiful, the conditions primitive and the pay minimal. Still, I soldiered on and taught my captive audience every children's song I knew, *with* the accompanying actions – no room for inhibitions in my class! I brought props to school and devised drama activities and games using TPR (total physical response) in an attempt to make the lessons as much fun and as interactive as possible. I was thankful for the fur hat, scarf and ear muffs that had somehow got left in my luggage from my winter trip to California, as these came in very handy for role plays and lessons on clothes. Games with boards and dice were always popular and it used to amuse me no end watching darling Titi, with his enormous wide eyes and outgrown crew cut, going through a little ritual, bowing and praying to the gods for luck each time he threw the dice. He would always ask '*May* I have a glass of water? *May* I leave the room, please?', unlike Don, who helped himself to water and left the room when he pleased, banging the door as he went.

Unfortunately, as the months went by Ms Hamster's manner cooled somewhat and in a letter to my mother, I actually referred to her as 'that vile woman I work for'! The comment, I believe, had been provoked by an interchange that had taken place after I'd been at the school for a few months. Out of the blue one day she suggested that I stop teaching at her school and take up a full-time job at a prestigious private school in Chiang Mai instead. She was quite sure the salary and conditions would be to my liking. I declined quite gracefully, I had thought, but the fury could be clearly detected simmering beneath her veneer of charm. She was not used to having her plans thwarted. No doubt she had already offered me up to an academic associate at a social gathering, as a favour owed, perhaps – and was incensed to find I couldn't be bought.

It was one Friday afternoon as I was walking home from school, relieved to have completed another week without mishap and even having enjoyed a few classroom successes, that I felt a sudden twinge in one of my back teeth. Over the years I have had dental work done in just about all the countries I have worked in

– all twelve of them. One dentist in New Zealand once quipped that I might consider having a small flag implanted in each tooth to indicate where the work on it had been done. I tried to put it out of my mind, but while drinking my second sundowner on the balcony that night I did a little tentative probing around the troublesome area with my tongue and, to my dismay, felt an ominous swelling just above the spot where one of my impacted wisdom teeth was. I'd been warned that I might have trouble with these wisdom teeth at some point and that I might even have to have them extracted. It had been explained that this would only be done if considered absolutely necessary, as I have a small mouth and there was very little room indeed for a dental surgeon to manoeuvre. Just my luck, I thought, of all the places to need complex dental surgery, here I was out in the sticks in northern Thailand. Already in my mind's eye, I could see myself laid out on an old operating table, surrounded by poorly trained, underage dental students wielding crude dental implements, eager to set to work on me. To my immense relief, the x-rays were reassuring and I left the dental surgery quite elated, having got away with nothing more than a five-pound scale and polish, performed through a crafty little embroidered flannel with a hole in the middle for the mouth. I'd been surprised to find the dentist was the friendly young woman we'd spoken to several times at one of our favourite evening food stalls in a little alley near our home run by the character we had christened the Ultimate Wok Man. I may have offended her slightly when I asked her if she was a dental student, as she swiftly put me right, telling me she'd had her own practice for five years. Her surgery was reminiscent of a teenage girl's bedroom with an overall theme of tropical sea life. The screen that separated the two dentists' chairs was a huge floor-to-head-height mirror engraved with fish and lurid green vegetation. The angle of the chairs was such that you could effectively check in the mirror to see whether your underwear matched the rest of your outfit – it certainly helped to keep my mind off the probing and prodding that was going on in my mouth.

Time slipped by, increasingly stickily as the temperature revved up and powered forwards towards full-blown summer, until at midday, when we ventured out of our air-conditioned room for lunch, it was hot as Hades. Our A/C unit was quite effective but expensive to run, so in the evening, when we were ready to call it a day, we'd stand before it like penguins, arms outstretched, absorbing each cooling particle before switching it off and diving onto the bed, hoping to get to sleep before the room warmed up unbearably once more. When we weren't teaching, we read, played cards and listened to music on our Walkman, taking it in turns to listen to the bootleg cassette tapes we'd bought in the street market – k. d. lang, Shane MacGowan, Van Morrison, Radiohead and others. We kept abreast of world affairs via the *Bangkok Post* and BBC World on our tiny TV and made vague travel plans, Vietnam for me being the carrot at the end of a quiet but by no means disagreeable stay in sleepy Chiang Mai. Sadly, our expedition to Vietnam was not to happen. The dastardly Cockney estate agent, John Carter, to whom I'd entrusted the keys to my Brighton flat, had been quietly pocketing my rent the whole period we were in Thailand, so instead of having a healthy travel fund sitting there ready to be drawn on when needed, I discovered to my horror, when I finally got to see my bank statements, I had a nasty overdraft both at the bank and on my Visa card. My dear friend in Brighton led a hectic life and it had taken her a little longer than expected to forward my mail. After a few sleepless nights tossing, turning and gnashing my teeth we decided to head back home to try and sort out the mess, returning not via Vietnam and Cambodia as planned, but via Laos, as it was a shorter and less expensive route.

On our return to Blighty in June 1998, just in time for the World Cup, I was plunged into what felt like an ever-widening whirlpool of worry and grief. Firstly, I had the bank to deal with along with solicitors' letters for non-payment of various bills and not least the smooth-talking, swindling swine, John Carter, who owed me the best part of £3,000, which was a lot of money for me back then. When I confronted the villain in his plush high street office, he blamed the whole fiasco on a non-existent alcoholic partner and told me that if I continued to cause a disturbance in his office, he'd call the police. We later heard the slimy character was a struck-off solicitor, so clearly knew the ins and outs of the law and all the useful loopholes for unscrupulous estate agents. When I continued to voice my dissatisfaction with his service, making no effort to lower my voice in front of other clients, he threatened to leave the office and lock me in for the night, telling me I was unbalanced and required a psychiatrist. The police, though mildly sympathetic, were not at all helpful and simply advised me to stay away from the man. Around a week later Mr Carter did a moonlight flit, owing around twenty people a month's rent. I'd been the hardest hit along with one other poor woman, who owned a string of properties with rent owing on each. Simon and I undertook some private detective work and managed to track down his ex-wife and new partner to a large art deco house in a London suburb. We were invited into the strangely sparsely furnished home, which we guessed had been visited sometime before us by the bailiffs. The only thing we learned that day was that this couple had no idea where he was and that they too wanted to get their hands on 'the little toe-rag'! It was starting to sink in that I would not get my money back. One thing that would have given me enormous satisfaction at that time would have been to see John Carter placed in the stocks in the centre of town and to join an avenging crowd hurling eggs and rotten tomatoes at him, duplicitous devil that he was.

Some years later I did a little research using the internet and got into a telephone conversation with a property developer, another John Carter from Hackney. As he chattered cheerily on about his days working as a dancer in Majorca and as a coxswain on the Thames, giving me a brief history lesson while he was at it on the origin of the name Hackney and its Hackney cabs, I listened intently to the Cockney accent, trying to detect whether the voice on the phone matched that of the individual I was trying to trace. I decided it did not and resolved to follow the fatherly sounding stranger's advice to write the money off once and for all, to remain a positive thinker and to believe that 'what goes around comes around'. I'd been hoping for a spot of instant Karma but failing this I can at least hope the fiend who swindled me and caused me so much anguish might be reincarnated in Antarctica as an emperor penguin, or perhaps a Galapagos penguin, as both of these are known to have particularly hard lives.

It was during the first few weeks after our return from Thailand that I travelled up to Shrewsbury with my mother to visit Doreen, a much-loved old relative of ours, a cousin of my grandmother's. She was an extremely colourful character and had led an interesting and eventful life, still possessing, even in her eighties, oodles of sex appeal and a wicked sense of humour. She was very much part of the family and had driven down to Berkshire in her snazzy little car to stay with us quite regularly. She always kept abreast of the times and when I once confided in her that I very much wanted to have a baby but couldn't find a suitable sire, she didn't hesitate to advise me: 'Just put your eggs on *ice*, my dear – I'm sure you'll find someone someday you like enough to ask for help with the rest.' On another occasion, I was bemoaning the fact that I've always been a dreadful sleeper and again the advice was immediate and clearly something she did herself: 'Just count your lovers, darling, and try to remember all their names and peccadilloes – that will soon get you off.' Since I had last seen Doreen, she had had a stroke and had given up her beautiful, stylish flat in the city centre for a rather drab, tiny room in a quiet old people's home. Half her face was paralysed and it was not easy for her to speak, though she did so briefly and quickly at chosen moments out of the other side of her mouth. Despite the sadness of the occasion, sad in that we knew the chances were that Doreen would spend the rest of her days in this rather soulless place, quite some distance away from us and away from many of the things she loved, we managed to have a jolly time, reminiscing about fancy-dress parties and good times we'd had and poring over a batch of photos Mum had brought. One of these photos in particular caused great merriment as it was of Mum lying asleep on a beach in Corsica earlier that year with her mouth open. It had been taken by her travelling companion, my aunt Rosemary, at such an angle that it looked very much as though Mum was heavily pregnant. It certainly wasn't the most flattering photo ever taken of her and we all got the giggles. We laughed so much that it provoked another mini-stroke in our dear relative and I had an awful feeling that it was going to finish her off. It didn't, as it turned out, but we left soon afterwards, cutting our visit short so that Doreen could rest and recuperate.

I got back to Hove that evening, exhausted and rather emotional. I slept badly and as I wearily drew back the bedclothes next morning saw a smallish, black spider making its way hastily to the edge of the bed. If I were superstitious, I might have taken this as an omen of some sort. Finding an itchy lump on my right buttock, I concluded that the wretched thing had just bitten me. Incredible though it may sound, it is quite conceivable that this insignificant creature was responsible for a condition that was to affect me for the best part of a year. That one small bite could possibly have been the thing that triggered what was later diagnosed as chronic urticaria. What started as localised hives gradually spread to each extremity of my body until I was practically covered in large, red, itchy spots. As urticaria is more commonly provoked by stress, of which I'd had more than my fair share since hearing of John Carter's shenanigans, Simon and I decided to leave dear old England with all its complications behind us once more and escape to what we imagined would be a peaceful life and a kinder climate on the quiet Canarian island of Tenerife.

Chapter 13

Tenerife – Heaven or Hell?

My father's parents, Jim and Kathleen, both always snowy-haired and laughing in my memory, had fallen in love with the island of Tenerife in the fifties and for many years would lock up their remote Yorkshire cottage in autumn and set off for the Spanish sun. My grandfather was an artist and I imagine loved the Mediterranean light and colours, which he captured beautifully in his oil paintings. My grandmother, like me, found English winters a terrible trial, and I suspect was the driving force behind their migratory habit. They would travel out by ship, the passage being paid for in a rather singular way – my grandfather would paint a picture for the captain, either a portrait or a Spanish scene, a happy arrangement that went on for many years. They loved their Spanish life – they taught themselves the language, made good friends and spoke of the old capital Santa Cruz so fondly it already had a place in my heart before I even set foot on the island. I have a black and white photograph of my grandparents standing under a giant Canarian cactus gazing steadily into the camera lens. My grandfather, tall, handsome and bearded, is in his bathing trunks and a loose white shirt – he has a tentative, slightly questioning look, though that could have been the sun in his eyes. My grandmother, tiny and composed beside him, is wearing a fashionable cotton frock with a string of coral beads and looks rather more assertive. I'd been told she'd had stunning auburn hair in her youth but that before she reached thirty it had turned pure white. She'd been working as a nurse when she met my grandfather, but in a different age, my mother always said, Kathleen would have become a doctor or an academic. I adored my grandparents and now feel sorry that I didn't see more of them when they were old and no longer able to travel. As I walked the dusty streets of their former Spanish home, watched the fountains play in the tranquil, sunlit, leafy squares with their exquisite Sevillian tiled benches and gazed up at the waving palms lining the wide pedestrian avenue of Las Ramblas, I often thought of them and wished they could see me there, wished they could know I thought of them, wished they could be there with me to share a *copa de vino tinto* and a saucer of olives. The closest I had ever come to visiting the Canaries up until this time was one winter in my early twenties travelling around Morocco in a Ford Transit van with a small group of friends. We had reached the port of Tarifa in the very south of the country and had made enquiries about taking a boat across the short stretch of Pacific waters to the islands, but as there was only one ferry a week and we'd just missed one by less than twenty-four hours, along with the fact that we were getting worryingly low on funds, we wisely gave up the idea.

During the hopeless and demoralising John Carter business, Simon and I had run into an old friend of his, who was settled in Santa Cruz and offered to employ us teaching in schools and companies in the north of the island. There was nothing to hold us in England, so it didn't take us long to decide. Simon took the overland route, enduring an interminable bus journey to Madrid, stopping off en route to see another old friend in the south of France, and then flying the relatively short distance from Madrid to Tenerife. I flew out to join him a few weeks later, surprised and delighted to be picked up at the airport by Simon and Patrick and whisked away in our new employer's comfortable soft top BMW 3 Series. We were driven at speed up the east coast with its dark volcanic beaches to the north of the island, then up into the mountains above Santa Cruz to a small, rustic restaurant, already packed with raucous families out for Sunday lunch. Here, Patrick informed us we would eat meat, assuring us that we would be served the best barbecued beef on the island. It was indeed a splendid meal and a fine prelude to our Canarian campaign. Happy to be reunited after some weeks apart, Simon and I were optimistic that our stay beneath the magnificent, snow-capped Teide volcano would be a good one.

To begin with we were to stay with Patrick in his unpretentious but comfortable home in the heart of the capital, which he shared with his dog George, an initially appealing but in fact quite aggressive terrier that resembled a small Chinese lion and would nip bare toes if you were foolish enough to go downstairs in the morning without shoes. We were given quite a pleasant room up at roof level with latticed shutters on the windows that cast an intricate pattern of shadows on the terra cotta tiled floor. The only drawbacks were the colony of termites in the ceiling, that I feared might lose their foothold and drop into my mouth while I was sleeping, and the incredible amount of street noise – cars and motorbikes zoomed up and down the hill day and night, almost all, it seemed, without silencers. Latin music was played at high volume, shrill voices rang out, fractious infants howled, and at weekends in particular there was lusty late-night singing and the babel of drunken brawling. It seemed unbelievable that older people put up with it all and that they didn't push for legislation to clamp down on offenders. Once I'd been put on heavy medication for my urticaria, despite the racket outside, I would fall asleep quite easily and invariably, according to my bedfellow, with a sweet, contented smile upon my face. I have several friends who are loath to take pills of any description. At that point in my life, I can only say I was grateful for the relief I was given by prescribed pharmaceuticals, though in days to come I was to pay the price for this temporary blissful solace.

Payment for our teaching work, we soon learned, rather to our dismay, was to be largely dependent on student numbers, so if word got around that our classes were fun and more people signed up, the fatter our pay packet. Many hours were spent in the sweltering sun queueing outside various offices to obtain social security numbers and all the other things required to make our employment legal. Patrick went to some trouble to help with this tedious process and even promised to buy a small car for us to get to the less accessible teaching venues he was lining up for us. Originally our vehicle was to be a brand-new Hyundai Atos – we went along to a promotional party at the showroom, where we eyed up the sophisticated, metallic orange run-around in some awe. As it turned out, Patrick reassessed his finances and we ended up with a tiny, white clapped-out Seat Marbella instead – an inferior model, I believe, of a Fiat Panda, a vehicle that would probably be considered unfit for use on UK roads – it became known to us as 'the death trap'.

At the first opportunity we planned a day trip with our newly acquired wheels to Masca, a quaint village and a great beauty spot, so we'd heard, way up in the mountains the other side of the island. Simon was keen to go via the Teide, as up until then we hadn't seen the famous volcano at close quarters and thought it would look all the more impressive with the summit still snow-covered. We set off at 9 am and by 10.30 am found ourselves high up above the city, having woven our way slowly to and fro around the many hairpin bends, through hushed dark pine forests, to a perfectly positioned lookout point, thankfully unblemished by droves of tourists. We'd noticed a bit of a whiff coming from the engine on the way up, but Simon seemed confident enough that the little beast was up to the trip. Not so – at just on 1,500 metres (higher than the highest point in the UK) the water tank boiled and spluttered and it seemed we were stuck, miles from anywhere, though with a stunning view of the Teide up above us and a magnificent panorama of the city and glistening sea far below. Waiting a good half hour or so, we tried the ignition once more, but it was obvious that the engine was not going to start, so – although no one in their right mind would have tried to steal the odious thing – we attached the steering wheel clamp and started heading down the hill. The walk back down must have taken at least a couple of hours. We did of course try to hitchhike, but the (mostly German) tourists in their hired cars quite definitely did not want to risk our company, and in the end, it was a Canarian road worker in his pick-up truck who reluctantly slowed down and gave us a ride to the nearest bus stop. The car was duly retrieved and the small hole in the engine repaired, but we had learned our lesson and didn't push our luck with a second attempt to reach Masca, opting instead to explore areas nearer sea level.

All too soon, work began and once more I found myself closeted in stuffy classrooms teaching unruly children, this time at a large, private school called Echeyde, high up on a mountainside, right the other side of town. I was quite happy for Simon to have use of the death trap for getting to and from work during the week. There was a reasonable bus service in Santa Cruz, so I resolved to make do with buses and my own feet for getting around myself. The bus to Echeyde, which was often late, took a long circuitous route across town, finally slowing to a laboured crawl in bottom gear up the lower slopes of the mountain and stopping at the end of its route quite some way from the top. The downward journey, by contrast, was like a roller-coaster ride, drivers often reverting to teenage exuberance and irresponsibility, cruising at ever more reckless speeds until someone would ring the bell and the vehicle was reluctantly reined in and brought to a jolting halt at the requested bus stop. The steep climb on foot from the bus stop to the school gate in the late morning sun with my heavy bag of books was not something I looked forward to, but at least must have kept me reasonably fit.

Before leaving Brighton, I had invested in a small library of new books containing innovative ideas for teaching young learners, all of which I had read keenly, determined to do better than previously with my least favourite type of learner. Although there were no suitable teaching resources at Echeyde and some of the classes were of very mixed ability, even mixed in age, I coped with the work after a fashion, mainly by putting in hours of work at the weekend, creating an extensive file of worksheets, games and activities for use at various levels. I also worked on my illustrations for board work and before long there wasn't an animal under the sun that I couldn't do a reasonable likeness of in less than thirty seconds. Fond though I have always been of children, it was in Tenerife that I came to the final conclusion that I simply didn't like teaching them. (Simon had known this about himself right from the start.) I couldn't believe my ears and eyes the first day at school when the break time came around. It was pandemonium – the children were allowed to simply run riot in the corridors, creating an almighty din, with no one even attempting to control them. It seemed to me there was rather a lack of respect for teachers in Spain, which contrasted strongly with the attitude in the Far East, where teachers of any description were generally held in high esteem. Teachers' day in Thailand and Taiwan, for example, had been an important event in the calendar long before World Teachers' Day (October

5) was established by UNESCO in 1994. In both Thailand and Taiwan, we had been showered with cards, cakes and gifts from grateful students on Teacher's Day – I don't recall this happening on any day of the year in Tenerife. Even though some of the girls in my classes were actually quite sweet, running up and kissing me tenderly on each cheek as I entered the classroom, gazing up at me wide-eyed and demure as I tried to teach them songs or poems, the majority of Canarian children I came into contact with were rowdy and cheeky, if not downright insolent. Many was the time I thought to myself as I left the school that my efforts were not paying off – that I was casting my precious pearls of wisdom before ill-mannered, ungrateful young swine. One of the few benefits of this job was that I qualified for free lunches in the school canteen – thankfully the teachers ate in their own room, away from the unholy hubbub in the children's area, and the food was surprisingly decent, even if Canarian salad, featuring sweet corn, white asparagus, tuna, boiled egg and pineapple, appeared a little too regularly for my liking. Every so often there would be a particularly fine paella, so fine in fact that I would return meekly to the serving ladies like Oliver Twist asking for more.

Though they were not as enjoyable as my classes in the Far East, I did find my adult classes in Tenerife significantly more rewarding than those with the young learners. One such job was at the bottom of this same mountain at Cita, a cigarette factory, teaching business English to four members of the admin and HR departments. The big bonus in this job, Patrick told me gleefully, was a free carton of cigarettes once a month. Not being a smoker, I failed to show enthusiasm at this announcement. None of the group appeared initially to be over the moon about being offered these afternoon English sessions at the company's expense. I expect it interfered with their routine work and might have meant they'd have to stay on late at the office. Of the four possible students on my register I could never be sure who might turn up. I had every conceivable combination – each one individually, each pair, each threesome and occasionally all four together. As the chemistry for each grouping was totally different, their work responsibilities and characters contrasting sharply, I would have to do some quick thinking and revision of lesson plans to tailor them to the particular individual or individuals. Fortunately, the most nervous and aloof of the four, Marina, the company legal advisor and PA to the president, had a few consecutive sessions on her own and I worked so hard at amusing her with anecdotes and getting her to reciprocate that she started breaking into peals of laughter at the drop of a hat. I was very touched one day at the end of class when she sweetly presented me with a beautiful little silver-framed handbag mirror in a velvet case, which I still have and treasure – either she thought I was doing a good job or possibly that I'd do well to check my appearance a bit more often. (The children were very quick to point out when I had whiteboard marker on my face, but it's funny how adults often didn't – I would sometimes reach home to find green or blue patches on my cheek and cringe to think how many people I'd spoken to while looking like a clown.) My work at Cita was mostly quite enjoyable and at the end of the course the pretty, sharp-witted younger female, Carmen, made a little speech about how much my classes had been appreciated and how they all wished I were staying on – they had just heard I was leaving and that their former teacher – actually Patrick – would be taking over the class once more. This was, of course, good to hear, though earlier in the course I'd invited the two females from this group to a small house-warming party, assuring them how very welcome they'd be, and neither had shown up. Nor had my two long-term private students, a jolly married couple, both air-traffic controllers from Galicia, who had promised they would come. If the island children I encountered in the line of duty were generally uninhibited and obstreperous, the adults, by contrast, seemed to be, initially at least, reserved, wary of foreigners and slow to make or respond to overtures of friendship.

My second adult class, part of a state-sponsored project to provide unemployed professionals with extra work skills, was made up of more outgoing individuals. They were a lively bunch, more relaxed and motivated than the cigarette factory employees, and I looked forward to my sessions with them. The only problem was that some extensive road works were going on just outside our classroom window – pneumatic drills alternated with the sound of bulldozers and tumbling boulders and drove us all to distraction, me in particular. Try as I might, I was unable to arrange a move to a quieter room. The beginning of the course coincided too with some truly atrocious weather; the island was pummelled by the worst storms since 1945, with thunder and lightning practically on top of one another. Gigantic waves crashed into the harbour with sea spray reaching halfway up the masts of even the largest ships. Small trees were buffeted and bent over in surges of wind-driven rain, sometimes until their trunks snapped. One evening, after a class that had been outrageously interrupted by a particularly vigorous bout of pneumatic drilling, I left the building exasperated and dejected. As I emerged into the driving rain, a gust of wind promptly broke my umbrella, and in the dark, I stepped into a deep puddle that drenched my best leather shoes. There was no doubt, we were unlucky with the weather, just as my mother had been the winter she travelled out to visit my grandparents. Ever a sun worshipper, as I too used to be, she'd been hoping so much for some winter sun and a golden tan to show off back home in North Wales. It rained just about the whole time she was on the island and the weather was said to have been unseasonably chilly. Still, in my memory, during our time in the Canary Islands, sunny days prevailed and it was only on the rare occasion that I felt the need to reach into my wardrobe for woollies.

One of the best things about our stay on Tenerife, I'm sure Simon would agree, was our friendship with Sally and Jess. Sally was an academic, a professor at La Laguna University, originally from Melbourne, the cultural capital of Australia, with an MA TEFL and PhD from Reading University, where I too had jumped through the hoops to acquire my own MA TEFL. Sally's academic achievements were not inconsiderable, but she was always endearingly modest about these and said she felt she'd got ahead and had lucky breaks not so much because she excelled in her work but more because people tended to *like* her. It was Patrick who told me I had to meet Sally Burgess, as he was quite sure we'd get on. We did indeed, and discovered that apart from having studied at the same university and being almost exactly the same age, we had all sorts of other things in common, our love of literature, our crush on Tom Petty and our sense of humour being the first to spring to mind. Apart from this, it transpired that we had both hung out in Crete during the winter of 1979 and had both had emotional traumas there on Palaiochora beach. We even had a mutual friend, Julia Walton, with whom I'd worked in New Zealand and with whom Sally had worked and shared a flat in London. Before Sally and I met face to face we had already become friends by chatting at length on the phone. While Sally was petite and pretty, slightly doll-like with jauntily wavy blonde hair and an infectious laugh, her partner Jess, an artist and photographer, was a slightly devilish-looking, wiry man, a little older than us, with spikey, sun-bleached hair and bronzed, weathered skin from playing tennis, running and mountain hiking in all weathers. One of Jess's ancestors, I learned, was the pilot who flew King Edward VIII over the channel to marry Mrs Simpson. Just after they'd flown over the white cliffs of Dover the king said to the pilot:

'Fly me over the cliffs one last time, would you, Charlie!' As far as I know, Jess hadn't flown aircraft but drove his new Peugeot 106 Rallye, which I learned from Simon had a very powerful engine for such an insignificant-looking car, with great verve and panache.

One weekend, when Sally was in the UK, escaping the carnival, Jess offered to take Simon and me on a gentle mountain walk. 'It's not hard,' he assured us. 'It's all downhill and should only take around three hours.' The hairpin bends on the ascent of the mountain above Arafo gave Jess plenty of scope to practise his advanced driving skills, and by the time we reached the snow level, where we were to start our walk, I was feeling extremely car sick. The black volcanic landscape, bright spring skies and sub-tropical vegetation (including, incongruously, masses of sweet chestnut trees) made for an interesting walk, helped along by enormous camembert-filled baguettes thoughtfully prepared by Simon that morning and consumed within the first twenty minutes. Although Simon was the one with the dicky knee, ironically, around hour two, it was me who started getting twinges, which developed into a fairly serious handicap for the rest of the walk. It did cross my mind that, being a highly suggestible type when it came to ailments, I might have been absorbing the pain on Simon's behalf, as he didn't have a spot of trouble on this walk and the pain in my knee was in exactly the same spot as his normally was. What with getting lost, my need for rest stops plus photograph taking, the three hours easily became four and a half.

The last lap was on a sealed road with an exceptionally sharp gradient, running through a rather picturesque village. For the final half hour or so, the only way for me to advance at all and make it back to civilisation was by striding backwards, bending slightly to the left so as to look down over my shoulder, arms outstretched in a balletic posture to keep pace with the others and maintain my balance. Naturally, this caused a little puzzlement in the locals who were dotted about and I felt obliged to stop and explain that I had rather overdone it, was really a bit old for mountain walking, and so on. Most of these rugged country folk were almost twice my age, yet were having no apparent trouble with the gradient themselves. They nodded sagely and sympathetically, watching me resume my somewhat idiotic performance. Needless to say, the following day Simon and I were both in a fair bit of pain but the days after that were so bad that we hobbled around quite pitifully. As luck would have it, I had hospital appointments on each of those days as well as my teaching duties, so there was no chance of putting my feet up with some good reading material, of which thankfully I had a constant supply from Sally, supplemented by the assorted dog-eared, second-hand books Simon picked up at the Sunday morning flea market.

Despite Sally's punishing workload from the university along with her various writing projects, she would always find time to meet up at weekends. We'd walk around the town talking about everything under the sun, sharing our joys and sorrows, gossiping about our tutors at CALS, both the charismatic and the less charismatic ones, taking it in turns to reminisce about our childhood and upbringing on opposite sides of the globe. I had always thought I had a good memory for detail, but Sally's was exceptional. We'd both been Brownies at the age of six or seven and I had very vague memories of our little brown tunics and badges, but that was about all. Not only was Sally able to describe a typical Brownie meeting run by Brown Owl in minute detail but she also remembered the very rhymes we used to chant around the toadstool – something about pixies always being there when people were in *fixes* and gnomes helping mothers in their *homes*! I was most impressed. The four of us would regularly meet for dinner, sometimes at our place but more often at theirs, a fifth-floor flat round the corner from Patrick's, with a lot of charm but no lift, which meant we would invariably arrive outside their door red in the face and gasping for air. We'd be given delicious prawn curries with cumin-studded poppadoms and would sit afterwards drinking Spanish wine beneath the bougainvillea on the roof terrace, watching their 'son', the beloved large kitten Max, retrieve balls as the sun set magnificently over the neighbouring rooftops.

Sally had a colleague at the university with an annual subscription to the beautiful old theatre in the town centre. She quite often had tickets to concerts, ballets and so on that she didn't intend using. Thanks to Sally, these tickets would be passed on to us and we saw some wonderful concerts performed by the Tenerife Symphony Orchestra – Debussy, Berlioz, Faure and, to Simon's delight, Mahler's Third Symphony. Several of the musicians were British and American expats and we would sometimes find ourselves chatting to them in the theatre bar in the interval. If I only quite enjoyed the Mahler evening (rather too much booming of drums for my liking), Simon was simply enthralled and sat on the edge of his seat gazing down from the front of the circle with rapt attention. The stage was so full of musicians, along with a fairly large choir of awkward-looking teenage schoolgirls, that one set of timpani was totally out of sight in the wings. I'm not sure if it was the actual appearance of the timpanist or his manner of playing but something obviously amused the girls. Each time the timpanist was about to start booming, all heads would turn to the left and we got the impression that there was much suppressed giggling. I could all too easily imagine my schoolgirl self and partner in crime, Charlotte, standing there in full view of the audience, desperately trying to stifle hilarity at hushed moments of the performance. The poor girls had to stand there for two hours, yet only sang for just over two minutes. As I sat listening to these concerts, I would find my mind wandering back to the ballet performances I'd taken part in as a child and young teenager – I would recall the smell of stage make-up, the fluttering butterflies of anticipation in the stomach as we stood in the wings, the roll of the drums, the surge of energy as we advanced onto the stage, the brightness and warmth of the stage lights, making the audience blend together in a golden, amorphous haze. I longed to be on the stage once more, the adrenalin pumping around my veins, moving sprite-like to the sound of flutes, stretching sinuously to the strains of violin and cello – I wanted the eyes of the audience on *me!* I wanted to hear the applause of a standing ovation – for *me!* I could but dream. It had been touch and go at one point in my early life as to whether I should follow my dance teacher Miss Lacy's advice and pursue ballet as a career, but a good set of exam results at grammar school swayed our decision against such a path. My pink satin ballet shoes and tutu somehow disappeared along with countless other childhood treasures while I was a student, when our family fortunes took a dramatic nosedive and our beloved rambling family house in North Wales, along with many of its contents, was sold.

We spent a brilliant Christmas with Sally and Jess along with some delightful, eccentric friends of theirs, the Slades. Also, a wonderfully boozy New Year's Eve party, at which we were treated to a long slide show of Jess's visit to Angkor Wat, which made me quite envious, as this was one of the places we'd intended going after finishing work in Chiang Mai. When twelve struck there was momentary panic as no one seemed sober enough to uncork the last vital bottle of champagne to mark the occasion. Somehow it was managed and as we stood outside together, the night air cooling our flushed cheeks, glasses replenished, watching the fireworks lighting up the inky sky, I had one of those waves of contentment when one knows that there is no other place on the planet one would rather be at that exact moment.

Carnival was approaching with all its weirdness and excesses. I found Sally's loathing for the event a little puzzling, but possibly if I'd lived in Santa Cruz for as many years as she had I might have found its allure wearing off a fraction too. It was certainly an extraordinarily noisy and frenetic affair, with much carousing and cavorting, which went on pretty much day and night for well over a week. The hype and scope of the Tenerife carnival was second only to the Brazilian one, with thousands of people flocking to the island in party mode from all corners of the earth. I think perhaps the first night was the one I enjoyed most, with its never-ending procession down the main street, people of all ages in wild and wonderful costumes strutting their stuff and gyrating to the drumbeat, flamboyant and fanciful floats with blaring Latin music, and all-night dancing in the main square beneath a fifty-foot model of Superman, fist outstretched and pupils flashing red, the overall theme of the carnival that year being comics. Never a lover of Latin music, Simon reacted, overall, to the whole thing with indifference and mild irritation but at least he stayed up with me the first evening until 1 am or so while I lapped it all up, dancing not with him but around him in my red sparkly wig and clingy cat outfit. Unfortunately, the wig I'd bought for the occasion was a bit big for my pin head and it tended to swivel around as I danced, which put me off my steps rather, but I refused to allow it to interfere with my enjoyment of the revelry and danced on into the early hours, happy as a clam. Another night I'd heard there was to be a magnificent firework display, so, continuing to embrace the carnival spirit, I borrowed a dalmatian costume. Sadly, what I'd thought to be a rather striking outfit became so unbearably hot amidst the milling throngs of revellers that I was compelled to spoil the effect by unzipping the top half and tying it around my waist, which made it very bulky but possibly saved me from the dangers of intimate dancing with fellow roisterers.

That would *have* to have been the evening I ran into some of my teenage Echeyde students, who seemed delighted to catch sight of their quirky English teacher dressed unbecomingly as an overheated spotted dog.

I was fascinated by the Burial of the Sardine, an event that marks the end of the carnival, on Ash Wednesday, and which some of my students claimed erroneously had originated in the Canaries. The parade parodies a funeral procession and culminates with the burning of a sardine, a symbolic burial of the past to allow society to be reborn and transformed with renewed vigour. There is a wonderful oil-on-panel painting of the event in Madrid in the 1810s by Goya. Masked and disguised revellers are seen dancing their way to the banks of the Manzanares River, where a ceremonial sardine is to be buried. Apparently, masks were worn to ward off the spirits of criminals and those who had died violently. In the overwrought gestures and expressions in the painting, one begins to feel the obscurely disturbing undertones of mass hysteria underlying the fiesta. In the Santa Cruz procession, streams of bizarre mourners filed past, weeping and wailing and tearing at their hair. Heavily made-up women and outrageous cross-dressers of all ages trooped by; on and on they came, clad in long, black, lacy garments and tight, satin, cleavage-enhancing bodices, blowing kisses and fluttering obscenely long eyelashes as they went. Close behind them came a motley assortment of men dressed as clergy, in cassocks and birettas, mostly rotund and florid with outsized crucifixes around their turkey necks, offering gaudy, bejewelled rings for people to kiss. They genuflected at chosen members of the roadside audience, occasionally revealing pages in their bibles with lurid depictions of naked women or lifting their tunics to show off toy rabbits attached to their crotch. A vulgar word for vagina in Spanish is '*conejo*', meaning rabbit. One particularly evil and lecherous-looking priest whispered to the woman next to me that his pink furry thing wasn't the real one – the real one was a *panda*! Many of the priests brandished dildos of various shapes, sizes and colours, using them in imaginative and startling ways. I found it all quite wild and wonderful, but then it was a novel experience for me and I was a great lover of theatre, Latin music and dancing – I wonder what my grandparents would have made of it all. I expect they'd have loved it too.

Winter turned almost overnight into spring and the town became ablaze with colour from the bougainvillea and flowering trees – purples, oranges, reds, yellows and pinks – and from the immaculate flowerbeds that lined the streets from one side of town to the other. The reason, I was told, for the roadside floral splendour was the upcoming elections – whatever the cause might have been, I was extremely appreciative as I spent around two hours a day on buses getting to and from work. Simon, poor thing, was too busy concentrating on negotiating the busy roads in the little death trap to notice the flowers along the way.

Keen to make as much headway as possible, not only in my Spanish but also in my Latin dancing, I entered into an arrangement with a dark and highly strung young Venezuelan woman I'd been introduced to called Norka (or Norks by Simon, who informed me casually when I asked that it was a slang word for breasts). The plan was that I would give Norka a one-hour English lesson and in exchange, she would give me an hour of Latin dance tuition – I was especially keen to improve my salsa and merengue moves. We soon discovered that I knew about as many dancing steps as Norka did, so we decided she would give me a Spanish lesson instead. As it turned out, Norka didn't have any observable Spanish teaching skills either, so between us we improvised and developed what I came to call the anecdotal method. Using the bits of Spanish that I'd taught myself from books and picked up on the street and in local hospitals, I'd launch into an account of the day's activities, concentrating on anything amusing or embarrassing that had happened to me – there was no shortage of such experiences. Norka would listen in pained silence while I struggled valiantly on, guessing wildly at vocabulary and mangling my tenses so horribly that her frown would deepen until she could bear it no more and would bark out a correction, 'Mala*con*, mala*con*, not *ma*la*con!*', sighing and writing out the worst of my mistakes with obvious reluctance, as though it was all a terrible chore and there wasn't a lot of hope for me. Actually, on days when we both had more energy, we'd have a lot of fun, particularly when joined by Patrick's stunning-looking Canarian girlfriend, Esther, for a drink at the local bar. Once we got started gossiping and telling stories there was no stopping us and we'd invariably end up crying with laughter on each other's shoulders, the jokes often being at my expense, which didn't bother me in the slightest. One of the better outcomes of my upbringing was that I believed it not only to be an advantage but also positively essential to be able to laugh at oneself.

Norka was blessed with a highly likeable husband, Jorge, a native of Tenerife with an MBA from New Orleans University. He was tall, dark, devastatingly good-looking and extremely witty, but incredibly sadly at the time we met him was going rapidly blind. Despite this, so we heard, he resisted help from Norka at home and as a result was constantly crashing into furniture, breaking things and sometimes hurting himself quite badly. Norka's nerves were shot to bits and, not having any rewarding occupation besides trying to look after her husband and shopping for clothes and perfume, she was anxious to get away – for how long, I wasn't sure – to the land of her dreams, England. She asked me if I knew anyone who wanted an au pair – all she required, she told me, was her own bathroom and she'd be off in a flash. I found their domestic situation and the state of their marriage rather puzzling and upsetting. They clearly adored each other but the stress they were both under on account of Jorge's deteriorating vision was taking a heavy toll. People with disabilities such as Jorge's, however, are well looked after in Spain and many of them make a living selling national lottery tickets on the pavement. This was, in fact, what Jorge was doing at the time we met. It seemed such a criminal waste of his intelligence and qualifications, but he never complained to us – on the contrary, he seemed to be one of the cheeriest people on the island.

One evening Norka invited us over to their flat for what she claimed was her absolute favourite Venezuelan food – corn griddle cakes, or 'arepas' – she was very keen that we should try this national dish and had built them up to be something very special indeed. We took wine and chocolates and looked forward to trying some Venezuelan home-cooking. Unfortunately, we were in for a bit of a shock – the arepas, when they were presented, looked and felt like flat, anaemic stones and frankly were about as appetising. A blob of margarine and a feeble filling of processed ham and cheese slices did little to mitigate the culinary ordeal. The meal consisted solely of arepas, and we quickly gathered that the idea was to eat as many of them as possible. We did our best, but I fear our performance was not impressive. Fortunately, the company more than made up for the pitiful meal. We cracked jokes and told anecdotes until the early hours of the morning, translating into Spanish or English for Norka and Simon's benefit, which, rather than becoming a bore, seemed instead on that occasion to add to the fun.

I told the story of the time my Parisian friend, Agnes, had come to visit me in Crete, when I was teaching at the little school in Chania. On my day off we'd taken a bus to the western tip of the island, where we discovered a deserted beach bordered by magnificent mature fig trees laden with fruit. Already being an experienced fig scrumper and connoisseur, I taught my friend which ones were the most succulent and desirable, and so, along with a few other choice picnic items I'd brought along, we had a rare al fresco feast. Taking advantage of our solitude, we discarded our clothes and had a glorious dip in the cool, turquoise waters, floating on our backs, lining up the soles of our feet so they touched each other's and swimming through shoals of tiny darting silvery fish. Unlike me, Agnes had never been one for sunbathing, so after a stroll to the end of the bay and back we headed back up to the bus stop. Halfway back to town, bowling along the coastal plain on a fully loaded local bus, the figs started to take their well-known laxative effect on my friend and before she knew it Agnes had an urgent call of nature. Seeing her distress and judging the problem to be travel sickness, a dear old couple, sitting beside us, kindly offered her a paper bag, to which Agnes rather rudely retorted '*Oh là là! Merde, dis donc!*', before rushing up to the front of the bus and begging the driver to stop the bus that instant. Visibly fuming and glowering at this foreign irritant, the driver reluctantly acquiesced and the bus ground to a halt. The only thing was there wasn't a bush in sight, so poor Agnes had to more or less climb a nearby mountain until she found a shrub large enough to hide behind, while the whole busload of curious passengers looked eagerly on. Some days later, Jorge told me that he kept thinking of the tale of Agnes and the figs as he sat on his street corner awaiting customers and found himself unable to stifle loud guffaws. I hoped people wouldn't avoid him, thinking he'd gone bonkers. During my tediously long commutes to and from work, I would think of Jorge laughing out loud on his street corner and would smile or even chuckle to myself, quite possibly causing fellow passengers to doubt my sanity too.

Another unforgettable evening with Norka and Jorge was the one we went to see a flamenco show. We had rather cheap seats right at the side near the front of the theatre, so had to lean forwards and peer to the right – even then we could only see about two-thirds of the stage. The main character Yerma was performed by a very dramatic and magnificent dancer of some renown, Carmen Cortes. Of course, it all ended in tears with histrionics and daggers and a pile of dead bodies but it was marvellous entertainment. There had been so much frenzied stamping of feet throughout the show that when we emerged from the theatre, we didn't even try to restrain ourselves. The three of us stomped and clapped our way down the road, inhibitions carried off into oblivion by the salty night breeze. Just as we calmed down and I thought we'd got it out of our system, Jorge would shout 'Hola, Carrie!' and off we'd go once more. Sadly, we lost touch with Norka and Jorge, but I feel sure that, wherever he is, Jorge at least will remember the figs and the flamenco every bit as clearly as I do and I hope he remembers us with as much affection as we remember him.

Sharing a house with Patrick and the dogs was not ideal. With my urticaria reaching its peak a couple of months after we arrived in Santa Cruz, I would have to get up several times during the night for a cold shower to stop the diabolical itching and I was worried I was disturbing our host. We started searching for a place of our own to rent – not a day too soon for Simon – and found a small but interesting one-bedroom flat down by the western edge of the seafront in a mainly residential area called Anaga. We had to pay quite a bit extra for a flat with a sea view, but we felt it would be worth it. From our balcony on the fourth floor, we looked down on rows of assorted flowering trees lining the seafront and the multi-coloured flags of the exclusive nautical club. The entrance to the club was illuminated in the shape of a huge cross, which, together with the fairy lights in the palm trees before it and the three wise men on camels, looked more like something out of Las Vegas than the sedate and slightly sophisticated place it was meant to be. Beyond the nautical club was the entrance to the port, which had a steady stream of boats and ships of every description, from inter-island jetfoils to huge, sleek, shining luxury liners and even – to Simon's delight – warships with 'stealth technology'. Some of the monster vessels were so colossal and approached at such a lick that the first few days we were there we felt they might come crashing into our very living room. We loved our nautical view and it seemed funny to me that one of my private students, Cololla, who lived on the other side of the building, couldn't see the attraction of a sea view at all. Just as we had felt in Auckland that the superb sunsets that we saw from our west-facing balcony were staged expressly for us, so here in Anaga the spectacle of the sea traffic, reminiscent of ballet in slow motion, was like an ongoing show choreographed for our own personal entertainment.

I have refrained up until now from mentioning the urticaria, except in passing, as ailments such as this don't normally constitute riveting reading. The condition did, however, dominate my life the whole of my nine months in Tenerife and it gave me some interesting insights into the Spanish medical system, even leading to a few curious encounters. We had thought that getting away from the UK to a more relaxed island lifestyle might be just what I needed to get the beastly thing out of my system, but we were wrong. From the moment we arrived, the hives increased in size and severity and before long they covered me pretty much from head to toe. Sometimes during the night my upper lip would swell up alarmingly and Simon would find himself waking up next to someone who looked more like Donald Duck than the fair female form he'd gone to bed with. What with the swollen lip and red patches, which sometimes resembled bruises, all over my face, I feel sure some of my colleagues at the school thought I'd come to the island accompanied by a vile British wife-batterer. Thankfully most of my classes were in the afternoon and early evening, the time of day when the hives tended to be a bit less angry and noticeable.

I started off talking to pharmacists and trying various antihistamine tablets, none of which were of any help whatsoever. Getting myself a GP in Tenerife proved to be a long test of patience and stamina that started to approach Kafkaesque dimensions. Being ill on this island, I was to learn, could become a full-time occupation and the queueing it required a way of life. Over a fairly short period of time, I must have walked many miles and spent dozens of hours in queues in countless old buildings, all teeming with people who generally looked a lot older and poorer than me – and visibly sicker. Each time I reached the front of a queue I would invariably be told that it was another department or another building altogether that I needed. My Spanish, admittedly, was not very good at this stage, but I have the feeling that the situation would not have been so different even if I had been quite fluent in the language. I learned the hard way that there were three hospitals in town, all of which I tracked down with some difficulty in driving rain before finding that the third and last one was the one I needed.

In the first hospital I had joined a long queue, resigning myself to an hour or so's wait. As I was standing there an old biddy came bustling in from the rain and started pushing her way to the front of the queue. Not a soul tried to stop her so I felt compelled to say – quite gently – I'm sorry, but we were all here before you. Her eye started twitching wildly and I wondered if she might lash out or start crying. Instead, she became quite submissive, mumbling 'Claro, claro!' (clearly), joining the end of the queue and meekly waiting her turn. When I finally found myself facing a receptionist, I was given short shrift and told the hospital I needed was elsewhere. The second hospital would have made a good setting for a Lowry painting – countless grey nondescript individuals milled around or sat hunched up and lifeless waiting for goodness knows what. An orderly told me authoritatively which line to wait in but it was the wrong line and even reaching the head of the queue in the right line proved fruitless, as, once again, I was in the wrong building altogether.

At the third hospital there were three women behind the reception desk, who didn't appear to be busy and there were no other patients waiting. Despite this, I had to ask to be served. The old matron who approached me was obviously against me from the start. Despite presenting my various documents carefully and politely for her to inspect, she sneeringly demanded the one paper I didn't have (my work permit), though what this should have to do with medical care I didn't see. At this point I began to get quite stroppy and started pointing out, possibly inaccurately, that when Spanish people need medical care in the UK it is immediate and free. To this she promptly turned her back on me and telephoned, I imagine, a superior. When she put the phone down her manner was still not encouraging but she started filling in forms and cards and it gradually sank in that at long last I was about to become a legitimate patient of the Spanish NHS. When she handed me the card and pointed to what looked like a doctor's surgery on the first floor above us, I forced a kind of smile and thanked her, apologising rather obsequiously for my poor Spanish. To my amazement, she responded in what appeared to be a very sincere manner, apologising for her lack of English and smiling almost sympathetically. I had never seen such a transformation. Sally had had so many of these strange changes of manner in colleagues, shop assistants and so on during her time in Tenerife that she'd formed various psychological theories, one of them being that with initial contact great formality, even curtness with shop assistants, is appropriate and commands far more respect than politeness and friendliness, which is often mistrusted and taken as being manipulative in some way.

Still smiling in bewilderment, I mounted the old wooden steps and, seeing a patient come out of the doctor's room, took the liberty of putting my head around the door expectantly. To my delight, I was invited in by a sweet, old, white-haired gent who couldn't have been a day under eighty. We soon established that our best common language was probably German, but I kept lapsing into Spanish and the doctor soon started throwing in a bit of English and by the time we came to say goodbye we were no doubt including French and Italian and anything else that came into our heads. The dear man was very keen to write me some prescriptions but as neither of us seemed sure what I needed he wrote out a referral note instead to see a dermatologist. When I asked how I should make the appointment he smiled and shrugged and said cheerily, 'I don't know!', which I took as a sign to leave and be grateful.

The staff at the allergy clinic were not a lot more help. After much queueing, form filling and waiting in cheerless waiting rooms, I finally got to see a consultant, who was extremely curt and cool at first, firing questions at me in reasonable English, reminding me constantly to answer *his* questions only. He really should have listened to me as I had informed him that I was currently taking two types of antihistamine, which made all the testing they subsequently did on my arm (leaving a pattern of black spots that the school children found intriguing) totally invalid. The second session with him, after I suspect he'd consulted his notes and noticed I'd been referred by the back door by his mate Dr de Vera, a brain surgeon and a miserly private student of mine, he was far more civil and informed me that he believed I wasn't suffering from an allergy at all but nevertheless a very real illness, mainly experienced by women, related usually to stress, philosophy of life and happiness. I was told that he'd have to wait for the results of the specimen analysis before drawing any conclusions, but in the meantime, I should try to relax and *be happy*!

I'm not sure if this is the case on the Spanish mainland but in Tenerife there seemed to be an obsession with collecting and analysing bodily fluids. On the various occasions when I entered into this rigmarole myself, the members of staff who received the specimens were so surly and nonchalant I was quite sure they regularly mixed them up. No frills such as the luxury of privacy for blood collection – again the inevitable queue, but this time with the novelty of being able to observe the dozen or so people in front of one sitting mournfully side by side on hard wooden chairs, while the nurses stabbed, dabbed and dismissed each in turn. Just as I was sitting down for my own ordeal, I was not reassured when one nurse appeared to fling a small bottle of blood to the floor, which smashed at my feet, narrowly missing my new crimson leather ballerina pumps.

Not feeling I was making any progress with NHS doctors, I finally decided to go private, signing up with a female dermatologist, who had been recommended by Sally and whose surgery was up above Santa Cruz in La Laguna, the former capital of Tenerife, home of the oldest university on the island. Each time I made the bus journey up the hill to see her, the waiting room was so packed some people had to stand and the waiting time was never less than an hour, sometimes nearer two. As I got to know her, I found it increasingly puzzling that her services were so much in demand. She was short, stout and imperious looking, with cropped dark hair and narrow calculating eyes that exuded malevolence. The woman was totally devoid of warmth or any other positive human attribute and I'd be really hard-pressed to think of a single redeeming feature. Halfway through each consultation a sadistic glint would come into her shark-like eyes and she would place the top meaningfully onto her biro. It was time for our strange little ritual. '*Quitate la blusa!*' (Take off your blouse!) she'd bark then would rise and rapidly approach my chair, standing directly behind me and making dramatic slashes with her capped pen on the exposed bare skin of my back, creating a giant cross like the mark of Zorro, waiting to see how quickly and angrily the weals would rise. I came to believe that her modus operandi originated in some horrific childhood trauma from which she would never fully recover.

Strangely enough, I had dealings with another female dermatologist a few years later in the UAE, who remarkably similarly appeared to take joy in inflicting pain on my back. I had developed a few small sunspots – actinic keratoses – that needed to be zapped with liquid nitrogen. She'd appeared bored and dejected when I entered her office and was almost slouching at her desk in an off-white lab coat. The minute I showed her the spots on my leg and arm, she came to life and rapidly instructed me to remove my blouse for a back inspection. Perhaps I should have read the warning signs. 'Return at the same time tomorrow,' I was told, and when I did so, it was as though a different person altogether stood before me. The doctor had applied make-up, had clearly been to the hairdresser and was dressed in a striking canary yellow outfit. Within minutes I was lying face-down on the operating table and the torture began. It was so painful the nurse had to practically hold me down and when I got home that evening and looked in the mirror, I was horrified to see my back was simply covered in red blisters where I'd been zapped, apparently at random. I should have got Simon to photograph my back before the 'treatment' as I can't have had more than four or five small spots that needed attention. I hadn't actually realised I had any at all other than on my legs and arms. I believe I counted almost twenty blisters and there wasn't a thing I could do to prove her crime – she had got trigger happy with her liquid nitrogen gun and I strongly suspect her motives had been mercenary, payment being, no doubt, per spot treated.

I always had a sneaking suspicion that the La Laguna dermatologist spoke perfectly acceptable English, but on the half dozen or so times I saw her she refused to speak a single word, which meant I was compelled to struggle to communicate in Spanish, unless her young assistant, who was able to interpret for us both and made life very much easier, was present. After examining a list of all the medication I'd taken over the past year, she had ascertained that my condition was almost certainly stress-related and had put me on a cocktail of around six pills, one of which was a powerful tranquilliser called Lexatin. This interesting drug is mentioned in some of the films of the legendary Spanish director Pedro Almodóvar, by various colourful characters living on the fringes of society, who use it for recreational purposes. After I'd been taking the shiny red and white capsules for a few months I happened to read the blurb on the notes inside the packet and was most perturbed to learn that it was described as a drug for use with 'severe psychiatric cases, only for short periods – no longer than four weeks'. I resolved to speak to the dermatologist about this at my next appointment. When I did so, the gorgon hit the roof and, turning an alarming shade of crimson, virtually shouted at me that *she* was the one who controlled the drugs, all I had to do was *follow* her instructions. This was not a request, it was a command. I decided to defy her and stop taking the tranquillisers, bringing upon myself what must have been a taste of cold turkey. During the day I felt distinctly edgy and at night would have the most terrifying dreams. It was as though I had stumbled unwittingly into a David Lynch film. Everywhere I looked there were bloodied knives, decomposing bodies and hideous ghouls intent on murder, rape and pillage. The atmosphere was one of dread, debauchery and downright evil. I'd awaken in a feverish state, trembling and disorientated, fearful of going back to sleep. After a couple of nights of this, I quietly resumed my drug regimen and was told much later, when I returned to Brighton and saw a dermatologist on the NHS, that in the UK Lexatin was categorised as a class A drug, that it was rarely used and most certainly not to treat urticaria. She told me that I would have to be weaned off it gradually, so that was what happened. At least now when one of Almodóvar's characters asks another if they have any Lexies I know exactly what they are talking about. I still have a few left in a little Chinese box somewhere in my bedroom, in case of emergencies.

On one of my weekend walks with Sally I must have been bemoaning the fact that Simon and I seemed to be doing a lot of running around working for not very much money. Once we'd paid the rent and other living costs, there was precious little left and the situation was not helped by the fact that some of my private students were very slow indeed to pay for their lessons. The wealthiest of the bunch, I had no doubt, was my brain surgeon, yet even after three polite letters reminding him of his outstanding bill he still had not coughed up. A little sleuth work had revealed his private address, so one weekend I had brazenly knocked on his door, enquiring politely after his health and asking what, if anything, was preventing him from paying me. As usual, he smelled of whisky and beat around the bush regarding payment, but did actually find a few notes in his wallet that covered what he owed. I learned from Sally that he had been going through an acrimonious divorce. His wife had just had an unbelievably expensive round of cosmetic surgery carried out at the doctor's expense, then had promptly left him. He may well not have deserved such treatment, but I'm afraid it was hard not to smile at hearing of his fall from grace.

Sally commiserated with me about our dismal financial situation then suggested – very tentatively – that I consider doing what another slightly impoverished yet well-educated, middle-aged Australian friend of hers had done – to bite the bullet and sign a three-year contract with the Higher Colleges of Technology in the UAE, an organisation that was recognised at the time as being the one that offered the 'best package' for EFL teachers. A couple of contracts and some careful saving should top up the kitty nicely and give us a lot more options about our future. I wasn't keen, but I knew she was right. Using one of her three computers, Sally helped me word process my CV and I sent it off to a former colleague and friend from the Brighton language school, Marie Louise, who was already working at Sharjah Women's College. She in turn passed my CV on to Tim Smith, then Head of English, apparently with the recommendation that I was 'a gifted English teacher'. It was duly reported back to me that all looked good but that I would need to attend an interview at the Emirati Embassy in London, before any final decisions could be made. I'd had a horrible feeling all along that I would be accepted, and it was with a heavy heart that I prepared to leave our Spanish island home, which held rather more happy memories than otherwise. Simon, not surprisingly, opted for the long route home via ferry and bus, leaving a little before me so as to be available for teaching during the peak period in Brighton. I took the early morning coach to the airport from Santa Cruz and was extremely touched when Sally materialised unexpectedly at the coach station to see me off. We had become quite close and the parting was all the more of a wrench as we both knew it could be many a moon before our paths crossed again.

Chapter 14

Full Circle

It was all very well the Head of English, Tim Smith, glancing at my CV in his office at Sharjah Women's College (SWC) and saying: 'Yep, we'll have her!', and then me learning of this pronouncement in Tenerife via my friend Marie Louise, now one of the SWC inmates. There were actually plenty of hoops to jump through before everything was signed, sealed and delivered. To begin with, there was a lengthy application form that needed to be completed using a word processor and submitted via email. This was 1999 and, as Sally had gently pointed out on her leafy terrace in Santa Cruz, I was not, as I had believed myself to be, PC literate and had never even set foot in an internet café. Within hours of touching down at Gatwick airport and reclaiming my little flat in Brighton, I had signed up for a Clait course (Computer Literacy and Information Technology) at an adult education centre in a scruffy old building somewhere near Brighton swimming pool. I motored through the two levels I'd paid for, in record time according to the tutor, and flew off to the internet café in Kemptown to attempt the online application form to SWC. I ended up in tears over the ropey old keyboard, having lost in the twinkling of an eye most of what I had so carefully composed and typed up during the hour I had paid for. The following day Simon came with me and helped. We had to race against the clock compiling suitably impressive lists of academic abilities and achievements, with the manager of the pokey, sweaty internet café hovering grouchily behind us, clearly keen to close up and get down to the pub for a pint of cold beer.

Our efforts were not in vain, however, as I was called for a video conferencing interview the following week at the Emirati Embassy. Aware that Sharjah was one of the most conservative of the seven emirates, having close links with Saudi Arabia, I decided to wear a long black skirt and a smart red tunic top with three-quarter-length sleeves. On the train from Brighton up to London I paid a visit to the loo and emerged with a dark horizontal stripe just below navel level, which I must have picked up from the grimy washbasin. Darned Southern Rail, not only do they fail to get people to their destinations on time, but they also skimp on cleaning services so that passengers emerge from their lavatories exasperated and in need of a dry cleaner. Fortunately, I had left myself plenty of time before the interview to find the building and as luck would have it a dressmaker's shop simply materialised before my very eyes almost as soon as I emerged from the Underground. On enquiring if the hem of the garment might be craftily turned up to hide the stain, I was greatly relieved to hear that it would be no problem at all – I could pick it up in a week's time. After hastily explaining my conundrum, I beat a hasty exit. Just a few doors down the road there happened to be a pharmacy, so in I dived, scouring the shelves for a DIY dry cleaning kit. I was in luck – they had exactly what I was looking for. Before the bemused-looking shop assistant had even handed me my change, I had shaken up the aerosol can and sprayed my midriff with a thick layer of foam. As I waited for it to take effect I strolled up and down the aisles explaining to curious onlookers what had necessitated this baffling behaviour and feeling rather pleased with myself for dealing with the catastrophe so calmly and competently. The sad thing was that the product was absolutely useless. Brushing the dried foam vigorously with the little brush provided did nothing whatsoever to remove the stain; it just teased the nap of the fabric in a very unsatisfactory manner. Strangely enough, I found myself sauntering up the street to the embassy in a philosophical frame of mind. I would puff up my chest, smile radiantly at the interviewers and hold my hands demurely over my middle – no one would be any the wiser. Besides, they would be so riveted by my clever and original answers to their questions, they would barely notice what I was wearing. I applied an extra layer of mascara in the embassy cloakroom and touched up my red lipstick, and, just as I had envisaged, it all proceeded swimmingly. Years later at a party in a grandiose apartment overlooking Sharjah corniche, I got chatting to Tim Smith, who had been one of the two interviewers that day at the Emirati embassy. I told him the story of the dirty red top and he was so amused he said he would dig the video out of his cupboard the following week and we'd have a good laugh over it in the morning break – sad to say this never happened.

A few days after my interview a formal offer of employment arrived in the post along with reams of paperwork, which I rapidly skimmed through, searching mainly for the starting date and salary. Curiously, I had turned down the original fairly decent salary I was offered, prompted, I believe, by Simon to ask for quite a bit more. It worked and at least I embarked on my stint in Arabia on what I felt to be rather a generous tax-free salary. I was not going to the UAE for the culture, the cuisine, or the carousing. I was about to make the ultimate sacrifice – my freedom and in all likelihood my well-being as a free spirit – in an attempt to make provisions for my old age. For the first time in my life, I was not following my heart, I was following my reasoning. It was a brave and grand experiment and, though friends wished me well on my Arabian adventure, painting romantic pictures of supping with Bedouins and their camels in the desert, mingling with sheikhs and their hawks beneath swaying date palms, dipping my toes in the tepid, turquoise Gulf waters, I knew before I set foot in the country that it was very probably not a place where I would be really happy. I would grin and bear it, work hard and save what I could. Anything good that came out of it would be serendipitous. The only thing I actually looked forward to was the warmth in winter.

Simon and I knew that cohabitation in the UAE was a risky business and, as I had applied to the Higher Colleges of Technology (HCT) as a single person, we thought it prudent for me to go on ahead to see how the land lay before he joined me out there. On the flight to Dubai with Emirates I found myself seated next to a balding, faintly roguish-looking engineer with beetling brows from Edinburgh, who at one point during the flight somewhat vainly compared himself to secret agent James Bond. He emanated, however, a certain *joie de vivre* that impressed me so we chatted away merrily for most of the journey, stopping only for dinner and the inflight movie, *The Matrix*, which, possibly due to our liberal consumption of inflight beverages, took on a fantastically surreal air, enchanting us both in equal measure. I learned from my new friend that professional expats in the UAE worked hard and played hard and that if I understood this, I'd be sure to have a ball. We exchanged contact details and Mr Bond, as I had come to know him, was later invited to our wedding do at Dubai Creek Golf and Yacht Club, accompanied by a very much younger French woman, who actually ditched him soon afterwards, I learned, claiming that he had behaved in an unacceptable and highly ungentlemanly manner. That was the last I saw or heard of Mr Bond.

Arriving at Dubai airport I had the forethought to buy a bottle of Harvey's Bristol Cream sherry (my first choice would have been Amontillado but unfortunately there was none to be had). With Sharjah being a dry emirate, it was not possible to just pop down to the supermarket to buy alcohol. One needed first to obtain a liquor licence from Sharjah police station, which involved messing around with ink pads while all ten digits were imprinted for eternity in their records, then one had to drive to a neighbouring emirate – in fact to the next but one emirate, Umm Al Quwain – to a liquor shop called the Barracuda, which stocked a good range of wines and spirits at very reasonable prices. Despite the Muslim ban on alcohol, many of the big spenders at the Barracuda were stout, sophisticated mature Emiratis in snow-white flowing robes. Cheerful and unabashed they could be seen striding through the sandy car park to their gleaming brand-new Toyota Land Cruisers, their trolleys piled high with every alcoholic libation known to man. One of my first questions to Tim Smith during our telephone interview had been 'Will I be able to drink legally in Sharjah?' 'Oh, yes,' I was assured, 'we all like a bevvy here. You can always get a drink at the Wanderers Club, just down the road from the college, and what you do at home is your own business.' As it turned out, a large percentage of the employees of the HCT were keen drinkers. Spirits were roughly half the price they were in the UK and though wine was rather more, what with tax-free salaries, free health care and no rent to pay, one could stock up on booze and party the night away at weekends without feeling the slightest pinch. Most of the really serious drinkers somehow got away with it, but a few didn't and ended up being escorted soberly to the airport, carrying whatever possessions they were able to grab on the way.

The first two weeks in the UAE as new recruits were what was known as the honeymoon period. We were put up at one of the better Sharjah hotels, in my case the Holiday Inn on the north shore of the emirate. We received a daily food allowance and were not expected to go into the college to work. Unless we had an appointment in the lobby with someone from HCT to fill in forms or sign papers, we were free to sunbathe, sight-see or even go shopping in the local souq for carpets, sequin-studded gowns or gold. After arriving on a morning flight, I had hastily unpacked, donned some swimwear and headed down to the hotel pool to sample a few rays of Arabian sun. Despite my time in Bahrain during the muggy, mid-year pea-soup season, I was not prepared for the extreme baking clamminess that awaited me beyond the overly cool air-conditioned inner areas of the hotel. After no more than ten minutes or so, I could feel my face turning a darker shade of puce and, admitting defeat, retreated into the shade of an umbrella, which actually was more or less the same temperature as it was in the direct sun. It was whilst I was gathering up my towel, book, sun-cream and so on that a Western woman of about my age with large green eyes and a reddish glint in her hair approached and addressed me confidently in a strong Northern Irish accent. She appeared to know my name and introduced herself as Maria Hughes, another newbie who had flown in from Belfast just after me that day. We became friends almost instantly and within half an hour of meeting discovered, to our amazement, that we had both almost gone out with the same intense-looking blonde English teacher, a certain Andy Harvey. Maria had met him working in Athens and he had later been on the first module of my MA course at Reading University. Some years later Maria and I stopped off for a week's holiday in Greece on our way back to the UAE for the Autumn term. We decided to give the poor man a surprise by turning up on his doorstep in Athens, unannounced. Not unsurprisingly, it being a weekday, he was not in residence. I don't think we left him a note, but we really should have done

– perhaps we were foolishly unequipped with paper and pen. We toasted our new friendship that evening in my hotel room before dinner with an aperitif from my dark blue bottle of Harvey's Bristol Cream – an appropriately named drink, we felt, after the discovery of our mutual friend earlier in the day. We headed down to the coffee shop for a light dinner and noticed something on the menu with the interesting name of *fattoush*. The waiter had some difficulty describing it, but as he assured us it was '*taïm*' and typical Emirati fare, we decided to give it a go. It turned out to be a wonderful choice – a crisp mixed salad, which included mint, parsley, lettuce, radishes, cucumber and red onion, strewn with small crunchy wafers spiced with sumac and zaatar. Health-giving and utterly delicious. The food in the UAE, we were soon to discover, was one of the better aspects of the country.

Our first appointment in Sharjah was to a clinic for an HIV test, courtesy of HCT. I also seem to remember having a chest x-ray in rather a primitive sort of shed; that didn't inspire confidence in the country's medical facilities. I later came to appreciate the medical system rather more. One could roll up at our local hospital, Al Zahra, with just about any ailment under the sun, see a GP, usually within ten minutes or so, sometimes less, and then be directed to the consultant who dealt with the part of the body that was posing problems. Most of this VIP treatment was covered by our medical insurance policy, even procedures that verged on the cosmetic – varicose vein or mole removal, for instance. The trouble was, some of the less scrupulous medical practitioners took full advantage of this situation with expats and recommended treatment that really wasn't necessary at all. On one occasion I went for a standard gynaecological check-up and was told I needed to be operated on immediately, as I had a suspicious-looking growth that had to be whipped out and analysed. Fortunately, when I got back to work my medical colleague and dear friend Nishi smelled a rat and arranged for me to be examined later that day at her husband's spanking new fertility clinic, Conceive, using state-of-the-art equipment. There was nothing wrong with my insides whatsoever – it would seem that this woman had forgotten her Hippocratic oath and had taken to worshipping at the altar of Mammon. It was at the same hospital that I came across the manic Syrian dermatologist who went berserk with the liquid nitrogen gun in an attempt to rid me of a large crop of non-existent sun spots. Funnily enough, I have rather pleasant memories of my regular visits to Al Zahra Hospital. To begin with, the GP I usually saw, Dr Abdullah, was a highly personable and excellent doctor, who took time to ask me about my life and travel plans as soon as the medical stuff had been dealt with. Added to this there was a magnificent frangipani tree just outside the main entrance that was covered in gorgeous fragrant flowers throughout the year. I would always choose a perfect one from the sprinkler-moistened grass below the tree on arrival and discreetly sniff at it as I waited inside to see a doctor.

Once the initial honeymoon period medical checks had been done, Maria and I were escorted by a good-looking but obsequious and vaguely shifty-looking accommodation officer, Yunis, to open a bank account into which a generous lump sum (around £5,000 sterling) was deposited to furnish our flats and villas, the latter generally being allocated to families only. Some of the more parsimonious colleagues managed to avoid buying brand-new furniture by keeping an eagle eye out for messages on notice boards written by departing colleagues, who would often sell the entire contents of their homes for laughably little. With stores like IKEA and Home Centre, however, as well as some of the funkier shops cum warehouses – Pinky's and Lucky's – that imported interesting ethnic furniture from places like Rajasthan, it was possible to furnish our spacious accommodation easily and tastefully for well under the allowance we received. It was the first and only time I have been in the position of furnishing a home from scratch at someone else's expense. Of course, the money was technically ours – it was part of the HCT package, only to be returned *pro rata* if we broke the three-year contract – but it somehow felt like a gift. The price we were about to start paying for this privilege was not yet known.

Maria and I would scour the shops together, loading our trolleys up at IKEA and the rather more exclusive The One in Dubai with gay abandon, staggering home to unpack our wares – it was a bit like Christmas, only we got exactly what we wanted rather than the so often disappointing choices others had made on our behalf. On one such outing we were examining beds at a Dubai department store when a desperately good-looking and extremely suave Emirati gent clad in a dazzling white dishdasha and sporting an immaculately trimmed, shiny black beard, approached us, permeating the air with expensive, spice-laden perfume. It was all we could do to remain composed and upright – I'm quite sure Maria would have tumbled onto the bed beside us with this magnetic stranger as happily as I would – we could hardly breathe for rampant pheromones. It transpired that our conversant was in the furniture business himself. He suggested in the subtlest manner possible that we might like to compare the beds at his shop, Pier Exports, before making our final decisions. 'Ah,' I exclaimed, 'so you work at Pier Exports! Are you by chance the manager?' (I knew of this shop as we had a branch in Brighton – I'd bought a couple of sale items there after a shop fire the previous year.) At this our Prince Charming handed us each a business card and it instantly became evident that he was not just the manager – he *was* Pier Exports he owned the whole caboodle and probably many more enterprises besides. We carried his card around in our purses for ages, daring each other to ring him up, as he had begged us to do, should we require help of any sort. It's one of those business cards I can never quite bring myself to throw away when I'm doing a cull. Dr Faisal remains firmly planted in my memory – and no doubt Maria's too.

As I've already mentioned, Maria and I were the last of the SWC new recruits to arrive that year, so were allocated the two flats no one else had wanted, the dregs lodgings wise, though smarmy Yunis hotly denied this when we verbalised our discontent. They were in Kalooti Towers, a new apartment block near the lagoon and its surrounding palm-fringed corniche. There was nothing really wrong with them; they were decent enough, spacious one-bedroomed apartments with well-equipped kitchens, shiny marble floors and large plate glass windows. The kitchens, however, were without windows, so not a room where one would want to spend any longer than one had to. More seriously, we felt, there were no balconies and the outlook was not out to sea or of the picturesque corniche but over a bit of waste ground with a sad little collection of corrugated iron-roofed workmen's shacks, a little like a mini shanty town. As Simon still smoked at that time I was rather counting on a flat with outdoor space or a balcony. Also, I suppose I was looking ahead to times we might have parties where again the smokers could puff away under the stars without fear of irritating others. I decided to take the bull by the horns and went to see our boss Farid's secretary the following day to ask if another flat might be found for me. Next thing I knew Farid himself came pouncing out of his adjoining office like a crazed jack in a box, his dark gimlet eyes boring into me like a drill: 'So, Ms Evans, I hear you are not satisfied with your accommodation!' To my muttered apologetic response, he took a slow audible breath and announced, 'Make do! We'll see what can be arranged in your second year,' before wheeling round and returning to his lair as suddenly as he had emerged. So, for that first interminable year, having little choice, I made do.

There were other HCT staff in the building, but though we passed them in the lobby most mornings and sometimes found ourselves closeted in the lift with them, no one asked if we were from the college or introduced themselves – they, the initiated, remained reserved and faintly supercilious, clearly choosing not to deign to befriend us mere fledglings. That was part of the trouble with SWC; our college was so large, and employed such a rapidly growing staff, there was an unhealthily competitive atmosphere with constant back-biting and tedious internal politics. There was no alternative but to become a rugged individual, ideally carving a niche for oneself and concentrating on doing what one did best, other than teaching, whether it was teacher development, academic research, management or something else. In my case, I decided to concentrate on materials writing, as it was something I enjoyed and that my colleagues seemed to appreciate. One of my lovely Irish colleagues, Claire, a tall willowy lass with striking pale blue eyes and corn-coloured hair, would occasionally ring me at my workstation from the other side of the campus with an anguished plea for a lesson on third conditionals or some such grammar point and I would send something over. Not only did she give me the honour of naming me Materials Queen, but would sometimes leave a box of the most exquisite hand-made chocolates, fresh from her husband's factory, on my desk the following morning.

Just before leaving the UK, I had spent an afternoon chatting to a former HCT employee, who had offered to give me 'the low-down' before I set off. The gist of her advice was basically not to trust a soul. 'It's a cut-throat world over there,' I was informed. 'Assume there is a tiger behind every tree, just waiting to stab you in the back.' An interesting mixed metaphor, I remember thinking, for an English teacher. Keep your head down and your mouth shut, particularly in your first year (a probation period apparently – I had no recollection of being told about any probation period). I'd been warned by others about our Palestinian director, Farid Ohan. He had a Jekyll and Hyde personality, by all accounts. Originally from Nazareth, a Doctor of Philosophy with Canadian nationality and a tendency to employ mild-mannered, line-toeing Canadians, he was a character to beware of, particularly in the smoking room, where one tended to be off one's guard. A throwaway comment uttered there when Farid had got out of bed on the wrong side could lead to instant dismissal.

At the end of our first academic year, an Irish wag in the English department, a certain Brian O'Nunan, organised a spoof talent contest, which verged on the obscene and, to some unfortunate individuals, was often downright insulting. One of the categories in this contest was for the most interesting Canadian member of staff – with a deadpan expression, gazing out across the entire assembled SWC staff, he announced that there were no nominees. Funnily enough, a Canadian couple ended up becoming very good friends of ours and I don't think it would be an exaggeration to say that Gail is one of the funniest and most outrageous people I know. She's always claimed to admire my eccentricity and diligence, and as I've always appreciated, apart from her ability to entertain, her kindness and generosity, we've had a sort of mutual admiration society going on over the years since we met. Gail's thing was management. She'd been a health information manager in hospitals in Canada, and in the course of her term at SWC, she trained up dozens of young Emirati women to be health information managers, sending them out into hospitals and clinics around the land to revamp their record systems and no doubt save lives in the process.

It was to the same Mr O'Nunan that I had recounted the tale of the day I showed one of my younger and more impressionable foundation classes a classic video of Mr Bean doing a maths test. In the sketch, he takes along a pink panther toy as a lucky mascot and before the start of the exam inadvertently bends the tail up between the animal's hind legs so that it resembles a monstrous pink erection. Thinking this a little crude for my young innocents I clasped the remote control leading up to this bit, planning to fast forward the video to safer waters the moment I saw Mr Bean picking up the offending animal. What actually happened was that I froze the video at the very worst possible moment, probably embarrassing myself a lot more than my Emirati girls in the process. Several of them were, after all, married already. I was not allowed to forget this incident. Sometime later, it became known that I was planning to marry my boyfriend when he joined me in the UAE from Germany and, with the staff still being small enough to do such things, the social committee fund had been drawn on to buy us a tasteful engagement present, a heavy glass-topped Rajasthani side table. A small group of teachers had assembled in the coffee break for the presentation and at the last minute I was called from my workstation to join the group, mildly alarmed to hear that my presence was required. A natural thespian, Brian announced to all and sundry that he was delighted to be making this presentation, especially as it had been touch and go for a while about my continued employment at the college after I had been caught showing pornographic videos to my students in their English class.

As far as I could make out, it was just a matter of luck as to what classes one was allocated on arrival at 'The Gulag'. School leavers entering the colleges were placed in either HD programmes (Higher Diploma) or CD programmes (Certificate Diploma). Naturally, the more academically inclined individuals were put into HD programmes, which ranged from business and graphic art to IT and health science courses, some of which led to a degree. I happen to have been placed at the higher end of the academic scale in the Health Sciences Dept. The benefit of having brighter, more serious, industrious young women in my classes was really outweighed by the disadvantage of having the most appalling amount of marking to do from one end of the year to the other. My life was simply dominated by marking – there was *always* a pile of essays, graph descriptions or dense, health-related assignments to deal with waiting at the end of my bed at weekends, and on any night of the week for that matter. Added to this was the pressure of having to prepare all my classes for the IELTS exam to the level required for graduation from college (students needed to get an average of band 5.5 out of a maximum of 9, equating to a good intermediate level in the four skills: reading, writing, listening and speaking). Unlike some other nationalities, Emiratis tend to excel at listening and speaking but find reading and writing a lot more challenging. The general standard of writing when the girls entered the college left a great deal to be desired. The only thing to do was to provide lots and lots of practice, which of course meant lots and lots of marking. As my old friend Charlotte's mother had said when I was a gauche thirteen-year-old, 'When Caroline does a job' (usually referring to washing up), 'she does it properly.' When it came to marking, not a word or punctuation mark escaped my attention – I marked with an eagle eye and didn't skimp on red ink. Many I know would question my method of error correction robustly, choosing instead to focus only on the more serious errors, but having written many an essay in a foreign language myself in the course of my education, and considered my own teachers' careful corrections, marks and comments sacrosanct, I found myself labouring on in the same rigorous vein, wielding my red pen ruthlessly with the courage of my convictions.

One of the first things Maria and I decided to do once we'd moved out of the honeymoon hotel and into our Kalooti apartments was to stock up on booze for weekend entertaining. We'd been told that there was a tiny, semi-legal shop in the neighbouring emirate of Ajman that sold a small selection of spirits and wines at competitive prices – it was closer and easier than making a trip across the causeway to traffic-congested Dubai at weekends. We'd been told that most taxi drivers, despite their religion forbidding it, would, for a small extra fee, take people to 'the Hole in the Wall' as it was known and wait for passengers while the transaction was taking place. Not yet possessing liquor licences and still feeling our way through the ins and outs of Emirati customs and laws, we were a tad apprehensive about this first foray into the vaguely illegal activities of the alcohol-consuming maverick ex-pat community. After flagging down a taxi from the dusty roadside outside our building, we anxiously enquired if the driver would be willing to take us to our destination. He eyed us up suspiciously and didn't seem at all keen but after a few moments' reflection quoted rather a large fee for the undertaking. Anxious to be out of the scorching late morning sun and on our way, we accepted and settled into the sagging back seat, searching, as our driver launched a little recklessly out into the flow of traffic, for the dirt-encrusted seat belts, most of which had disappeared down the back of the seats into the vehicle's unsavoury innards.

Our journey took us past the scenic Sharjah docks, where dozens of quaint old wooden dhows were berthed, laden with spicy cargo, waiting to depart for other Gulf destinations or to have their cargo brought onshore by wiry dockers of all ages, their dusky skin glistening in the punishing sun. The port is one of the oldest in the country. It was a meeting place in the 1900s where traders dealt in charcoal in return for rice and materials brought by traders from India and Iran. The whole area was ablaze with colour and teeming with activity – hulking great packages were lowered jerkily by cranes onto the oily rope-strewn dockside; fearsome foremen hurled abuse at young slackers, no doubt threatening them with instant dismissal unless they threw down their beedies and jumped to it. Although we were hardly travelling in luxury, we were at least out of the sun and enjoying a coolish breeze through the open windows of our hired vehicle. Maria and I didn't need to verbalise our feelings of gratitude for our lot in life. We sat in silent contemplation of the lives of the dock workers and their gruelling, hazardous work. After twenty minutes' uncomfortable, bouncy drive we drew to a halt in the sand at the side of the road beneath a crumbling wall that had once surrounded a patch of scrubland. There was an entrance of sorts and our driver indicated with a gnarled, tobacco-stained index finger, barely disguising his disdain for such unprincipled heathens, that we would find what we were after if we took ourselves off through it.

The 'Hole in the Wall' was aptly named as that is precisely what it was. There was barely room for the two of us at the chipped Formica counter, but eager to see what potent brews were on offer we peered into the dimly lit space within, smiling politely at the swarthy, oily-haired vendor, who leered back at us, staring brazenly at Maria's slightly low-cut top and recently bronzed cleavage. Spurning the wine on account of its almost certain mistreatment since leaving the shores of France, we opted for a dusty bottle each of Martini and some good old Gordon's gin, which was so cheap we took two bottles each. The tonic we had bought previously at Spinney's supermarket had cost roughly the same as the spirit itself, though the lemons and limes were a bargain. When we piled back into our taxi, bearing plastic bags bulging with clanking bottles, our driver inspected us in the rear-view mirror with what looked like something akin to fear and set off at some speed, weaving his way frantically through dusty deserted suburbs as though the police were hot on our tail. Green though we were in this alien land and having already heard rumours of expats being deported, sometimes after incarceration in dire conditions, for lesser offences than buying liquor without a liquor licence, we remained silent, each wrestling with our own creeping consternation and willing the whole episode to be over as soon as possible.

Before we got back to our Kalooti home, the driver came to an abrupt halt at a tiny makeshift mosque that we guessed serviced the poor construction workers, whose shantytown we looked out on from our spacious lounges. Hurling himself from the car, he rushed off without a word of explanation. We could only guess that as a devout Muslim, assisting infidels to purchase alcohol, a forbidden substance – absolutely '*haram*' – he felt tainted in the eyes of Allah on account of his collusion in our crime and was taking the very first opportunity to beg for forgiveness, even though he had not yet deposited us at our destination. We were already starting to see the funny side of the whole business, especially as it appeared we had not been followed by zealous police and our building was now actually within sight. After some minutes our driver returned, visibly relieved and almost jovial, fired up his engine and cruised around the corner to Kalooti Towers. 'Oh, madams!' he exclaimed in a heavy south Indian accent. 'I was needing very urgently to *go toilet*! Now is fine. Everything is fine. Which entrance are you requiring – the front side or the back side?' It was all we could do to contain our hysterics until we had decanted ourselves and our illegal liquor from the taxi. After lugging our haul up the steps into the deliciously cool air-conditioned foyer with its tinkling fountain, shining marble floor and potted palms, we summoned the lift, and on arrival in my flat I fixed us a large G and T with some thoughtfully pre-prepared ice cubes and fresh limes. This, we were to learn, was somewhat typical of life in the UAE – lashings of heat, dust and frustration followed by moments of great relief and comfort, if not sheer bliss.

It was rather unfortunate that there were well-polished mirrors on all three sides of the lifts at Kalooti Towers. During those first few months after the honeymoon period, Maria and I would return from work each evening to confront our reflection. The faces that looked back at us had tense, haunted expressions and the cares of the day were etched out in ever-deepening wrinkles. We'd take it in turn to have crises, tearful outpourings behind the safety of closed doors, during which we'd swear it was just not worth it, that we would pay back our furniture money and hand in our resignation the following week. We did our best to bolster each other up and point out that the weekend was only a day or so away, that we should start making plans to paint Dubai red. Mr Bond had not been wrong when he described the work hard, play hard regime. With Maria being that bit younger than me, when it came to weekend partying, there's no doubt, she had more stamina. No excuses, however convincingly they were made, were tolerated on Wednesday night (the equivalent of our Friday night, though the weekend changed, discombobulatingly, to Friday and Saturday at some point during our stay, when the Emiratis decided it was in their interests to partially synchronise with the rest of the international business world). Glad rags would be donned and war paint applied before we hit the nightlife in Dubai, often joined by another feisty English teacher from Belfast, who became another dear friend, the bold Barbara Forbes. A pokey G and T or two, usually at mine, would kick off the weekend then into a taxi we'd clamber and head for the Irish Village for an open-air drink by the fountain and a spot of supper – nothing too heavy, though, as we needed to be fit for dancing at Savage Garden. We were all moved by the rhythms of Latin America, so after a fairly basic dance class led by a flamboyant Costa Rican couple, we'd mingle with the crowd, hoping for a Latino male, or at least someone dark and Middle Eastern or Mediterranean-looking rather than one of our pasty compatriots with visibly damp armpits and two left feet, to materialise and lead us to the dance floor. Apart from Savage Garden, which sadly closed down sometime during our first year, there was no shortage of buzzing night spots and musical events in Dubai with a steady stream of visiting pop stars, everyone from Bryan Adams and Boney M. to the Bootleg Beatles. By far the most spectacular open-air evening show Maria and I went to was that put on at the tennis stadium starring Enrique Iglesias, then at the height of his fame. As we sat in our seats bursting with anticipation, a shining apparition appeared suddenly illuminated high above us, as if created at that very instant in the inky firmament. Slowly descending towards the stage, reclining in a giant crescent moon, he crooned away to an enraptured audience that would have had his father, Julio, turning green all over with envy.

Since my days in Tenerife, where I had once been unable to restrain myself from dancing in a shoe shop when his song 'Suavemente' came on the radio, I had been a big fan of the sexy Puerto Rican hip-swiveller Elvis Crespo. Hearing he would be one of the performers at a small two-day Dubai music festival, Desert Rhythms, I didn't hesitate to buy a ticket. Our very good friends Steve and Debbie were up for it too, along with a lovely couple I'd met originally in Brazil, Nick and Ozzie. Massive white tents with Moroccan-style lanterns and billowing silks hanging from the ceilings created an extravagant and sultry ambiance. Reclining beneath the whirring ceiling fans on comfortable white linen-covered sofas with brightly coloured silk cushions, we congratulated ourselves on lining up what promised to be a great weekend's entertainment. The event can't have been properly advertised as, to our surprise, it was sparsely populated on both days, despite some really outstanding singers, Algerian raï giant Cheb Khaled being one of them. His song 'Aïcha' is a classic and I shall be eternally grateful that I saw him perform it live. By the time Elvis Crespo came on stage, Debbie and I had sampled at least two blue margheritas and were fired up with the heady atmosphere and pulsating Latin music. Grabbing me by the wrist, Debbie pulled me to my feet and dragged me through the crowds to the front of the stage where mainly scantily clad far younger women were dancing. Next thing I knew Elvis himself was leaning forwards towards me as he sang with an outstretched hand, willing me to lean forwards and upwards and touch fingers, which of course I did. Another moment to cherish. Whether he recognised me as the ardent fan I was, whether he felt we had a spiritual connection or if he just had a thing about older women, I shall never know. Thank you, Debbie, for helping to make this happen.

Wherever we girls chose for our Wednesday night revelries, somewhere around midnight, a tall, dark, bespectacled and earnest-looking character would appear looming above the merry throng and join our group – the infamous and enigmatic Gerry Griffin. He'd been at university with Gail in Canada many moons before our UAE days – he was highly intelligent but lived on the edge, always feeling the challenge to go that bit further out away from the accepted and the commonplace. His marriage was dissolving and he had reverted to the life of a discreet single man about town. One weekend, to our dismay, Maria and I spotted our bookish colleague by the pool at our Sharjah Sports Club, where we enjoyed a few quiet hours at weekends without any reminders of our taxing workplace. Fortunately, we were not spotted and as I later walked past Mr Griffin's abandoned sun-lounger I saw he was halfway through reading a considerable paperback tome by Anthony Trollope. The following morning at work I couldn't resist pulling Gerry's leg: 'You didn't see us, but we saw you at the weekend, Gerry… with your big, fat trollop.' Such was Gerry's look of dismay, if not momentary horror, I slightly regretted such a cruel jest. My enduring memory of Gerry is of him driving a gang of us in the early hours one weekend in his old jeep from Kempinski's beach bar in Ajman back to Sharjah, his foot flat down on the pedal as we hurtled over road bumps, everyone being thrown up in the air, whooping and screeching as our heads hit the roof. All too soon the working week would be upon us, our sparkly dresses and dancing shoes would be banished to the wardrobe and moments such as these would be pushed to the back of our brains, to be retrieved with great fondness years later when focusing on the positive aspects of our Middle Eastern days.

The one and only time Christmas coincided with the Muslim *Eid Al Fitr* holiday was that first year in the UAE. Naturally, Simon and I planned to spend the time together. I winged my way towards him with a certain amount of apprehension as I had just been to a Sharjah beauty salon for a bikini wax and somehow had emerged mistakenly with a Brazilian, which involves removal of every single hair in the nether regions. The pain was such that I screamed the place down. Despite Simon's final verdict that he preferred 'a little foliage', we spent a romantic week in Paris, and on my return to Sharjah, we found we missed each other so much that we decided over the phone that he would resign from his job in Germany, join me in March and that we'd make arrangements to get married straight away. My students were delighted to hear of the development and when I expressed my fears about Simon having to overcome his growing phobia about flying, one of them piped up, 'Don't worry, Miss. Love will help to get him here!' A few days before his flight, I sent him an email – then still quite a novel form of communication – wishing him well on the journey and saying I'd be thinking of him every second of the way until he set foot on Emirati soil and so on. To my great dismay, the following day I got an email back starting with 'I'm so sorry to have to tell you this, but I shan't be able to join you in the UAE...' I could hardly believe my eyes.

What on earth could have happened to make him change his mind? Surely it wasn't the Brazilian. Reading on with pounding heart I gradually realised that this email was not from Simon at all, but from someone else with exactly the same name – Simon Cummings – and a very similar email address. The impostor actually sounded rather nice – and had thought from the heartfelt words in my message that I did too. He greatly regretted that he would not be coming to join me but wished me a very happy life with his namesake. More entertainment for my classes that day when I filled them in on the mishap.

One class in particular became quite spellbound when I told them of my fiancé's safe arrival and of our plans for the wedding. It was the same class who had begged me to tell them over and over again about the moment I fell in love on our first date at a Mondrian exhibition at the Tate. Romantic love and even the word boyfriend were taboo at that time in my college, and quite probably still – most marriages in the UAE were arranged ones, often to first cousins – hence my students' delight hearing me describe my feelings as Simon took my hand in his on setting out for Brighton station, how the whole day took on a dreamlike quality and how, on the journey home, the sun shone into his remarkable green eyes with the hazel flecks, mesmerising me and stealing my heart... by the time the train pulled into Brighton station once more I was in love. Normally a noisy bunch, my class at this point were so quiet you could have heard a pin drop such was their involvement in the tale. It was in moments like this that I felt incredibly close to my girls – I knew and they knew that if word got out about the content of some of my lessons, I'd be given my marching orders. My transgressions created a bond between us and it was the relationship I had with this class in particular that I probably treasure most from my time in the UAE. Finding our idea of getting married under a frangipani tree in the Abu Dhabi embassy garden to be unfeasible, we settled for a simple church ceremony in Dubai followed by a Thai-style seafood buffet at Dubai Creek Golf and Yacht Club. It was an exuberant affair with plenty of champagne (Simon splashed out on twelve bottles at club prices – by far the most expensive round he had ever bought) and there was laughter and dancing under the stars until the early hours, with Simon acting as DJ and very gracious host.

Lovely though it was to have Simon back in my life, work at SWC didn't get any easier. On the contrary, the noose seemed to be getting tighter. Unused to having our freedom restricted in virtually every aspect of our lives, we found ourselves on a non-stop roller-coaster, locked into our seats for the duration of our three-year contracts. The stresses and strains at work were ongoing. It wasn't just the amount of work we were grappling with, but the unusual technological demands placed on us along with the whole ambiance at SWC. I had been warned before I even set foot in the country that the Palestinian director at Sharjah Women's College was a tartar and that he monitored the arrival and departure of each employee from the campus to the extent that one felt Big Brother was watching you each minute of the working day. The number of contact hours increased alarmingly during my first contract, class sizes were often around twenty, which is a lot for a language class, so what with three or four different classes of higher-level students, all being prepared for the IELTS exam, and content teachers expecting English teachers to mark and often render intelligible several project reports a year, a phenomenal amount of marking had to be done, which was made all the worse as friends teaching lower-level students often failed to appreciate what we were up against. My cool, handsome, reserved Australian colleague, Brett, and I slogged away day in day out, while our supervisor, Tony, a master of delegation, who always reminded me for some reason of Rupert Bear, would tend to disappear mysteriously when there were significant numbers of exam papers to be marked and if there was no marking to do would dream up huge academic projects for those in his department. Being a glutton for punishment, I would take on such projects whole-heartedly, going way beyond the call of duty, staying regularly at my workstation when most people were long gone and spending large chunks of my weekends poring over them when I should have been switching off completely and 'playing hard', as Mr Bond had advised. Perhaps the most absurd situation I found myself in with regard to work was the weekend we went on a camping trip to Oman with a group of friends. We chartered a small dhow, an old Gulf cargo ship, in Khasab on the Musandam peninsula, and made our way up through the fiords, past deserted, remote sandy coves and craggy, crumbling mountains. While people dived from the boat and stretched out on the deck to sunbathe, I found myself tackling a large pile of health science projects on – of all things – venereal diseases. Not surprisingly I ended up with the swirling vision that precedes a migraine, warning me in no uncertain terms that sea cruises and marking simply don't mix. Catching sight of a pair of dolphins swimming alongside our vessel, leaping alternately into the air for sheer joy, I cursed the day I was allocated HD classes and I'm sure the thought crossed my mind to fling my wretched projects into the sea and hand in my notice.

Decadent though it now sometimes seems, eating out in the UAE with our tax-free salaries was something we did quite regularly in the early days, before guilt at the appalling inequality between the haves and have-nots in the country took much of the pleasure out of it. Several of the larger hotels had breathtaking buffets that included almost every conceivable type of cuisine, laid out in sections in cleverly designed labyrinths with culturally related decor, artwork, artefacts and so on, for each nation. One generally had the option of paying a little more for unlimited standard alcoholic drinks to accompany the food and a bit more again for premium alcoholic drinks. As one of our favourite types of food in these food halls was Japanese, expertly prepared by Japanese nationals, we generally went for the premium alcohol deal as it included warm sake, the perfect accompaniment to soothe the taste buds after a blast of wasabi. The only thing was the sake glasses were extra small ones, which necessitated frequent trips to and fro through the labyrinth to maintain the effect. Grilled lobster tails were another item not to be missed, though the Indian chefs needed to be watched like hawks or they would fill your plate with over-cooked ones waiting at the side of the griddle when what you wanted were the fresh, lightly grilled ones. During our first years in the UAE, we often feasted on the most divine local fish, hamour, as this and red snapper were then plentiful and quite affordable. As time went on the fishermen had to go further and further out into the Indian ocean to catch the fish and hamour became a lot more expensive and generally not as good. Of course, there was always the temptation at such buffets to overindulge and make a thorough pig of oneself, but we learned to be very selective, to pace ourselves and to limit ourselves to the tiniest taste of a few items from the vast array of beautifully decorated desserts. Having inherited my mother's sweet tooth, I have had a lifelong battle to resist sugary, fattening food, but surprisingly, despite these not-infrequent weekend binges, I don't remember having any particular problems remaining a size ten in the UAE. I expect the excess calories were burned up in nervous energy during the week toiling away at the workhouse.

Once a week, on average, I would ring my mother, who at that time was living rather a good life in Berkshire, which involved horse riding, dog walking, foreign travel, and frequent trips to the theatre in London with female friends, my stepfather being more of a stay-at-home type. She also kept remarkably fit by attending classes and putting on performances of Margaret Morris dancing, which has nothing, as many guess it does, to do with morris dancing. Besides being an artist, writer, educator, physiotherapist and choreographer, Margaret Morris was a highly gifted pioneering dance teacher whose avant-garde ideas of the 1920s and 1930s paved the way for modern and contemporary dance. Far ahead of her times, she took Isadora Duncan's six Classical Greek ballet positions and devised a system of movement, enshrined in the Margaret Morris Movement (MMM), which encompasses recreational, therapeutic, athletic and creative elements of dance and exercise for all ages. I'm convinced that it was her MMM activities that kept my mother so supple and youthful right up until her eightieth birthday, when very sadly she fell over her Jack Russell in the kitchen and broke her hip, which put paid not only to her dancing days but also to her horse riding. I swore to her that if she ever reached ninety, I would get her back on a horse, even if it meant hiring a small crane to do so. I promised her a lovely gentle ride with me over the Sussex downs. 'Oh no, I don't think so,' she replied, looking wistful. 'If you get me on a horse again, I won't be going on a gentle ride, I shall gallop!'

I suppose I did a fair bit of complaining to Mum about the rigours of my work and the obscene amount of marking I had to do and she would invariably respond, 'Oh yes, darling, I know, but you must remember you really do have a *very* good social life.' It was true that barely a weekend went by when we weren't invited to some sort of party, outing or social gathering. I have to say I attended some of these less than wholeheartedly, as I felt that having spent the whole working week with one set of people, I really would have preferred to spend the weekend with an entirely different set, if not alone with my dear Simon, but of course one didn't have that option – Maria, for a start, would not have permitted me to hide away at home like a wallflower.

Moving to the UAE we had entered a typical ex-pat community with all its cliques, gossip, intrigues and bitching – I had never experienced such a lifestyle before and I have to say that, being something of a free spirit if not an out-and-out loner, it didn't really suit me at all. I made an effort, however – what else could I do? I'd spruce myself up on party nights, down a glass or two of something potent with Simon before we set off and joined in with the merry-making. Funnily enough, in the end, I must admit I generally did end up enjoying myself… after a fashion.

One of the most regular party-givers and one of the most generous, a provider of extravagent banquets who slaved away for hours on end in her tiny kitchen producing veritable feasts of mouth-watering dishes and exotic salads, was the intrepid Jay Butler, whom I'd first met at the Emirati Embassy in London for our HCT interviews. The condition of attending these wild and wonderful parties was that one was expected to participate in a whole battery of games, which often required dressing up, some sort of performance and generally making a fool of oneself. One game at Jay's I recall involved a small wooden milking stool with a photograph of our Palestinian director Farid Ohan looking particularly manic stuck to the seat. I expect the milking stool formed some sort of penance, being made to sit in the corner whilst singing a song, for example, feeling the awful man's beady, satanic, laser eyes burning through your nether regions. The parties I enjoyed most, though, were those given by our Cornish flower child friend, Debbie, and her bodybuilding scientifically minded husband, Steve, who was a great influence on Simon with regard to fitness and with whom he would talk far into the night about quantum physics, string theory, parallel universes and so on. Of all the parties we went to, theirs were the most laid-back, populated with guests from all walks of life, not just the same old HCT crew, and always involved fantastic food created by their Sri Lankan live-in maid, Genna, and, most importantly, dancing. No one would get out of Debbie's parties alive if they hadn't had a spin on the dance floor.

Despite the wonderful social life my mother assured me I was having, despite being on the best salary I was ever likely to be on, despite for the most part enjoying my time in the classroom and despite having a kind, loving, considerate partner and some dear friends, I became quite depressed during my first year in the Emirates and ended up consulting a highly recommended psychiatrist, who advised me to first see a gynaecologist to make sure that my weekend weeping bouts weren't simply hormonal. The Australian consultant he sent me to at one of the large Dubai hospitals – let's call him Dr S – was a stocky, blonde, jovial type with fingers like Cumberland sausages. He spent a good hour or more quizzing me in great detail about all aspects of my life, including my love life. I was reasonably frank in my replies and in return I was treated to a confident analysis of my type, as well as Simon's, according to the Karma Sutra – Elephant Man/ Rabbit Woman, if you are any the wiser. He seemed if anything even more surprised than Reverend Gurney, who had officiated at our wedding in Dubai, that we had decided to get married so late in life. He believed that it generally worked out rather better if the mature couple kept their own accommodation and just met for sex however many times a week suited them. I could hardly believe my ears. Still, as he seemed to be a kind, genuine, almost fatherly individual, I tolerated what others might not have and agreed to take the progesterone tablets he had a strong hunch might 'do the trick'.

Tiny and innocuous though the tablets appeared, I found myself pleasantly relaxed much of the time and almost sedated by the time I got home from work. If I stretched out on the sofa for a few minutes I would find myself slipping straight off to sleep. The weekend blubbing mercifully subsided and I managed to become a little more dispassionate about my UAE existence.

After a few weeks on the prescribed medication, I returned to the gynaecologist for a follow-up appointment and tried to describe the bizarre state of limbo I seemed to have been living in since embarking on the course of medication, as well as my tendency to 'rest' when previously I had been more inclined to keep busy. 'Ah yes,' Dr S replied, nodding with satisfaction, 'that's good, that's good – that's why we call them "the docile old cow pills".' It amazed friends I told of our conversation that the man was able to hang on to his job, talking to patients in such a manner. In the end, however, Dr S actually didn't manage to hang on to his job. He was obliged to 'do a runner', back to Australia I presume, after an Emirati baby he'd delivered died soon after it had arrived in this world. The parents were convinced that the baby could have been saved, so were claiming blood money for 'the murder' of their child. I was shocked to hear the news. Despite his rather unconventional style, unacceptable according to some, I liked Dr S, trusted him and believed his interest in and concern for his patients to be completely genuine. I hope he was able to pick up his career where it had left off, back in his native land.

When I really stop to think how very hard that first year was at Sharjah Women's College – the lack of suitable materials at the upper end of the academic spectrum where I found myself, the lack of academic support of any kind, minimal technical support and the feeling that Big Brother was watching you every step you took and so on – it is a wonder I got through it, let alone the first contract. The fact that I signed on for and completed three three-year contracts amazes me still today. Between the second and third contract I headed off to Cambodia solo, as Simon, being a British Council employee, rarely had holidays that coincided with mine. I intended to fulfil a lifelong ambition of seeing the magnificent ancient temple complex of Angkor Wat and at the same time to decide if I had it in me to stick it out for a further three years at the gulag.

As always when I land in South East Asia, I started to relax and switch off from worldly concerns and, on stepping from the tarmac into Siem Riep airport, acclimatised almost instantly. Picking out a moped rider from the small assembly waiting hopefully outside the terminus, I agreed on a daily rate for transporting me around the temples and out to Tonle Sap Lake, where I hoped to see pelicans and other birds in their natural habitat. It was a sublime experience, even if my camera battery did die on me minutes before the sun set at the main temple on the first evening and I failed to get the shots I'd longed for. I remained philosophical, however, reminding myself what Anthony Bourdain had written about his experience of Angkor Wat in his *A Cook's Tour* a few years earlier – that no camera is adequate to the task of capturing the magnificence of the temples. 'There's no way to convey through simple images the sense of wonder when you encounter the cities of Angkor looming up out of the thick jungle'. Puttering along the tranquil, leafy jungle roads between temple complexes, helmetless and feeling all the better for having the breeze play around my ears, I decided – no, enough was enough. I would *not* sacrifice another three years during the prime of my life in a country I had no love or even liking for. To hell with the tax-free salary; I'd rather work once more for peanuts in a South East Asian country – Thailand, Laos or Cambodia. This is where my heart was, I felt at peace with myself and the world. I'd hand in my notice, visit my family in the UK then head back out East, with Simon of course, and together we'd create a simple but fulfilling life for ourselves amongst the Buddhas and banana trees and gentle folk, a place where we could feel at one with our environment, something simply not possible in a barren land of mosquitos and mosques with their fanatical-sounding muezzins and moustachioed, macho Emirati youth, many of whom considered themselves so superior. And yet, I returned to Sharjah a few days later and signed another three-year contract – I have no recollection of making any conscious decision to do so; I just went and did it. I think the main reason, if I'm honest, was that Simon and I had been thinking of buying a flat for ourselves back in Brighton – the little garden flat I owned was really too small for the two of us. My mother had been quite astute in her remark on her second flying visit to the UAE that we would soon become accustomed to such palatial accommodation. My Cambodian trip was followed by a brief one to the UK during which I succeeded in getting a mortgage on a lovely Regency flat in Hove, which gave us the impetus to continue the UAE slog.

The best years in the UAE for us were undoubtedly the first three, when there were far fewer cars on the roads, meaning for instance that we could get over to Dubai to shop and dine out at weekends relatively easily. Without traffic, the run westwards to Dubai City Centre shopping arcade used to take a mere ten minutes. As the years went by, the volume of traffic became unimaginable, roads became hopelessly congested until, towards the end of our stay, it could take up to two hours to make the same journey to the wealthier and in many ways more interesting emirate of Dubai. In our final year or so, Simon, leaving home at six in the morning to reach his work at the British Council in Dubai, would have to make a huge detour, tripling his mileage to avoid the busiest roads. Sheikh Zayed Road, which runs all the way from Dubai to Abu Dhabi, was said to be the most dangerous road in the world at that time – almost daily fatalities, many caused by wealthy young Emirati men racing each other in brand-new vehicles, high on cocaine or some such drug, lulled into a false sense of security by the comfort of their plush four-wheel drive Toyota Land Cruisers. Barely a month went by at our college when we weren't disturbed during the day of study by the heart-rending sound of wailing mourners, alerted mid-lesson to the death of beloved brothers, cousins, even husbands.

They simply wouldn't learn. If young men were snatched from this life in the most horrific of circumstances, it was the will of Allah.

Although the diversions of Dubai went some way towards alleviating the boredom at weekends of living in a land with little accessible culture, what was rather more exciting, and in every way more memorable, were the weekend camping expeditions we went on, mostly in the early days, when the roads eastwards were clearer too and the idea of sleeping under the stars far away from the madding crowds was all quite a novelty. We soon understood the merits of buying our own camping equipment rather than accepting offers from friends to lend us stuff after a rather superior camping chair, belonging to a Canadian couple we didn't know very well, was blown by a sneaky sea breeze into the campfire embers during the night and melted beyond recognition. It took us ages to find an exact replica to replace it. Our destinations varied according to the time of year and who our travelling companions were. A rather odd British couple who lived in our building, and whom Simon had befriended, were fired up with the idea of camping in the wilds and led us to a place they'd been to before, a remote spot in the vicinity of Niswah in Oman. It lay amongst dramatic, towering mountains and was reached by narrow, crumbling, unsealed roads that wound around the sides of steeply inclining slopes for mile upon mile until one wondered if one would ever arrive. Finally, a small settlement built around an oasis came into sight, with neatly kept fields of crops and tethered livestock, their bleating the only sounds to be heard once our engines had been turned off. Coming across young men, mere boys really, out hunting with their hawks, armed with shotguns, seeing the expressions of wonder on the faces of village children as we changed a flat tyre on our Land Rover, encountering a jolly band of plump red-faced housewives attacking heaps of steaming laundry in an underground hot spring – all of these form vivid and precious memories that I'm sure will outlast those of consuming caviar, crayfish and cava in fancy Dubai hotels.

On other occasions, we headed for the golden beaches of the unspoiled, remote east coast of the UAE. The one we picked on our first trip turned out to have treacherous sinking sand in the middle, necessitating an alarming plunge down from the dry sand dunes at the top of the beach followed by loud revving and a furious spurt across the suspect area, all of which I found so nerve-racking I had to get out and let Simon operate solo. Once we reached the desired spot and had pitched camp, the top priority was creating a campfire on which to barbecue fish, chicken kebabs and other such meaty morsels. Simon once brought a huge pot of pre-cooked green Thai chicken curry that was a big hit amongst our comrades, Steve, Deb, Nick, Ozzie and co. It was with the same merry crew that we later travelled to Liwa way down in the southwest of the country in the Empty Quarter of the desert, tantalisingly close to the Saudi border. Liwa is known for its magnificent, colossal, other-worldly sand dunes. We had seen pictures of the dunes but nothing really prepared us for their awe-inspiring beauty when standing astride them. After several hours' drive, we congregated at Moreeb Dune – a whopping three hundred metres high – where drag racing competitions were in progress on a fifty-degree slip face. Even from a distance, the vehicles made an incredible racket and it was impossible not to share their exhilaration when drivers reached the top of the dune.

I'll never forget climbing the gigantic sand dune that flanked our camp first thing in the morning before breakfast on our last day – it must have been well over a hundred metres high – with Simon and Alex, Steve and Deb's son, then a tough little lad of six, with an intense gaze and a mop of thick curly hair. Once we got up there the view was quite stupendouos – our vehicles beside the camping spot looked like Dinky toys and the figures around the campfire matchstick men. The dunes stretched as far as the eye could see. No two dunes were the same and the patterns made in the sand by the wind were exquisite. Here and there you would see the tracks of small animals and if you were lucky a desert beetle making its way purposefully to a distant appointment. Between many of the dunes were massive craters that you felt might mesmerise you and draw you into their sandy depths to meet almost certain death, as how would you ever get out without the help of a helicopter? As I contemplated the deceptively benign golden slopes, I remembered reading in one of Wilfred Thesiger's accounts of his time in the Empty Quarter how nomadic women dug deep holes in the sand looking for water in times of scarcity and many were buried alive when the sides caved in on them. The thought filled me with dread.

The preparation involved for such trips, buying and packing all the food, hauling the camping gear out of the cupboards, loading up the car, getting out onto the road before the sun heated up on the first morning of the weekend, sometimes after a latish, boozy night the night before – all this called for a fair bit of effort and willpower, but the wonderful thing was that once we got away time seemed to expand and after the pressures of the working week the feeling of release and freedom under the desert skies sometimes verged on euphoria. One thing one could depend on in the Gulf, whatever the season, was blue skies and almost constant sun, making colours more vivid, birds sing with more zest and the sea glint with extra allure. Walking in my orange Birkenstocks and cut-off jeans across the wasteland that lay between our flat and Carrefour shopping centre on winter evenings, I'd savour the balmy salt-laden breeze coming off the corniche and think with sympathy of all the poor souls back home battling British blizzards and whisper to myself a little prayer of gratitude.

So, now I have come full circle. What started off all those years ago as a way of letting off steam, a way of getting through one of the most difficult periods of my life, has become an account of my passage through the years, seen either through the eyes of a youthful learner myself or through the eyes of an EFL teacher, attempting to conduct lessons that would convince my students, if not myself, of their worth. As Simon went zooming off back to the UK in May 2008, a few weeks before my HCT contract ended, to start work at the English Language Centre in Hove, where we'd first met, the task fell to me to supervise the team of mainly Filipino workers who packed up the entire contents of our flat to ship back home in a twenty-five-foot container. I had sold or given away quite a lot of stuff before the frenzied packing process started. There still remained, however, an alarming amount of furniture and possessions that we had acquired over our nine years with an unusually generous amount of disposable income. The polite posse of workers went through the flat like a swarm of locusts, madly enveloping everything in sight in swathes of bubble wrap, bandaging up bundles of every shape and size with giant rolls of Sellotape, which made a loud high pitched screeching noise each time a packer cut a strip off the dispenser. Although I tried to monitor what was going on, there was activity at each end of the flat, so a few items slipped through that really shouldn't have. I remember weeks later opening with some puzzlement four white plastic loo brushes in their holders, a large dead plant in a cracked pot and some slightly sticky, half-empty bottles of chilli, soy and teriyaki sauce.

Just like the induction period nine years previously, the extraction process from UAE life was tedious and time-consuming, involving much queueing to pay off the phone company, the electricity company and so on. As it turned out, my friend Maria had decided three contracts was her limit too, so, just as our feet had touched the dusty desert ground on the very same day many moons ago when we were comparatively young and innocent, so we stepped from the hot muggy air out on the tarmac into the acclimatised cabin of an Emirates aircraft on exactly the same day too. To mark the occasion and celebrate our survival, with sanity more or less intact after all the blood, sweat and tears, we downed a bottle of champagne and set out for Sharjah Gold Souq in search of a few mementos of our desert experience. We both ended up buying not one but several magnificent carpets, which we hauled with some difficulty out to the roadside below, where taxi drivers gawped at us rudely, cruising on by rather than attempt to get us and our bulky wares into their vehicle.

The ambiance at Dubai airport was even more dreamlike than usual the day of our final departure – the larger-than-life gold palm trees, the great mounds of pistachio-stuffed dates and macadamia nuts at the dried fruit counter, the wafts of heavy oil-based Arabian perfumes, bearded Emirati men in their dazzling white dishdashas gliding about as though they owned the world. I would pass through this airport from time to time in years to come, usually en route to or from my beloved Thailand, but in a very different frame of mind. Whilst working in the UAE, I would return at the end of the summer break, uplifted by my new travel experiences and by all the art I had managed to cram into my vacation, but filled with a kind of dread at the prospect of the workload, the meetings, the endless paperwork and all the other demands that were just waiting to clamber up onto my shoulders. I would leave the country, as in fact now, with an overwhelming sense of relief that I had 'got through it', stayed on target and stuck it out right up to the bitter end – or sweet, sweet end I should say. A change in currency exchange rate meant that our nine-year bonus had plummeted abysmally, but it was still a sizeable sum and, along with my savings, enabled me to pay off in one fell swoop my half of the mortgage on our new

Regency dream home in Hove, still leaving me with a reasonable financial cushion and even a bit left over for future travels. I had applied for and been accepted on a training weekend to become an English examiner for Trinity College London, a job my friend Zoe had done for several years and to which we both felt I'd be remarkably well suited, as it involved lots of overseas lone travel and language work with both children and adults. Funnily enough, the bold Maria Hughes was accepted onto the very same course that November at windswept Wyboston Lakes in Bedfordshire – there's no doubt our destinies are linked and I often hear her lilting Irish voice in my head when I'm in need of a word of commiseration or encouragement. She was always particularly enthusiastic when I had just made a highly extravagant purchase of some kind.

After what I can hardly believe was three full decades, my days in the classroom had come to an end. Looking back, I think the standard of my teaching over the years was slightly erratic, though, hopefully, it improved considerably as time went by. Being an open, expansive type of communicator myself, I think my idiosyncratic style of teaching probably appealed to less conventional types of learners, those comfortable about sharing experiences, opinions, ambitions and aspirations. Like my learned great-uncle Lionel, an influential relative who had me down as a worker from an early age and encouraged me to embrace art and literature whenever possible in life, I have always had difficulty with spelling and one of my constant fears in the classroom was of misspelling – sometimes quite common words – on the board. If my errors were spotted, or my inability to give a handy rule on a tricky grammar point when asked was evident, I think I must have been forgiven as I believe my sincerity in the classroom was never in doubt. If I expected my students to fight their inhibitions and open up about their lives, I made myself open to them too. I would always attempt to answer questions truthfully and I think my willingness to share confidences and admit to failures and mistakes was appreciated and sometimes won over individuals who might initially have been unsure of my unorthodox *modus operandi*. I don't think anyone who attended my classes could doubt that I put my heart and soul into my teaching and that I cared about my students. Of course, there were those I didn't take to, even actively disliked, and a handful I dearly wished I could have banished from my class right from the start, but my professionalism, I certainly hope, enabled me to disguise these negative feelings and I would at least attempt to show extra kindness and concern for the progress of these undesirables. Kill them with kindness, I'd tell myself. Many of my students, from as far back as the seventies, remain firmly planted in my mind – the stories they told, opinions they expressed, their quirks, mannerisms and foibles. They will accompany me, I feel sure, throughout my life, so I can only assume that the same is true for some of them – that I will remain part of their lives, embedded in their memories. I just hope these are good memories, that I brought some sunlight into their days, some understanding when they felt misunderstood, and above all that they remember the fun we had.